TECHNOLOGY OF SWEETS (MITHAI) WITH FORMULAE

TECHNOLOGY OF SWEETS (MITHAI) WITH FORMULAE

Written By :
EIRI Board of Consultants & Engineers

ENGINEERS INDIA RESEARCH INSTITUTE

4449, Nai Sarak, Main Road, Delhi-110 006 (India)
Ph.: 91-11-23918117, 23916431, 45120361, 45626431
Fax :91-11-23916431, 23918117
★ **E-Mail**: eiribooks@yahoo.com & eiriprojects@gmail.com
★ **Website**: www.eiriindia.org, www.eiribooksandprojectreports.com

Printed and Published by :

ENGINEERS INDIA RESEARCH INSTITUTE

4449, Nai Sarak, Main Road, Delhi-110 006 (India)

Ph.: 91-11-23918117, 23916431, 45120361, 45626431

Fax :91-11-23916431, 23918117

★ **E-Mail**: eiribooks@yahoo.com & eiriprojects@gmail.com

★ **Website**: www.eiriindia.org, www.eiribooksandprojectreports.com

Marketed By:

EIRI PROJECT CONSULTANTS & PUBLISHERS

Roop Nagar, Delhi—110007

ISBN : 978-93-80772-00-4

Printed in New Delhi (India)

Rs. 1050/-

Printed and Published by Sudhir Gupta for "Engineers India Research Institute", 4449, Nai Sarak, Main Road, Delhi-110 006 and Printed at Swastik Offset, Delhi

Preface

The Book **Technology of Sweets (Mithai) with Formulae** covers almost all the basic and advanced details to setup own Unit. The book covers details of raw materials used for Sweets Manufacture, Making of Milk Based Sweets, Raw Material the Milk Used for Making Sweets, Technology of Bengali Sweets, Technology of Dahi and Yogurt, Technology of Mishti Doi, Shrikhand Manufacture, Chakka Powder, Shrikhand Wadi, Kheer Manufacture, Dried Kheer Mix Manufacture, Payasam Manufacture, Phirni Manufacture, Sevian Manufacture, Sohan Halwa, Gajar-Ka-Halwa, Kaju Burfi Manufacture, Ghevar Preparation, Rasogolla, Kheer and Pal Payasam, Preparation of Lassi, Shrikhand Preparation, Technology of Khoa Manufacture and Storage, Peda, Khoa Based Sweet - Kalakand, Khoa Based Sweet - Gulab Jamun, Milk Based Sweet - Burfi, Chhana based sweet - Rasogolla, Preparation of Kulfi, Yoghurt, Production of Sandesh, Manufacture of Shrikhand by Ultrafiltration Process, Preparation of Traditional Sweets, Gulab Jamun/ Rasgullas, Winter Products, Dessert Powders and Puddings, Ice Cream etc.

The book has been written for the benefit and to prove an asset and a handy reference guide in the hands of new entrepreneurs & well established industrialists.

ENGINEERS INDIA RESEARCH INSTITUTE

4449, Nai Sarak, Main Road, Delhi-110 006 (INDIA)
E-mail : eiribooks@yahoo.com & eiriprojects@gmail.com
www.eiriindia.org, www.eiribooksandprojectreports.com

Contents

1

Details of Raw Materials used for Sweets Manufacture

SWEETENERS GUR (JAGGERY), KHANDSARI, BURA, CHINI

Sugar is extensively used as a sweetener in various Indian milk products. Generally used as a macro-nutrient ingredient, sugar imparts a number of other properties to the products. Possessing multi-faceted functionality, sugar is used as a bulking agent, preservative, texturizer, humectant, dispersing agent, stabilizer, fermentation substrate, flavour carrier, browning agent and decorative agent. Brown sugars and molasses provide additional flavours.

Consumption-wise, refined cane sugar is a major sweetener in India. However, the indigenous varieties of sugar produced by the cottage industry in the rural sector also account for about 37 per cent of the total sweetener consumption. After the extraction of sugarcane juice in a country crusher (kolhu), it is boiled down to a series of major products: namely phanita (thickened juice, now called rab), gur (jaggery), shakkar (brownish sugar or bura, or gur crystals obtained by thoroughly draining of molasses without refining), and khand (crystal sugar in the form of large lumps or small, faceted grains). Khand is refined to yield almost white crystalline sugar. Small crystals product is called chini while the product having considerably large crystals is called misri. Gur or jaggery is a major sweetening agent, whose solution may be thickened over a fire to yield semi-dry material. Residual material is pressed by hand to obtain lumps of gur. Besides sugarcane, juices from khajur (date) and tala (Palmyra palm tree) are highly valued for production of gur.

Traditional confectioners mostly use khandsari, a less refined form of sugar. Jaggery (gur), an unrefined sweetener, is mainly used by rural folks. Both these products are valued in traditional milk product formulations for their characteristic flavour, texture and colour, and also for providing vitamins, iron, calcium and carbohydrates.

Gur (Jaggery): The most common form of sugar sweeteners in rural areas, gur is considered as the most nutritive sweetener. It is used by halwais at the cottage level in preparation of traditional sweets where a dark brown colour is also desirable.

Jaggery is a crude type of raw sugar made by the heat desiccation of sugarcane juice. It is hygroscopic and is produced in the form of lumps of varying size. Its colour may vary from golden yellow to dark brown, depending upon the molasses content and the heat treatment imparted during the manufacturing process. For obtaining bright golden yellow colour, sulphur dioxide or $NaHSO_3$ is often used in the production process.

Table 1.1 : Indian standards for gur (jaggery).

Parameters	Specifications
Total sugar (expressed as invert sugar)	Not less than 90 per cent and sucrose not less than 60 per cent
Extraneous matter insoluble in water	Not more than 2 per cent
Total ash	Not more than 6 per cent
Ash insoluble in hydrochloric acid (HCl)	Not more than 0.5 per cent

Annually, about 8 million tonnes of jaggery is produced, mainly on small scale in rural areas, from nearly 50 per cent of the total sugarcane produced in India.

Regulatory Status: The Prevention of Food Adulteration (PFA) Rule *A.07.05* defines gur or jaggery as the product obtained by boiling or processing juice pressed out of the sugarcane or extracted from the Palmyra palm, date palm or coconut palm. It shall be free from substances deleterious to health and shall conform on dry weight basis to the analytical standards given in Table 1.1.

Dextrose and fructose, present in jaggery, in varying amounts (depending upon the molasses content), impart hygroscopic character to it. Begasillo and earth mainly constitute the insolubles in jaggery.

As defined in PFA, gur or jaggery, other than that of liquid or semi-liquid variety, shall not contain more than 10 per cent moisture. It may contain sulphur dioxide in concentration not exceeding 70 ppm. Sodium bicarbonate, if used for clarification purpose, should be of food grade quality. Table 1.2 lists some physical and chemical parameters of jaggery.

Technology: Jaggery is mostly made from the sugarcane juice or occasionally from the juice of certain types of palms or dates. The purified juice is boiled in an open pan to produce sugar crystals lightly coated with molasses. During prolonged heating, sugar undergoes caramelization resulting in development of caramel flavour and colour. Moisture control is critical as it affects the shelf life of the product during storage. Sometimes, sulphur dioxide and sodium bicarbonate are used to give jaggery a light colour so as to appeal mainly to urban consumers.

Khandsari (Khand): It is light to dark brown sugar having uniform crystals. Also known as khand, khandsari sugar carries the natural sugarcane flavour as well as the aroma of natural caramel and it is enriched with several nutrients. It has a crude appearance and its natural brown colour comes from the sugarcane molasses, which also impart a unique flavour to it. Depending upon the molasses content, colour of khandsari varies from light golden brown (low molasses content) to deep brown (high molasses content). Since it is manufactured mainly in small scale units, it does not undergo any harsh chemical refining process. It is also not subjected to sulphuring, usually done to whiten sugar. Khandsari is mainly used in traditional sweet making because of its easy availability at a reasonable cost. It is more suited for syrup preparation for sweets like gulabjamun.

Regulatory Status: As per PFA Rule A.07.02, khandsari sugar obtained from sugarcane juice by open pan process may be of two varieties:

(a) Khandsari sugar (desi);

(b) Khandsari sugar (sulphur), also known as "sulphur sugar".

It may be crystalline or in powder form. It shall be free from dirt, filth, iron fillings and added colouring matter. Extraneous matter shall not exceed *0.25 per cent* by weight. Khandsari shall also conform to the standards given in Table 1.3.

Table 1.2 : Additional quality parameters for three grades of gur (jaggery).

Parameters	Special grade	A grade	B grade
Physical			
Colour	Light brownish yellow	Medium brownish	Brown
Texture	Granular	Semi-granular	Very small granular
Hardness	Hard	Soft	Soft
Taste	Sweet	Sweet	Sweet
Chemical (%)			
Non-reducing sugars	80	75.1—80.0	70.1—75.0
Reducing sugars	10	10.1—15.0	15.1—20.0
Moisture	Upto6	6.1—8.0	8.1—10.0
Extraneous matter	Uptoi	1.1—2.0	2.1—3.0

Khandsari sugar can be distinguished from white sugar by difference in conductivity. A 5 per cent solution of khandsari shows conductivity reading of 100 to 300 millimho/cm², while the conductivity of white sugar solution does not exceed 106 milimho/cm².

Table 1.3 : Indian standards for khandsari.

Parameters	Khandsari sugar (Sulphur sugar)	Khandsari sugar (Desi)
Moisture (when heated at 105°C for 3 hours)	Not more than 1.5% by weight	Not more than 1.5% by weight
Ash insoluble in dilute hydrochloric acid	Not more than 0.55% by weight	Not more than 0.7% by weight
Sucrose	Not less than 96.5% by weight	Not less than 93.0% by weight
Sulphur dioxide	Not more than 150 parts per million	Absent

Technology: Khandsari is manufactured on a small scale by open pan process in which juice of sugarcane is concentrated by continuous heating at atmospheric pressure to crystallize sugar particles. In most cases, khandsari sugar does not undergo any refining and whitening process. Hence, its colour also varies. Khandsari production in the organized sector involves sulphuring treatment to decolourize it.

Bura: Another form of indigenous sugar, bura is mainly produced and consumed in western Uttar Pradesh and Haryana. It is in powder form and can be made from any kind of khand or gur. Bura is white to light brown, with a fine granular appearance.

Regulatory Status: According to the PFA Rule A.07.02, 01, bura sugar means the fine grain sized-product made out of any kind of sugar. It shall be free from dirt, filth, iron fillings and added colouring matter. Extraneous matter shall not exceed 0.1 per cent by weight. It shall also conform to the standards given in Table 1.4.

Table 1.4 : Indian standards for bura.

Parameters	Specifications
Sucrose	Not less than 90 per cent by weight
Ash insoluble in dilute hydrochloric acid	Not more than 0.7 per cent by weight
SO_2 content	Not more than 150 ppm

Technology: Raw khandsari or sugar is dissolved in water to prepare syrup, which is boiled vigorously. Final product is superior to starting material in terms of colour and flavour. In traditional methods, during boiling, gummy extracts of some plants like fruits of okra, leaves of simul or red silk cotton, phalsa and sukhali or karaya, are used to remove impurities as scum. Alternatively, "hydro" (a crude blend of sodium carbonate, sodium sulfate and sodium chloride) may be used for clarification purpose. Due to vigorous boiling, the syrup thickens and the process is continued till a semi-solid mass is formed (when the mass leaves the sides of the pan without coating it). Constant stirring is carried out with the help of a wooden handspade to avoid charring/ sticking on the heating surface. The contents are turned into a circular plate. During the cooling process, the stirring continues till the whole mass is transformed into small powdered granues (bura) that are removed continuously.

Chini (Refined Sugar): This crystalline sugar is either refined from crude raw sugar or processed from sugarcane or sugarbeet juice. Both these sources give identical sucrose with no chemical, physical or structural differences.

Technology: The first step in the industrial production of refined sugar is to extract juice from sugarcane using a series of roller presses. Thereafter, non-sugar impurities are removed by mechanical filtration, followed by limecarbon dioxide purification step. The juice is allowed to settle and then filtered to get purified juice. In some factories, this step involves limephosphoric acid floatation procedure. Further purification of the juice is achieved by treatment with activated charcoal and ion exchange reactors. This juice (12—15% total solids, 91—92% purity) is evaporated in multi-stage vacuum evaporators to get sugar concentrate containing 65—71% solids. Thereafter, crystallization of sugar is effected in vacuum pans under conditions of controlled temperature, pressure, density and viscosity. The resulting sugar crystals are separated from mother liquor by centrifugation. The semi-dry sugar is rinsed with water and dried with hot air in a rotating drum, cooled, classified on vibrating screens and packaged. The mother liquor goes through a series of crystallization steps to harvest maximum yield of premium quality sugar. The left-over liquor is a by product of sugar industry, called blackstrap molasses. The molasses are 38—15% purity, and 82—88% dry solids. Typically, high purity granulated sugar is 99.90—99.95% purity and 0.02—0.04% moisture.

The sweetness rating of refined sugar varies according to the crystalline form and size. It is related to the stereo-chemistry of the structural units in sugar. Table 1.5 lists various grades of refined sugar.

Table 1.5 : Grades of refined sugar and their physical characteristics.

Grade	Physical characteristics
Cube Sugar	Crystallized sugar cubes
Loaf Sugar	Crystallized in loaf shapes
Powdered Sugar	Coarsely powdered sugars
Finely Powdered Sugar	Very finely pulverized sugar
Confectioner's Sugar	Very finely pulverized sugar with added starch
Brown Sugar	Cane sugar with small percentage of molasses
Yellow Sugar	Cane sugar with traces of invert sugar and colouring matter

Table 1.6 : Quality requirements of refined sugar.

Characteristics	*Quality requirement*
Appearance	Crystalline, white, odourless and free from dirt and other extraneous matter
Colour in ICUMSA* units, max	50
Sucrose, per cent by weight, min	99. 8
Moisture, per cent by weight, max	0. 10.5
Reducing sugar, per cent by weight, min	0. 03
Specific conductivity (w/v) aqueous solution of 35°C, max	15. 0

*International Commission for Uniform Methods of Sugar Analysis (ICUMSA).

The quality requirements for sugar to be used in milk products and Indian sweetmeats are given in Table 1.6.

Storage: Dried refined sugar has about 0.2 per cent moisture. Even at this low level, there can be problems in its storage. It is usually conditioned to prevent its caking during long storage period. Conditioning is essentially a holding period of perhaps 24 hours in which any moisture released from the crystal can pass into the surrounding air and be blown away from the sugar. It is usually carried out in a silo. In some cases, dehumidified air is passed through the sugar in the silo.

Packaging: As per good manufacturing practices, refined sugar is packed in clean, sound and new At-will jute bags, lined preferably with polyethylene film. These bags are machine or hand-stitched. The net weight of the refined sugar in each bag is 100 kg. It is also packed in smaller consumer packs.

GRAINS

Chawal (Rice), Maida, Suji, Rava

Rice (Chawal): Rice *(Oryza sativa* L.) is the staple food of over half the world's population. In India, rice in all its forms is revered as a symbol of plenty, purity and fertility. When a Hindu bride steps over the threshold of her new home, she kicks a measure of rice into the house in an attempt to make as big a mess as possible. The bigger the spray, the more auspicious, as the rice is symbolic of the good fortune she brings to her new home. It is consumed as cooked, parboiled whole grain, puffed, roasted whole grain products, or in the form of flour. Rice is also used as an adjunct with milk for preparation of traditional Indian dairy products such as kheer, payasam, phirni and rice puddings.

Aromatic rice varieties such as Basmati, Muskan, Badsha and Bhog are classified (Table 1.7) on the basis of kernel dimension, with a premium in price for their aroma. However, the superior quality rice is seldom useful for producing traditional cereal-milk based dairy products. Generally, short, broken rice or rice flour is used in kheer or payasam or phirni.

Quality Characteristics: Market quality of rice depends upon the size, shape, degree of milling (whiteness), aroma, foreign matter and shelf-life. The cooking quality depends upon the amylose content, gelatinization, water intake, gel consistency and the texture of cooked rice grain. To assess the suitability of rice for use in kheer, payasam and phirni, different quality indicators may be employed. For various rice desserts and rice puddings like kheer, waxy milled rice may be the best because of its lower rate of retrogradation or hardening when cooked. High-amylose rice is not desired in such products. The soft sticky nature of low-amylose waxy rice serves the purpose.

The high-priced quality Basmati rice from Punjab in India is not preferred for kheer making because of its low gelatinous temperature (GT) of the strarch, high-amylose content and hard gel consistency. For industrial production of ricebased indigenous milk products, quick cooking rice varieties may be preferred. Parboiled brown rice may be made quick cooking by scouring about 1 per cent by weight of the pericarp to remove the outer water impervious layer.

Packaging: If normal climatic conditions allow the grain to dry during storage, it may be packaged in jute or sisal packs. If rice is transported to a more humid area, it may be necessary to pack it in polythene packs. Retail bags include heat-sealed polythene bags.

Table 1.7 : Systematic classification of rice and their length (L) and breadth (B) ratio.

Classifications	Specifications
Long Slender (L.S.)	Length ≥ 6 mm; Length/Breadth ratio (L/B) > 3
Short Slender (S.S.)	Length < 6 mm; L7B ≥ 3
Medium Slender (M.S.)	Length < 6 mm; L/B 2.5 to 3.0
Long Bold (L.B.)	Length ≥ 6 mm; L/B < 3.0
Short Bold (S.B.)	Length < 6 mm; L7B < 2.5

Maida and Suji or Rava (Wheat Flours): Wheat (Gehun) is classified into two types: hard and soft. In comparison to soft wheat, hard wheat has higher protein and gluten content, yielding strong flour for more elastic dough, which is better for bread-making. Strong elastic dough is obtained from flour containing over 12 per cent protein, essential for high leavened volume. In contrast, soft wheat is lower in protein and yields weaker flour that makes weak dough or batter.

Wheat flour is the most important cereal food and is the vital part of bread and bakery products. It is exceptionally rich in gluten, the essential protein.

Three basic types of wheat flour are: (a) whole meal flour consisting of the whole of the wheat grain obtained from milling or grinding of cleaned wheat; it is termed 100 per cent extraction flour (atta); (b) brown flour containing about 85 per cent of the cleaned wheat grain; and (c) white flour consisting of approximately 72-78 per cent of the cleaned wheat grain (maida).

Maida (Refined Wheat Flour): Maida is the fine, white, inner flour of wheat obtained either by selective grinding in a chakki, or by segregation using specific gravity principles during the milling of whole wheat. It is obtained by milling cleaned hard or soft wheat or blends thereof in a roller flour-mill and bolting. Maida comprises mainly the inner endosperm, with a large part of the bran and germ layers removed during milling. Maida is used for making bread, different types of biscuits, pastries and a number of other products. In India, its largest use is in home kitchens and in the preparation of the traditional Indian sweet gulabjamun.

Characteristics: Maida for use in indigenous milk products should have a characteristic taste and smell. It should be free from insect and fungus infestation, rodent contamination, dirt and other extraneous matter.

Microscopic appearance: This appearance can serve as an additional aid for checking the quality of maida. Micrograph of maida should show more small starch granules than large ones. The diameter of good quality maida granules varies between 5 and 50 μ.m.

Grades: Based on its gluten content, maida is grouped into three grades. The required gluten content in maida varies according to its usage. For making bread and biscuits of certain varieties, a minimum gluten content of 10 per cent is required. For cakes, pastries, Indian sweets and domestic preparations, the required gluten content is between 7 and 10 per cent. Table 1.8 lists the specifications of three grades of maida formulated by the Bureau of Indian Standards (IS: 10091-968).

Packaging: The packages used for packing 1,10,20 and 40 kg maida may be polyethylene bags or polyethylenelined jute bags. For maida above 65 kg, single A-twill oi B-twill jute bags are used, the mouth of the bag being machine or hand-stitched.

Suji or Rava (Semolina): Grits of wheat are in either coarse or fine form for different endusers. Its other names are suji, rava, semolina and cream of wheat. Semolina is used as an ingredient in many Indian sweet dishes including a variety of kheer. It is the coarsely ground endosperm

Table 1.8 : Indian standards for the three grades of maida.

Characteristics	Specifications		
	Low grade	Medium grade	High grade
Moisture, per cent by weight, max.	13.0	13.0	13.0
Total ash (on dry basis) per cent by weight, max.	0.70	0.70	1.0
Acid insoluble ash (on dry basis), per cent by weight, max.	0.05	0.05	0.05
Gluten (on dry basis), per cent by weight	7.0 to 8.0	Above 8.0 and up to 10.0	Above 10.0
Alcoholic acidity (as H_2SO_4) in 90 per cent alcohol, per cent by weight, max.	0.1	0.1	0.1

of wheat. It is generally made from hard, durum wheat, which facilitates a high yield of semolina with minimal production of flour. Semolina production process resembles that of maida. Purified semolina is uniformly sized by passage through a succession of sizing screens and graded accordingly.

Characteristics: Semolina is obtained from clean wheat. It has a characteristic taste and smell. It should be free from musty or other off-odours, insect or fungus infestation, rodent contamination, dirt and other extraneous matters. Its appearance, taste and odour can be judged by organoleptic tests. Table 1.9 lists Indian standards for semolina.

Table 1.9 : Indian standards for semolina (IS: 1010-1969)

Characteristics	Specifications
Moisture, % by weight, max.	13.5
Total ash (on dry basis), % weight, max.	1.0
Acid insoluble ash (on dry basis % by weight, max.	0.05
Gluten (on dry basis), % by weight, min.	6.0
Alcoholic acidity (as H_2SO_4) with 90% alcohol, % by weight, max.	0.1

Microscopic Appearance: When subjected to microscopic examination, the micrograph of semolina shows starch granules with characteristic appearance revealing concentric rings and more small granules than large ones.

Grading: In most parts of the country, the terms suji and rava are used as synonyms. In some parts, suji is available in two grades, differing only in particle size, viz.: (a) Large particle (LP); and (b) Small particle (SP).

Large Particle Grade: When tested by the method prescribed in IS: 1010-1968:

(a) All the material shall pass through a sieve of silk or nylon bolting cloth 20 GG (aperture 1.16 mm) or 1.18 mm IS sieve;

(b) Not less than 90 per cent of the material shall be retained on a sieve of silk or nylon bolting cloth 30 GG (aperture 0.73 mm) or 710 micron IS Sieve; and

(c) Not less than 98 per cent of the material shall be retained on a sieve of silk or nylon bolting cloth 70 GG (aperture 0.24 mm) or 250 micron IS sieve.

Small Particle Grade: When tested by the method prescribed in Appendix A of IS 1010-1968 :

(a) All the material shall pass through a sieve of silk or nylon bolting cloth 20 GG (aperture 1.16 mm) or 1.18 mm IS sieve;

(b) Not more than 10 per cent of the material shall be retained on a sieve of silk or nylon bolting cloth 30 GG (aperture 0.73 mm) or 710 micron IS sieve; and

(c) Not less than 98 per cent of the material shall be retained on a sieve of silk or nylon bolting cloth 70 GG (aperture 0.24 mm) or 250 micron IS sieve.

Packaging: Suji should be packed in polyethylene bags or polyethylenelined jute bags or any other suitable material, in 1,2,10,20,40,65,75 or 90 kg packages. For packages above 65 kg, packing material should preferably be A-twill or B-twill jute bags or DW-flour bags conforming to IS: 1943-1964, IS: 2566-1965 and IS: 3984-1967, respectively.

Storage: Recommended conditions for storage of semolina are same as for maida.

DRY FRUITS AND OTHER NUTS

Badam, Kaju, Copra, Pista, Khaskhas, Akhrot, Kishmish

Almonds (Badam): They find extensive use in the Indian epicurean cuisine in various forms, ground with honey or sugar and fashioned into confections (badam ki burfi, badam milk, badam ki jali); beaten after grinding, into sweetened milk (badam kheer); as a flavourant for tea, or for dressing halwa and the like. Almonds are valued both for their nutritive value and for providing a typical flavour and richness to food products. They are mostly used as a minor ingredient to bring desirable aroma, flavour, crispness, tenderness, rich colour to servings or garnish them.

Description: Despite the availability of only a few cultivars, almonds are available in many sizes, shapes and forms. Green almonds are oval in shape, with a downy succulent cover enclosing a hard shell, in which the edible kernel is borne. In India, no attempts have been made to categorize or standardize green almonds because of their scanty and unorganized production. In most almondgrowing nations, nuts are classified in terms of the size of kernel, type of shell and processing treatments. Table 1.10 lists the categories of cut almonds as graded by the US Grower Exchange.

Table 1.10 : US Grower Exchange's grades of cut almonds.

Grades	Characteristics
Sliced natural unblanched	Cubed, unblanched, cut cross-wise
Sliced blanched	Steel cut, medium unblanched
Slivered blanched	Steel cut, fine unblanched
Broken blanched	Meal unblanched
Split blanched	Diced, roasted, buttered unblanched
Halves, unblanched	Cut length-wise

Quality Characteristics: Important appearance characteristics for almonds marketed in the shell include shell integrity, suture opening and kernel colour. Kernel defects include damage from insects, mould growth and mechanical injury, gum, callus growth, shrivelling and doubling. These defects are generally encountered if proper handling and transportation guidelines have not been followed. Quality criteria, used for grading, involve freedom from dust particles and other foreign materials and uniformity of shape and colour.

Textural attributes of firmness and crispness are governed by moisture content in nuts. Roasting not only improves flavour of nuts but makes them crisper than the raw ones. Flavour depends on sweetness, oiliness, intensity of almond flavour, and absence of off-flavour, resulting from rancidity, staleness or other causes. Wet conditions and higher temperature encountered during temporary storage may sometimes cause a problem in roasted nuts known as "concealed damage", manifested by internal darkening and poor flavour.

Safety steps relate primarily to counter the potential of almond contamination with mycotoxins, especially aflatoxin produced by the fungus *Aspergillus flavus.* Proper pre and post-harvest management is required to check this contamination. For effective marketing, infected nuts are removed from the lot. Pesticide residues (used to control "Navelorange worm", *Any elois trasitella)* can be reduced by adopting integrated pest management control.

Shelf Life: Almonds have a higher shelf-life than other nuts. This is attributable to their low moisture and the presence of relatively low levels of polyunsaturated fatty acids. Besides, the protective tocopherol present in almonds acts as an anti-oxidant and enhances their oxidative stability. The USFDA guidelines for tree nuts define 'a safe moisture level' (i.e.

the moisture content which will not support mould growth) as a water activity level not exceeding 0.70 at 25°C. This is equal to moisture content of 7 per cent. The optimum range for unroasted almonds is 4—6 per cent moisture. A temperature range between 0°C and 5°C has been recommended for almonds storage—the lower temperature allowing longer shelf-life.

The storage life of raw almonds can be extended up to 2 years under low-oxygen atmosphere at 0°C. Low-oxygen (05 per cent) atmosphere enhances the keeping [quality and flavour, delays rancidity and checks the insects effect on the stored product.

Propylene oxide, the only sterilizing agent approved for nuts, is generally effective against bacteria, but less effective against moulds and yeasts. Propyleneoxide treated almonds are recommended for incorporation into high-moisture foods like Indian milk products or in other microbially sensitive applications.

Nutritive Value: The nuts contain low levels of saturated fatty acids. They contain predominantly unsaturated fatty acids that are considered desirable for cardiovascular health. Studies have shown that almond diets significantly reduced total serum cholesterol by 8 to 12 per cent and LDL (bad) cholesterol by 9 to 15 per cent. People eating an ounce or more of nuts five or more times a week had significantly lower risks of heart attacks and heart disease, as compared to those who did not consume any nuts or consumed them less often. This protective effect is attributed to the vitamin E, unsaturated fatty acids and phytosterol content of the nuts. The proximate nutritive composition of some nuts is given in Table 1.11 while values of almond nutrients is presented in Table 1.12.

Applications: Almonds find application in a wide variety of foods including sweets, health foods, baked foods, cereals, ice cream, dry mixes, garnishes for food entrees and packaged snacks. It is directly used as a whole nut, or chopped, diced, sliced, split, halved, slivered or cube cut. Its powder, paste and oil are also used.

The largest usage category is in confectioneries. Almonds enhance their flavour and acceptability by lowering their sweetness, adding crunch, enhancing the nutritive value and adding sales appeal. In Indian dairy products, almonds have been used since ancient times as a flavouring and nutritional agent.

Table1.11 : Nutritive value of one ounce (28.4 g) of selected nuts.

Nuts	Calories	Total fat (g)	Saturated fat (g)	Fibre (g)	Phytosterols (g)
Almonds	160	14	1	3	34
Cashews	160	13	3	1	45
Pine nuts	160	14	2	1	40
Pistachio	160	13	2	3	60
Walnuts	180	18	1.5	2	20

Source: United States Department of Agriculture Nutrient Base for Standard Reference, Release 13, 1999.

Table 1.12 : Nutritive value of almonds.

Components	Concentration
Moisture (%)	4.4
Protein (%)	19.9
Fat (%)	52.2
Carbohydrate (%)	20.4
Sugar (%)	4.4
Fibre (%)	2.7
Ash (%)	3.0
Fatty acids:	
Saturated (%)	4.9
Monosaturated (%)	33.9
Polyunsaturated (%)	11.0
Vitamin A (IU)	Nil
Thiamin (mg)	0.2
Riboflavin (mg)	0.8
Nicotinic acid (mg)	3.4
Pantothenic acid (mg)	0.5
Vitamin C (mg)	0.6
Calcium (mg)	266
Phosphorus (mg)	520
Iron (mg)	3.7
Potassium (mg)	732
Magnesium (mg)	296

Source: United States Department of Agriculture Nutrient Base for Standard Reference, Release 13, 1999.

In several traditional indigenous beverages, almonds constitute a prominent ingredient such as in 'almond milk' and *thandai.* These are mainly consumed for their cooling and health-promoting qualities. Similarly, almond burfi, made from almond paste, sugar and khoa, is a connoisseur's delight. It is served on special occasions. Broken or slivered nuts are used mainly to garnish dairy products like kheer, beverages, sweets and frozen desserts. The powdered form of almonds can be utilized in burfi mix and thandai mix.

Almond Oil: Both sweet and bitter almonds varieties are used for the extraction of oil. The oil is strawcoloured, nearly odourless and of non-drying type. The essential oil of almonds is obtained from bitter almonds. It is colourless and owes its characteristic flavour to benzaldehyde. It also contains hydrocyanic acid that has to be removed before flavouring. The resulting oil is called as the oil of bitter almond. This oil is high in unsaturated fatty acids and very susceptible to oxidative changes. Almond oil has considerable potential as a flavouring component in certain dairy products. However, high cost, bitterness and poor stability during processing and storage limit its application in Indian dairy products.

Kaju (Cashew): These are kernels of dry seeds of *Anacardium occidentale,* curved in shape of the letter 'C. The unprocessed nut tastes starchy with the characteristic flavour of cashew. It is dried and sometimes smoked to give a shelf-life of six to seven months when kept dry. Cashew seeds are picked when fully ripe or after falling to the ground. Cashew kernels are extracted from cashew nuts by roasting, shelling and peeling. Extracted kernels are then graded. Ninety five per cent of India's total output of cashew kernels is exported to USA, Western Europe and Australia. Their grade characteristics according to IS: 7750-1975, are presented in Table 1.13.

Quality Characteristics: The cashew kernels should be kept reasonably dry. These may be either scorched or unscorched and in the form of whole kernels or pieces. The kernels should be free from insects (living, dead or fragments), moulds and rodent contamination. Extraneous matter such as stone, dirt or any other foreign matter should be absent in food-quality kernels.

Preservation: The process of drying removes water from the kernels thereby inhibiting the microbial growth. The smoking process is quicker at higher temperatures leading to destruction of some enzymes and contaminants.

Packaging and Storage: Cashew nuts are packed in polythene or sold loose from large boxes or bags. The containers should be new, clean, dry and lea-proof. The product keeps well for several months if securely sealed/packed in air-tight and moisture-proof bags in atmospheric

Table 1.13 : Grade designations, trade names and characteristics of cashew kernels.

Grade Designation	Number of kernels Per kg	Per lb	Characteristics
A-1. Cashew Kernels (whole)			
W180	265 to 395	120 to 180	Cashew kernels should have the characteristic shape, should be white, paie ivory or light ash in colour; reasonably dry and free from damaged kernels and black or brown spots. They should be completely free from rancid kernels. The kernels should be completely free from testa.
W210	440 to 465	200 to 210	
W240	485 to 530	220 to 240	
W280	575 to 620	260 to 280	
W320	660 to 705	300 to 320	
W400	770 to 880	350 to 400	
W450	880 to 990	400 to 450	
W500	990 to 1100	450 to 500	

Grade designation	Trade name	Blemish	Characteristics
A-2. Scorched Cashew Kernels (whole)			
SW	Scorched wholes		Cashew kernels should have the characteristic shape, should be reasonably dry, free from damaged kernels, black spots and testa. They should be completely free from rancid kernels. The kernels may be light brown, light ivory, light ash or deep ivory in colour due to scorching as a result of overheating.
A-3. Dessert Cashew Kernels (whole)			
SSW	Scorched wholes second or scorched wholes IA	Slightly shrivelled kernels	Cashew kernels should have the characteristic shape, should be reasonably dry and free from testa. Slightly scorched kernels and kernels with slight speckling and discolouration are permitted. They should be completely free from rancid kernels. The kernels may also be immature. The kernels may be light brown, light blue or light ivory in colour due to scorching.

Grade designation	Trade name	Blemish	Characteristics
DW	Dessert wholes		Cashew kernels should have the characteristic shape, should be reasonably dry and free from testa. Scorched, discoloured, speckled and shrivelled kernels permitted. Rancid kernels not permitted. The kernels may show deep black spots.
A-4. Cashew Kernels (white pieces)			
B	Butts	Kernels broken cross-wise and naturally attached	Cashew kernels should be white, pale ivory or light ash in colour; reasonably dry and free from damaged kernels and black spots. They should be completely free from rancid kernels. The pieces should be completely free from testa.
S	Splits	Kernels split naturally length-wise	-do-
LWP	Large white pieces	Kernels broken into more than two pieces and not passing through a 4.75 mm IS Sieve *Note: Equivalent to 4 mesh ASTM or 16 SWG sieves.*	-do-
SWP	Small white pieces	Broken kernels smaller than those described as LWP but not passing through a 2.80 mm IS Sieve (see IS: 460-1962) *Note: Equivalent to 10 mesh BS or 24 SWG sieves.*	Cashew kernels should be white, pale ivory or light ash in colour and should be reasonably dry and free from damaged kernels and black spots. They should be completely free from rancid kernels. The pieces should be completely free from testa.
BB	Baby bits	Plomules and broken kernels smaller than those described as SWP but not passing through a 1.70 mm IS Sieve (see IS: 460-1962) *Note: Equivalent to 10 mesh BS or 24 SWG sieves.*	-do-

Note: Broken kernels or kernels of the next lower grade, if any, should not together exceed 5 per cent by weight at the time of packing.

conditions, provided that the processed nuts are low in moisture (lower than 12%). They should be stored in a cool dry place.

Copra (Dried Coconut Kernel): Coconut (Narial) is called Sriphala, the blessed fruit. The dehusked coconut is used as a sacred symbol in Hindu rituals. It is offered to guests and used in wedding ceremonies. Auspicious occasions often begin with the breaking of the coconut and for offering to Gods. Gifts are given with a coconut to symbolise respect.

The coconut is one of the defining flavours of South Indian cuisine. The fresh tender coconut yields water, a delicious, natural refreshing drink. Coconut milk is a hand extract of fresh kernel gratings with hot water. It is also used in various dishes, including for making chutney, garnish, or added to various curries, appams or uttappams (rice-flour and coconut milk pan-cakes), dais and rice dishes.

Copra (dried coconut kernel) is pressed and made into coconut oil, a popular cooking medium in Kerala, as well as used as hair oil and as a base in medicated pastes and oils. Shavings of copra form a food ingredient to make confections like laddus that have a pleasant chewiness. They are also now widely used in biscuits, cakes, sweets and a variety of indigenous dairy products.

Description: Copra is made by drying shredded pieces of pared kernel of fully mature fresh coconut. Nuts are stored for three to four weeks before being dehusked in the field and carried to the factory. The brown testa are removed by hand. Kernels are then washed and sterilized to avoid risk of Salmonella contamination. After sterilization, disintegrators reduce them to a wet meal or cutters produce fancy cuts such as threads or chips. Drying is done by indirect drier at 75—80°C or by direct firing at 120°C.

Quality Characteristics: Copra should be pure, white and crisp with a fresh natural taste of coconut, free from rancidity. It should not show fat sweating and should be free from cheesy, smoky, musty or other objectionable odours, fungus and insect infestation. Desiccated coconut should not contain any coconut shell, testa, starch, added sugar, papaya stem tissues or other foreign material and added colouring or flavouring agents. The presence of more than 6-7 per cent sucrose is an indication that sugar has been added.

Protein content of dried coconut is about 6 per cent, unavailable carbohydrate content about 18 per cent, crude fibre about 4 per cent, along with some mineral contents. To be of superior quality, copra should conform to the following specifications:

Characteristics	Specifications
Moisture, % by mass	0.3
Fat, % by mass	65
Fat acidity, as % lauric acid	0.3

Microbiological Quality: The desiccated coconut should be processed in premises, maintained under hygienic conditions. The coliform count of desiccated coconut should not exceed 10 CFU/g. It should be free of Salmonella.

Grades: On the basis of particle size, dried coconut is classified into three grades according to IS: 966-1975 (Table 1.14).

Table 1.14 Grading of desiccated coconut according to BIS standards

Grade	Particle Size	Percentage
I	425 to 850 microns	70—75
II	250 to 425 microns	25—30
	425 to 850 microns	30—35
III	2.36 to 4.00 mm	75
	1.18 to 2.36 mm	25

Packaging and Storage: Desiccated coconut should be packed in suitable moistureproof and grease-proof containers, e.g. low density polyethylene bags, sealed at both ends and placed in aluminum foillined plywood boxes to protect it from moisture, fat seepage and ultraviolet rays.

Pistachio (Pista): A delicacy, pistachio figures prominently among the nuts due to its characteristic flavour and nutritive value. It is consumed as roasted or salted nut. It is also used in appreciable amounts in the manufacture of milk-based sweets and frozen desserts. Pista-kulfi, a traditional Indian frozen dessert, delights the palate of consumers.

Pistachio grows in grape-like clusters, encased in an outer skin called hull, which turns rosy when the nuts are ripe and ready to harvest. The nuts appear red from outside but green inside. The white fruits are 1.5 to 2 cm (0.6 to 0.8 inch) long and tend to split at one side without discharging the nut, which is a greenish kernel enclosed in a thin, tightly adhering and reddish skin. The single, solid kernels have a pleasing mild resinous flavour.

Processing: For industrial processing, pistachio is mechanically shaken from the tree on to a catching frame, without touching the ground.

They are immediately transported to the processing plant where they are hulled, washed, dried and sorted. The nuts must be processed within 8—12 hours after harvesting. Otherwise, tannin in rosy hulls will stain the ivory-hued shells. Pistachio is dried from an initial moisture content of about 3—5 to 5—6 per cent. Forced air-drying is carried out at 35—37.5°C. Later, the nuts are roasted and salted. A small portion of the harvest may be dyed red by dipping in synthetic colouring solutions of FD and C Red 40 for those consumers who prefer colourful nuts. The nuts are placed in a tumbler and the dye is atomized onto them to ensure an even coating. Electric-eye sorters have the capability of removing pistachio nuts with blemishes and of colour sorting them as well.

Regulatory status: There are no regulations for pistachio in India. However, as per USDA standards for shelled 'pistachio' to be labelled as 'whole' kernels, 80 per cent of their weight must consist of three quarters kernel. Whole and broken kernels must contain 40 per cent whole kernels.

In shell pistachios are graded by weight (number of nuts per ounce = 28.4 gms):

Size	***Number of nuts***
Extra large 19 or less	
Large	20—25
Medium	26—30
Small	31 or more

The Codex committee on additives and contaminants has laid down maximum residual limits of aflatoxin B_1 in pistachio.

Shelf Life: Nuts require proper storage, both prior to manufacture and when used in processed foods. The high fat content (53%) makes the kernel susceptible to odour absorption and rancidity. Storage of nuts in dark, cool, dry areas under carbon dioxide and inside protective containers enhances their shelf Life. At water activity of 0.50.6, the nuts have a two year shelf-life.

Another problem associated with improper storage of nuts is aflatoxin. The predominant flora on stored pistachio nuts is *Aspergillus, Penicillium, Cladosporium* and *Rhizopus*. Growth *of A.flavus* occurs mainly on the shell surface. Growth of fungi and insect infestation cause shell discolouration, which is used as criteria for grading of nuts.

Nutritive Value: Pistachio contains 20 per cent protein, 53 per cent fat, 15.1 per cent sugar, 6.1 per cent moisture, 3.1 per cent fibre and 3.1

per cent ash. It also has most of the vitamins like vitamin A, B_1 and B_2 are in appreciable quantity. One hundred grams of pistachio generate 630 calories. The fatty acid composition of pistachio nut is presented in Table 1.15.

Application: Consumers once viewed pistachio only as an upscale nut for snacking due to its short supply and high prices, but this is no longer the case. About 90 per cent of all pistachios are salted and roasted in shell for consumption as snacks. This trend has changed dramatically, as consumers have discovered that the pistachios' rich buttery flavour and vivid green colour provide exceptional flavour, texture and colour to many food products. Pistachio butter's high protein content allows it to be used as a natural thickener, emulsifier and binder. As a heavy cream replacer, it can help reduce saturated fats and eliminate cholesterol in confections. Kernels can be used in whole, dried, sliced and slivered forms. The choice of size depends primarily on the application.

Table 1.15 : Fatty acid composition of pistachio nut.

Fatty Acids	Percentage
Palmitic acid	8.2
Myristic acid	0.6
Stearic acid	1.6
Oleic acid	69.0
Linoleic acid	19.8
Unsaponifiable matter	0.8

Khaskhas (Poppy Seeds): It is a common spice in Indian kitchens and also converted with jaggery syrup into laddus. Its origin is the small black seeds of poppy, obtained from the opium plant, *Papaver somniferutn.* Poppy seeds, however, have no narcotic properties because the fluid in the bud that becomes opium is present only before the seeds are fully formed. In India, var. album of poppy with white seeds has been cultivated for many years for production of seeds. Poppy seeds have found application in sweets, confectionaries and curries. Best poppy seeds are obtained if the capsules (fruiting body) have not been incised for the extraction of opium. In Europe, var. nigrum, which has slate to blue coloured seeds and known as "Maw seeds", is exclusively cultivated for this purpose.

Poppy seeds are tiny, about 1 mm in length, kidney shaped and greyish blue to dark blue in colour. Due to their small size, a thousand poppy seeds weigh just 0.25—0.5 grams. They possess a faint nut-like aroma and a mild, nutty taste especially popular in breads and other baked goods.

Application: Poppy seeds are utilized as food and as a source of oil. They are considered nutritive and are used in breads, curries, sweets and confectioneries. They are also used as thickening agent in curries and milk based cereal desserts. Khaskhas kheer is a popular dish of South India. The drying oil, obtained by cold expression of poppy seeds, is a colourless to pale-yellow liquid. The cold, white poppy seed oil is used in foods.

Akhrot (Walnuts): One of the oldest tree foods known to man, they have been in use since 7000 BC. Considered as the food for gods in the early days of the Roman Empire, walnut was named *Juglans regia* in honour of God Jupiter. It is indigenous to the region from Persia to Kashmir. Its trees occupy more land in Kashmir than any other fruits except apple. They are also grown in small quantities in other Himalayan States. The nuts keep for months at ambient temperatures and are not subjected to bruising.

Walnuts are harvested from late August to November. After harvesting they are pulled, washed, mechanically dehydrated and separated by size and colour. Once purchased, they should be kept under refrigeration (0—4°C and 65% relative humidity) to maintain their freshness.

Quality characteristics: Walnuts are available in two forms:

Inshell Walnuts: Inshell walnuts are creamish brown in colour, clear and dry, containing the nut inside the shell. The grade designations and quality characteristics for inshell walnuts are given in Table 2.3.16.

Shelled Walnuts: Shelled walnuts are obtained by shelling selected walnuts. The kernels are dry and white, cream or brown in colour. Good quality walnut kernels should possess the characteristic taste and be free from foreign taste including rancidity and mustiness. Walnuts in shell or their kernels should be free from insects (living, dead or fragments) and rodent contamination. The extent of extraneous matter like wood splinters; husk, dirt, walnut meal, shell pieces and any other foreign matter should not exceed 0.25 per cent by weight.

Applications: Walnuts are a good source of several vitamins including thiamin, vitamin B and folacin. They are naturally low in sodium and contribute substantial amounts of dietary fibre. They contain no cholesterol and are high in unsaturated fats. Walnuts are used in many indigenous dairy products. They add a slightly bitter taste that contrasts well with the sweetness of dairy products. They also make excellent toppings by giving a unique crunch and the desired mouthful to the consumers.

Kishmish (Raisins): The word 'raisin' comes from the French word 'raisin sec' meaning dry grape. In the present context, raisin refers only to the 'seedless dry grape'. Produced by natural shade drying of grapes, raisins are very sweet, small, round, plump and light brown in colour with a coat of natural bloom. India used to import raisins from Afghanistan, Iran and Australia, but is virtually self-sufficient now. Green-coloured raisins fetch a premium price in India, since it is difficult to produce raisins of Afghanistan under Indian climate. However, the Indian market does accept raisins that are yellow in colour, sweet and fleshy. They are used to dress such dairy delicacies like kheer, halwa, kesari-bath and the like.

In India, though grapes are primarily used for fresh consumption, in recent years the production of raisins is gaining popularity. India produces 12,000 tonnes of raisins annually, utilizing 40 per cent of seedless grapes produced in the country. Raisins are extensively used in India in the preparation of various sweets and bakery products, whereas lexiors (monakka, dry seeded grapes) are used in Ayurvedic medicines.

Quality of raisins is determined to a great extent by the variety and composition of grapes used, and maturity or stage of harvest. Therefore, apart from being seedless, the variety should have very high solids content, preferably greater than 20—22° Brix, moderate to low acidity; thin skin, crisp, fleshy and small in size, with round to oval shape. It is desirable to schedule the harvesting 12—15 days later than normal. This delay may increase solid content of berries by 1.73 to 2.05° Brix and reduce the acidity.

The raisins for international trade are made mainly from three varieties, viz., 'Thompson seedless', 'Black Corinth' and 'Muscat of Alexandra'. Raisins prepared from the Indian 'Sundekhani' variety of grapes compare favourably with imported raisins.

Processing: Raisin production involves the following steps:

Sulphur Fumigation: Sulphur fumigation is done before drying of grapes to give a golden yellow colour to raisins and protect them during storage. Sulphur dioxide is a selective antiseptic and temporary preservative, since it is easily oxidized to sulphate. Sulphur dioxide is required to prevent fermentation than to inhibit growth. *Drying and*

Table 1.16 : Grade designations and quality characteristics for inshell walnuts.

Grade Designation	Minimum Size	Quality Characteristics	Tolerance Limits
Indian Super Special	32 mm	(a) The walnuts should be of the current year crop only. (b) They should be free from live pests, grubs, and eggs. (c) They should be well developed, well washed or bleached, should present a clean and attractive appearance and should have bright shells. The nuts should be reasonably dry so that the loss in weight should not exceed one per cent on arrival at destination. (d) They should give over 90% good cracking and yield edible kernels of agreeable taste and aroma. *(e) Invisible or internal defects:* The lot should be fairly free from nuts having invisible defects like kernel darkening, oil seepage or bleeding, mould or fungus attack, rancidity, shrivelling and insect pest infestation and powdering (meal formation). The lot should not contain stony (hard or fragmented) or empty nuts. (f) *Visible or superficial defects:* The lot should be fairly free from nuts showing visible defects like undersized, partially developed or deformed nuts, damaged or cracked shell, splits or perforations, oil stains, sunburns or blight marks, residue of chemical bleaches, and the like. The lot should be clean, well graded and fairly free from foreign matter like cobwebs, shell grits, hull remains, rodent excreta and human hair.	— — — — Invisible or internal defects: 10%, stony nuts (hard or fragmented exceeding 2%.
India Special	30 mm		-do-
India I	26 mm		-do-
India B	24 mm		-do-
XGrade*	24 mm		-do-

Note: All percentages for calculating tolerance should be on the basis of count.

* 'X' Grade as per contract for grade designations and qualities not covered above.

Postdrying processes: The drying of grapes is carried out till the moisture content of around 15 per cent is reached in raisins. Raisins used in bakery and cereal products are often treated with coatings to prevent excessive drying and hardening. The fruit dried to around 15 per cent moisture are separated from cluster stems, washed in lukewarm water to remove the dust, pesticide residues and excess of chemicals which may be present on the surface. Thereafter, the fruit is allowed to dry in a well ventilated/aerated place. Further, these raisins are put in a big air-tight container and left for three-four weeks for what is known as curing or equalization of moisture. Depending upon the total solid level of grapes used and final moisture content of raisins, 20—35 per cent of yield is obtained. Higher the total solids, more will be the yield and better the quality of raisins.

Packaging and Storage: The cured raisins are packed in 15—400 gauge polythene bags, placed in small-corrugated boxes and stored. Sulphur dioxide is better retained in glass jars or plastic bags than in cardboard or paper bags. Storage at low temperature is the best method to retain the golden yellow colour as well as organoleptic quality. Zero energy cool chambers increase the shelf-life of raisins to nine months. In general, a cold chamber maintained at 12—15°C, with maximum humidity is recommended for storing raisins.

FLAVOURINGS AND COLOURINGS

Chhoti Elaichi (Cardamom), Gulab Jal (Rose Essence), Kesar (Saffron), Cocoa

Chhoti Elaichi (Cardamom): India is the world's largest producer of cardamom, a spice which originated in the country's southern region. It is one of the important commodities exported from India. Cardamom is used in most of the indigenous milk products like kheer, payasam, phirni, burfi, peda, gulabjamun, sandesh, shrikhand, etc., to impart flavour and enrich taste. Its substitute is the large Bengal cardamom, badi-elaichi, from *Ammomum aromaticum,* grown in Bengal and Assam. Cardamom is the nearly ripe fruit of a large-leaved perennial plant, *Elettaria cardamomum* (chhoti elaichi) in the form of capsules that have been dried.

The colour of cardamom capsule ranges from light green to brown, cream and white. The capsules are globular in size, three-cornered and with ribbed appearance. The capsules are 1—2 cm long, and contain 15—20 brownish black seeds. Good quality capsules should be well formed containing robust cardamom seeds. These seeds enhance the sweet aromatic flavour of cardamom. The cardamom seed capsules may also be decorticated and the separated seeds packed for trade purpose.

Characteristics: To enhance the quality of indigenous dairy products, cardamom should have the following characteristics :

(a) *Physical Characteristics:* The taste and aroma or flavour of cardamom should be original and fresh, free from foreign taste and aroma or flavour, including rancidity and mustiness. Its capsules and seeds should be free from visible moulds and insect infestation. The percentage of different types of abnormal capsules/seeds should be as follows:

- *Empty and Malformed Capsules:* The proportion of empty capsules (without seeds) or malformed capsules (scantily filled with seeds) should not be more than 5 per cent (tested by opening 100 capsules).
- *Immature and Shrivelled Capsules:* Their proportion should not exceed 7 per cent by mass.
- *Blacks and Splits:* Capsules having blackish to black colour and open at corners for more than half the length should not be more than 15 per cent by count (tested by counting 100 capsules).
- Light seeds: Seeds brown or red in colour, broken or immature and shrivelled should not exceed 5 per cent by mass.

(b) *Extraneous Matter:* In capsules and seeds, it (including stalk bits) should not exceed 5 and 2 per cent by mass, respectively.

Grading: There are 25 grades of cardamom with capsules based on colour, clipping, size mass, bleaching or otherwise, extraneous matter and place of origin (Table 1.17). Apart from the large Bengal cardamom (badi-elaichi), three cardamom types are at present recognized in the trade: the inferior Sri Lankan, the pale green and more delicate Mysore, and the larger and more robust Alleppey green (now grown in Kerala, but originally derived from Mysore).

Packaging: Cardamom capsules or seeds are usually packed in clean, sound and dry tinplate containers or wooden cases suitably lined with polyethylene or water-proof paper or kraft paper or in new jute bags lined with polyethylene.

Table 1.17 : Grade designations of cardamom with capsules and their requirements.

Grade designation	Trade name	Extraneous matter, per cent mass max.	Empty and malformed capsules, per cent count max.	Unclipped capsules per cent count max.	Immature and shrivelled capsules per cent weight max.	Blacks and splits, per cent count max.	Size (dia of holes in mm of the sieve on which retained)	Mass in g/1 min.	Colour	Characteristics
Alleppey green AGEB	Cardamom extra bold	Nil	2.0	Nil	2.0	Nil	7.0	435	Deep green, green or light green	Kiln dried; 3-cornered and having a ribbed appearance
AGB	Cardamom bold	Nil	2.0	Nil	2.0	Nil	6.0	415		
AGS	Cardamom superior	Nil	3.0	Nil	5.0	Nil	5.0	385		
AGS1	Shipment green 1	Nil	5.0	Nil	7.0	10.00	4.0	350		
AGS2	Shipment green 2	Nil	5.0	Nil	7.0	12.0	4.0	320		
AGL	Light Coorg green	Nil	—	Nil	—	15.0	3.5	260		
CGEB	Extra bold	Nil	Nil	Nil	Nil	Nil	8.0	450	Golden to light creamy	
CGB	Bold	Nil	2.0	Nil	3.0	Nil	7.5	435	Creamy light greenish to greenish, or brownish to brown	Global shape, skin ribbed or smooth; the pedicels separated
CG1	Superior	Nil	3.0	Nil	3.0	Nil	7.5	435		
CG2	Coorg green or motta green	Nil	5.0	3.0	7.0	Nil	6.0	385		
CG3	Shipment	Nil	5.0	5.0	7.0	10.0	5.0	350		
CG4	Light	Nil	—	—	—	15.0	3.5	280		
Bleached or half bleached										
BL-1	Nil	Nil	Nil	Nil	Nil	Nil	8.5	340		
BL-2	Nil	Nil	Nil	Nil	Nil	Nil	7.0	340		
BL-3	Nil	Nil	Nil	Nil	Nil	Nil	5.0	300		
Bleachable white										
BW1	Mysore/Mangalore bleachable cardamom. Clipped	Nil	1.0	Nil	Nil	Nil	7.0	460		

Gulab Jal (Rose Essence): Among all the floral derivatives, rose is undoubtedly the most used in a wide range of flavour formulations. Rose with its intensely scented flowers has always attracted the imagination of chefs. The use of rose plants is found in old recipes for sauces and other delicacies. This is also true for some classic liquor and sweet cordial formulations and rose flavoured sherbets. In India, the application of rose essence in traditional culinary preparations was introduced by the Mughals.

Rose essence is traditionally obtained from the petals of rose flowers. Two rose varieties, *Rosa damascena* and *Rosa centifolia,* are most frequently used for this purpose. Rose derivatives include concrete, absolute, essential oil (otto of rose) and cohobating waters. These are different forms of rose essence. The absolute is used in flavour work, while the distilled essential oil is more suitable for use in perfumery. Sometimes rose water is used to dissolve the soluble and essential oil-based flavours.

Rose water or gulab jal, the most favoured form of rose essence among Indian sweets makers, is a clear liquid, distilled from fresh rose petals. It is a flavouring that can be subtle, when used lightly or soapy when added in larger quantities. Rose water is considered as a by product of the distillation process. In Morocco and France, the two big producers of rose flavours, rose oil is obtained by distillation. However, solvent extraction from the flower petals of *Rosa centifolia* yields a better quality product.

Chemical Composition: Main components of rose flavour derivatives include linalool, (β–phenethyl alcohol, C-citronellal, nerol, geraniol, aldehydes, esters and stearo phem (paraffin). The choice of rose derivatives for flavour application is determined by the proportion of (βphenethyl alcohol, a water-soluble component. This component is generally present in large quantities in the extracts, but almost absent in distillates and can, therefore, have a significant effect on the resulting aroma.

Imitation Rose Flavours: Rose flavour is successfully employed in the formulation of compounded flavours, such as sour cherry, mango, raspberry, sweet cherry, strawberry, tutti-frutti and pistachio. Synthetic rose flavour may also be developed. However, flavour substitute for true rose must contain only those constituents of rose absolute which have a pleasing flavour. Typical composition of rose flavours is given in Table 1.18.

Table 1.18 : Typical composition of imitation rose flavours.

Ingredients	Parts by weight
Geraniol	4.0
β–Phenethyl alcohol	3.0
Linalool	1.25
Rhodinol	1.25
Citronollol	0.5
Aldehyde µg	0.05
Citral	0.04

Table 1.19 : Industrial uses of rose derivatives in processed food products.

ppm

Product/derivative	Rose oil	Rose absolute	Rose water
Baked goods	1.02	1.86	228
Frozen dairy	0.89	1.67	155
Pudding (milk)	0.98	1.47	50

Application: Rose derivatives impart a deep warm rich rose fragrance with a slightly bitter sharp flavour at higher concentrations. Some uses of rose derivatives in processed food products are listed in Table 1.19. Pleasant aroma can be obtained by dilution with water. In Indian traditional sweets, rose water is mainly used for flavouring purpose, especially in kheer, gulabjamun, rasogolla, milk-based beverages and sherbets.

Kesar (Saffron): Saffron (Kesar) evokes images of wealth and rarity unparalleled in the culinary lexicon. Spain and India are the only major producers of this flavoursome, fragile spice. Saffron and zafaran of Persia is acutally the gently dried stigma of the nargis (narcissus) flowers, *Crocus sativus.* Saffron is probably native to Greece, being recorded in the 4th century BC. Saffron cultivation in Kashmir dates back to 550 AD. It has lately been introduced in Himachal Pradesh as well as in Kumaon and Uttaranchal with a relatively higher yield. The plant flowers for a couple of weeks in October, when the blossoms are plucked at dawn before the heat can wilt them, and then the delicate stigmas are dried.

Saffron is widely used in savoury and sweet dishes. Its powerful fragrance and orange colour are prized in Indian cuisine among the wealthy. Even a couple of stamens, soaked in warm water or milk, are sufficient to infuse the dish with colour and a rich, fragrant flavour to milk delicacies like kheer, kulfi and shrikhand. It takes more than 1,500 hand-plucked stigmas to yield just one grain of saffron. It makes for a wonderful gift.

Packaging: Saffron (filament or in powder form) is usually packed in water-tight, hard plastic box with lid so that the quality is preserved.

Grading: Saffron is presently sold as selected quality and unselected quality. Selected quality, also known as mongra, is all red and consists of mainly broken stigmas and excess in flavour. The unselected quality, generally known as lachcha, contains some yellow filaments besides the stigmas and floral wastes. Internationally, saffron is graded into four categories on the basis of floral waste and extraneous matter content. The Bureau of Indian Standards (IS: 5453 (Part 1)-1996) has also classified saffron filaments into four grades (Table 1.20).

Table 1.20 : BIS classification of saffron filaments.

Quality	Characteristics per cent by mass, max.	
	Floral waste	Extraneous matter
Grade 1	0.5	0.1
Grade 2	4	0.5
Grade 3	7	1.0
Grade 4	10	1.0

Given below are some quality requirements and definitions associated with saffron:

Flavour: Good quality saffron has a characteristic flavour, described as slightly bitter and slightly pungent.

Freedom from moulds, insects etc: Saffron should be free from mould growth, insects (dead/living/fragments) and rodent contamination. It should not be adulterated with turmeric or safflower seed.

Saffron in Filament: These are stigmas of the flower, dried, dark red in colour and trumpet shaped, serrated or indented at the distal end. The length is between 20 and 40 mm. The stigmas may be isolated or joined in twos or threes at the end of a portion of the style, which is white/ yellow in colour.

Saffron in Cut Filaments: These are stigmas with styles removed and completely detached from each other.

Yellow Filaments: These are dried yellow stamens of the flower.

Floral Waste: These are yellow filaments that are unattached and separated, pollens, stamens, parts of ovaries and other parts of the flower.

Extraneous Matter: These are leaves, stems, chaffs and other vegetative matters including mineral matter such as sand, earth and dust.

Saffron Powder: This consists of saffron obtained by crushing the filaments.

Chemical Requirements: Chemical requirements of saffron are listed in Table 1.21.

Cocoa (Cocoa, Cocoa Powder & Coatings): Cocoa powder is obtained by mechanical transformation of cocoa pressed cake into powder form. The cake is the result of partial removal of fat from the ground nib of well-fermented sound and wholesome roasted beans of *Theobroma cacao.*

Cocoa powder is used as a natural colour and flavour in a wide variety of sweet foodstuffs including Indian sweets (example burfi), ice cream and in the confectionery industry. When de-fatted, it is used as a beverage or ingredient in bakery products. The product has an excellent shelf-life. Even after ten years, the flavour is good when packed in air and moisture-proof containers. Only some fading of the colour may be noticed, comparable with fat bloom on chocolate. This disappears when the cocoa is used in milk.

Cocoa Coatings: Cocoa is used in indigenous milk products like burfi in the form of cocoa or chocolate coatings. The material may be of the following two types:

(a) *Plain Cocoa Coatings:* This is a homogeneous product obtained by processing a mixture of one or more of cocoa mass, cocoa powder (high or low fat types), sugar and solid vegetable fats.

(b) *Milk Cocoa Coating:* This is the homogenous product obtained by processing a mixture of cocoa liquor, cocoa powder (high or low fat types) with sugar, milk fat and vegetable fats.

Characteristics: Good quality cocoa product is obtained by grinding cocoa from mature, sound and wholesome cocoa beans, which have been properly fermented, dried and roasted. It may also be obtained by dispersing cocoa butter in low-fat cocoa powder. It may also contain one or more of these ingredients: sugar (sucrose), milk solids, and cocoa butter, permitted flavouring agents, emulsifying agents, sweeteners and

Table 1.21 : Chemical requirements for saffron, in filaments or in powder form.

Characteristics	Requirement		Test method
	Saffron in filaments	Saffron in powder form	
Moisture and volatile matter, per cent by mass, max.	12	10	9 of IS: 5453 (Part II)-1996
Total ash, per cent by mass on dry basis, max.	8	8	10 of IS: 5453 (Part II)-1996
Acid-insoluble ash, per cent by mass on dry basis, max			
(a) Grade land 2	1.0	1.0	
(b) Grade 3 and 4	1.5	1.5	
Solubility in cold water, per cent by mass on dry basis, max.	65	65	11 of IS: 1797-1985
Bitterness, expressed as direct reading of the absorbance of picrocrocine at 257 nm, on dry basis, min.			
(a) Grade 1	70	70	
(b) Grade 2	56	55	
(c) Grade 3	40	40	
(d) Grade 4	30	50	
Safranal, expressed as direct reading of the absorbance at 330 nm on dry basis			13 of IS: 5453 (Part 2)-1996
Minimum	20	20	
Maximum	50	50	
Colouring strength, expressed as direct reading of the absorbance of crocine at 440 nm on dry basis			13 of IS: 5453 (Part 2)-1996
(a) Grade 1	190	190	
(b) Grade 2	150	150	
(c) Grade 3	110	110	
(d) Grade 4	80	80	
Total nitrogen, per cent by mass on dry basis, max.	3.0	3.0	IS: 5194-1969
Crude fibre, per cent, by mass on dry basis, max.	6	6	13 of IS: 1797-1985

vegetable fats. Good quality cocoa coatings have a colour, taste and flavour characteristic of good chocolate. These should be free from rancidity or other off odours, insect or fungus infestation, filth, added colouring matter, adulterants, or harmful ingredients. Ideally no pathogenic organisms should be present in cocoa. The requirements for cocoa coatings are listed in Table 1.22. *Packaging and Storage:* Cocoa powder is hygroscopic and needs to be protected, especially in humid climates. Lidded tins maybe used but a cheaper alternative is sealed polypropylene bags. The powder contains a high proportion of fat and therefore should be stored away from heat, light and moisture to reduce the development of rancidity. The cocoa coating meant for covering purpose should ideally be packed in clear, sound and odour-free containers made of tin plate, plastic, or grease-proof paper or aluminium foil.

MISCELLANEOUS

Makhana (Gorgon Fruit): Makhana (gorgon fruit or fox nut) is obtained by roasting seeds of the plant *Euryale ferox.* It is an important aquatic fruit of the family Nymphacaceae. It is grown in shallow ponds and lakes in the eastern and North-eastern States of India, Bangladesh and China. In North Bihar, it is one of the cash crops for livelihood of the poor fishermen. Makhana plant is characterized by its huge thorny elliptic or orbicular leaves floating on the surface of water like the leaf of lotus. Fruits are spongy and covered with stout prickles. Each fruit contains 20—50 seeds. The seeds measure 5—15 mm across. The seeds are collected and processed into the edible form —makhana.

Makhana is fried or converted into powder. Although India's total annual makhana production is not known, it is estimated that approximately 150 tonnes of popped makhana are dispatched annually from Darbhanga (Bihar) alone to other states of India and partly abroad.

It is rich in carbohydrate, protein and minerals. The popped *makhana* contains: 12.8 per cent moisture; 9.7 per cent protein; 0.1 per cent fat; 76.9 per cent carbohydrate; 0.02 per cent calcium; 0.9 per cent phosphorus and 0.5 per cent other minerals. According to BIS standards (IS: 3155-1965), makhana seeds should have not less than 8.0 per cent protein (on dry basis), 0.5 per cent crude fibre on dry basis, 10 per cent moisture by weight, 1.5 per cent total ash and 0.1 per cent acid insoluble ash.

Cultivation of makhana in North Bihar has been going on for centuries. It is a multi-purpose aquatic fruit, perhaps the only aquatic variety that has an industrial use, besides being a food item. It can be used as starch in the textile industry. The Mysore-based Central Food Technological Research Institute (CFTRI) and the Indian Institute of Technology (HT), Kharagpur, have developed two popping machines for makhana. The Rajendra Agriculture University of Samastipur (Bihar) has also developed a machine for this purpose. A 'kheer-mix' with makhana of Madhubani has been developed at the National Dairy Research Institute (NDRI), Karnal.

Harvesting and Processing: On ripening of fruits, the pedicles and petioles along with the leaves start rotting, leaving the fruit afloat. After a few days, even the fruits rot and seeds with their hard seed coat enveloped in a thick membrane separate to settle at the bottom of the pond. The seeds are collected from the pond and threshed by feet to remove their membranous covering.

Roasting and Popping: About 300 g of conditioned seeds are taken and roasted over fire in an open pan at 280—335°C with continuous stirring. After one-two minutes, a crackling

Table 1.22 : Requirements for cocoa coatings.

Characteristics	Specifications	
	Plain coating	Milk coating
Moisture, % by mass, max.	3.0	3.0
Total fat (on dry basis), % by mass, min.	29.0	29.0
Milk fat (on moisture-free and fat-free basis), % by mass, min.	—	2
Cocoa solids, moisture-free and fat-free basis, % by mass, min.	12.0	2.5
Sugar (sucrose) on dry basis, % by mass, max.	65	55
Sulphated ash, moisture and fat free basis, % by mass, max.	5	5
Acid insoluble ash (moisture, fat and sugar free basis), % by mass, max.	0.2	0.2
Milk solids, moisture and fat-free basis, % by mass, min.	—	10.5
Sfaphy/ococcus (cfu/10 g)	Absent	Absent
Salmonella (cfu/25 g)	Absent	Absent
E. coli (cfu/10 g)	Absent	Absent
Yeast and mould count, cfu/g, max.	100	100

Note: The cocoa solids content shall be checked from the records maintained by the manufacturer.

noise indicates the end of roasting. The moisture content of these roasted seeds is about 11 per cent. The hot roasted seeds, 57 in number, are scooped from the pan, kept on a hard surface and sudden force applied with the help of a wooden hammer. When the hard seed coat breaks, the inside pops out in expanded form. The seed coats are separated manually. The yield of popped makhana varies from 35 to 42 per cent on raw seed weight basis. Makhana should be manufactured in sanitary conditions. If sand is used for roasting, care should be taken to avoid contamination. The final product should be free from extraneous matter and added colouring matter.

Polishing, Grading and Packaging: Popped makhana is polished by rubbing it on the surface of a basket made of bamboo splits. This is done soon after popping, because the popped makhana absorbs moisture very quickly. It is finally grouped into two or three grades, based on size and whiteness. A polyethylene-lined gunny bag (with a capacity to store a quintal of sugar) may be used to pack 89 kg of quality makhana.

Uses: Fried or popped makhana, salty or sweet, is widely consumed as a snack food. Makhana is commonly used in milk-based food preparations like kheer and puddings. It is also used for making excellent curry and indigenous tonics.

Sabudana (Sago): It is a processed food starch marketed in the form of small globules or pearls. In Hindi, it is known as sabudana. The name sago is derived from the original product manufactured from the starchy core of the stem of the sago palm *(Metroxylon sagu* and *Mrumphite)* found in the Indonesian Islands. Sago is manufactured in India from the starch obtained from the tubers of tapioca *(Manihot Utilisima Pohl, Mesculenta).*

Characteristics: Sabudana is white in colour and is available in the form of small hard globules or pearls. The material should be free from fermented or musty or any other objectionable odours, added sweetening or colouring matters, adulterants, fungal contamination and insect infestation.

Gelatinization: Sabudana to be used as an ingredient in dairy products should be cooked and tested by the method prescribed in Appendix A of IS: 899-1971. For a good quality product the quantity of starch that passes into the gruel should not exceed 30 per cent by weight of the material taken for the test. Moreover, the individual globules or pearl should retain the globular shape.

Some additional requirements for sabudana enlisted by the Bureau of Indian Standards (IS: 899—1971) are shown in Table 1.23.

Table 1.23 : BIS requirements for sago (sabudana).

Characteristics	Requirement
Moisture, per cent by weight, max.	11
Total ash (dry basis), per cent by weight, max.	0.4
Acid insoluble ash (dry basis), per cent by weight, max.	0.10
Starch (on dry basis), per cent by weight, min.	98
Protein (N x 6.25) (on dry basis), per cent by weight, max.	0.30
Sulphur dioxide, ppm, max.	100
Crude fibre (on dry basis), per cent by weight, max.	0.20
pH of aqueous extract	4.5 to 7.0
Colour of gelatinized alkaline paste in porcelain cuvette on the Lovibond Scale, not deeper than	IR + 3 Y

Applications: Sago starch is used in making a variety of dessert puddings including indigenous dairy products, like sago payasam, sabudana kheer, various starchy food products, and in some bakeries as a component in certain breads and pastries. A blend of milk or cream with soft-boiled sago granules and sometimes fruit juice topped with ice cream goes to make a rich beverage called falooda, popular in Mumbai and other metro cities.

Packaging: Clean, sound and dry new A-twill jute bags, with their mouths stitched make good packaging material for sago.

WATER

Water is used in indigenous milk products for making syrups for gulabjamun, rasogolla, and for cooling/ texturizing of paneer after setting as well as for preparing various kinds of doughs. When used as an ingredient, it is important to ensure that water is clear, colourless, odourless, tasteless and free from soluble impurities. It must also conform to the micro-biological quality requirements.

The impurities generally found in water are dissolved mineral salts, dissolved gases, sediments and turbidity, organic matter and various micro-organisms. Salts commonly found are bicarbonates, sulphates, and chlorides of calcium, magnesium and sodium. They impart hardness to water. Water hardness is generally expressed in terms of equivalent calcium carbonate measured either as parts per million or as grains per gallon. One grain is equal to 17.1 ppm. The US Geological Survey has developed a classification for water (Table 1.24).

Table 1.24 : US Geological Survey developed classification for water.

Class	ppm of calcium carbonate
Very hard	>180
Hard	120-180
Moderately hard	60-120
Soft	0-60

The tolerances for radioactivity of water are given in Table 1.25. Additional requirements for total hardness as calcium carbonate are 30 mg/litre; for iron 0.1 mg/ litre; and manganese 0.1 mg/litre.

Table 1.25 : Tolerances for radioactivity of water.

Characteristics	Tolerance
α-emitters, μc/ml, max.	10^{-9}
β-emitters, μc/ml, max.	10^{-8}

Water used for dairy processing operations should conform to the bacteriological quality standards as given in Table 1.26.

Table 1.26 : Bacteriological tolerances of water.

Characteristics	Tolerance
Coliform bacteria, MPN index cfu/100 ml	Less than 1
Standard plate count, cfu/ml, max.	50
Proteolysis and lipolytic organisms, combined cfu/ml, max.	5
Thermophillic bacteria	Absent
Slime forming organisms	Absent

According to quality requirements stipulated in the "Indian Standards for quality tolerances for Water for Processed Food Industry" (IS: 4251-1967, reaffirmed 1977), the physical and chemical tolerances are given in Table 1.27.

Table 1.27 : Physical and chemical tolerances of water.

Characteristics	Tolerance
Colour (Hazen units), max.	20
Turbidity (units), max.	10
Odour	None
pH	6.5 to 9.2
Total solids, mg/l, max.	1000
Total hardness (as $CaCO_3$), mg/l, max.	600

Sulphate (as SO_4), mg/l, max.	200
Fluoride (as F), mg/l, max.	1.5
Chloride (as Cl), mg/l, max.	250
Cyanide (as CN), mg/l, max.	0—01
Selenium (as Se), mg/l, max.	0.05
Iron (as Fe), mg/l, max.	0.03
Magnesium (as Mg), mg/l, max.	75.0
Manganese (as Mn), mg/l, max.	0.2
Copper (as Cu), mg/l, max.	1.0
Lead (as Pb), mg/l, max.	0.1
Chromium (as Cr^{6+}) mg/l, max.	0.05
Zinc (as Zn), mg/l, max.	15.0
Arsenic (as As), mg/l, max.	0.2
Nitrate (as N), mg/l, max.	20
Phenolic substances (as C_6H_5OH), mg/l, max.	0.001

Hard water is the chief cause of scale formation in boilers, leading to a serious problem of reduction of efficiency of heat transfer. Hardness is also undesirable in bottle washing, equipment and lines cleanup, process cooling and air conditioning operations, because it is involved in their corrosion. When hardness exceeds 85 ppm, a water softening system should be considered.

The presence of excessive iron leaves brown spots on equipment. Iron in processing water (> 0.1 ppm) can interfere in the flavour and colour of food product being produced. Iron and magnesium favour the growth of certain bacteria as well.

Turbidity in water results from suspended solids. Normally municipal water is clear and suitable for use. Some rasogolla syrup manufacturers clarify their syrup by adding a small amount of milk during syrup boiling and removing the scum formed on the surface.

Colour in water is ascribed to the presence of decayed organic matter and may be accompanied by odour from gases like hydrogen sulphide. Micro-organisms are always present, but are easily controlled by chlorination at the plant level. During paneer manufacture, generally, water containing 5-10 ppm of chlorine would be effective in controlling contamination with extraneous bacteria. The pH of water should be in the range of 6.5-9.0.

In certain locations, water quality may require treatment to remove suspended matter, undesirable odour or flavour, and reduce dissolved solids. Various processes are available and their selection depends on the severity of the problem. A general water treatment process to obtain potable water may involve a combination of certain processes. Physical processes entail filtration through sand and activated carbon beds or reverse osmosis/micro-filtration membrane system. Ozonation and ultraviolet radiation based processes are also available. Chemical processes include precipitation with alum, lime treatment, demineralization using cationic and anionic ion exchange, iodine or bromine or chlorine treatment and electrodialysis.

2

Making of Milk Based Sweets

From time immemorial, milk and milk products have been part of the heritage of India, dating back to the Indus Valley Civilization (c. 2500 to 1500 BC). Today, the Indian sub-continent is heir to this magnificent legacy. Milk products like kheer, ghee, dahi, paneer, shrikhand and buttermilk continue to delight the palate with their rich and distinctive aroma, flavour and taste, as they did in the pre-historic times.

Scriptures from the early Buddhist and Jain period have documented sweets made from heat-desiccated milk such as sihakesara and morandeka. These were used as dessert at the end of meals among the well-to-do. Lord Buddha allowed his followers to take milk sweets as a portable ration for journeys on routes where it was difficult to get foodstuffs. In the Maurya Period (268-233 BC), sweets were prepared from concentrated milk and honey or jaggery. The post-Gupta Period (750-1200 AD) literature also describes varieties of milk sweets.

Milk sweets have been an inseparable part of the socio-cultural life in the Indian sub-continent. They reflect the wealth and status of people, while forming an important part of their cuisine. These are offered on special religious occasions (yagna, homa and sacrificial rituals), social events (birthdays, weddings) and festivals. In the vedic period, as also now, milk sweets offered to guests constitute an expression of the warmth of hospitality.

One is fascinated at the amount of science and technology that gastronomical artists of the yore inter-mixed in these delicacies so effortlessly while retaining their basic goodness to delight the epicurean, without getting lost in the bylanes of logic and "logies", including technologies. They took care to preserve and promote the romance of food.

One of the basic tenets that guide people in their search for good life and zest for living is this: "You are what you eat". So, much care and thought have been given to the daily diet and nutrition that forms part and parcel of the folk wisdom, passed on from one generation to another for ages in this sub-continent. As Dr. K.T. Achaya has noted in his book, *The Story of Our Food:* "The ethos of food preparation and the attention to cleanliness and purity are, in a large measure, an Aryan inheritance that goes back three thousand years."

These concerns extend beyond the sensual, as reflected in the uncanny ingenuity shown to preserve the perishable nutrients in milk through the application of heat treatment and the like. Thus, the culinary craftsmen of the by-gone days created an impressive array of heat-desiccated milk products such as khoa—an intermediate concentrate—that is the base for a wider range of mithais, including gulabjamun, burfi, peda, kalakand, rabri, kulfi and their variants.

The heat processing and accompanying reduction in water activity result in a substantial destruction of pathogenic and spoilage micro-organisms as well as inactivation of enzymes. Besides, desirable heat-induced chemical interactions among milk constituents result in reduction of redox potential and water activity, thereby extending the product shelf-life under the ambient temperatures of tropical climate. Also, novel flavours, textures and portability attributes were added in these milk foods.

KHOA/MAWA

As a versatile intermediate base for a wide range of sweets such as burfi and peda, khoa occupies a prominent place in the traditional dairy products sector. It is also known as khoya, khawa, khava, kava, palghoa or mawa. It has been defined under the PFA as the product obtained by rapid drying milk of cow or buffalo or goat or sheep or milk solids or a combination thereof. The milk fat content shall not be less than 20 per cent of the finished product. Khoa may contain citric acid not more than 0.1 per cent by weight.

Khoa contains fairly large quantitites of muscle building proteins, bone-forming minerals and energy-giving fat and lactose. It is also expected to retain most of the fat-soluble vitamins A and D, and also fairly large quantities of water-soluble B vitamins contained in the original milk. Addition of khoa to sweets further increases the calorific value of the product.

Product Description: Khoa is obtained by boiling milk (buffalo milk preferred) in a large, open, bowl-shaped metal frying pan with two handles

2.1 : SENSORY PROFILE OF TRADITIONAL DAIRY PRODUCTS.

For millennia, traditional dairy products have been contributing to the health, nutrition and delight of discriminating consumers in the Indian subcontinent. To establish an efficient, economic and profitable system for their industrial scale production, a proper understanding of these products' sensory profile is essential. This knowledge will help design and develop product innovations and variations to meet the new demands of the market. The desirable sensory attributes of major traditional products are tabulated below:

Product	Flavour	Body and texture	Colour and appearance
Khoa	A typical mildly cooked flavour similar to that perceived from boiled milk is most acceptable. The taste should be pleasantly sweet.	Soft and uniform body and granular texture is most desirable. Pindi khoa shall have smooth, compact, homogeneous texture with very fine grains, Dhap khoa shall have granular texture and slightly soft body. In Danedar khoa, presence of big grains with brown colour is desirable.	Cow milk khoa shall be pale yellow with a tinge of brown having moisture surface, whereas buffalo milk khoa shall be white with a tinge of brown having slightly greasy/oily surface.
Gulabjamun	Typical heated fresh aroma, taste moderately sweet, free from doughy feel and fully saturated with syrup.	Soft and thin crust, smooth granular texture, soft and spongy, free from lumps and hard central core.	Light to yellowish brown, uniform, round/elongated shape, smooth, glossy, moderate size.
Chhana	Mildly acidic smell and pleasant sweetish taste are considered desirable flavour attributes.	For rasogolla, chhana should have moderately soft and uniform texture and shall show slight springiness, when pressed with thumb; upon rolling between palms, it should yield round ball of even surface and no cracks. It should not release fat on kneading/working.	It should have uniform yellow colour (cow milk) to whitish colour (buffalo milk, calcium lactate as coagulant). It should be neither too moist nor dry, and absence of visible soil of burnt particles,
Rasogolla	Pleasant flavour, moderately sweet, free from doughy feel and fully saturated with syrup.	Soft body and maximum sponginess, free from lumps and hard centre.	White colour, round shape, smooth, moderate size,

Sandesh	Typical cooked and heated aroma, sweet, fresh creamy taste.	Soft grade is cohesive, smooth and little grainy. Hard grade is crumbly, smooth and has fine grains.	Yellowish white and uniform in colour. Attractive size and shape, free from mechanical holes.
Paneer	A characteristic blend of flavour of heated milk and acid, i.e. pleasant, mildly acidic and sweet (nutty).	It should be sufficiently firm to hold its shape during cutting/slicing yet tender enough not to resist crushing during mastication. The texture should be compact, smooth and velvety.	Uniform, pleasing white colour and greenish tinge (buffalo) and light yellow for cow milk paneer.
Dahi	Pleasant sweetish aroma of diacetyl and clean acid taste is desired. Skim milk dahi lacks this.	A weak gel-like junket, a creamy layer of fat if whole milk is used. Homogeneous body, while cut surface is trim and free from cracks and gas bubbles,	Creamish yellow for cow milk and creamish white for buffalo. It should have smooth and glossy surface and no free whey separation.
Shrikhand	A clean, pleasant sweet-sour flavour representing blend of sugar and fermented milk solids.	Typical semi-solid uniform consistency showing a characteristic firmness and pliability and shall show a smooth texture and no graininess.	Uniform colour and glossy appearance and devoid of free fat and syrup separation.
Ghee greenish	A natural sweet, pleasant, nutty, slightly cooked/caramelized aroma and an agreeable taste.	A good textured ghee requires large and uniform grains with very little liquid fat. A greasy texture is objectionable.	When melted, it should be clear, transparent and free from sediment and uniform throughout. It should be bright yellow for cow and white with tinge for buffalo milk.

Source: Dr. H.K. Desai, Managing Director, Vidya Dairy, Anand, Gujarat.

called karahi, resembling the Chinese wok. The liquid milk is stirred at first and later its solidified portion is constantly scraped with a long-handle flat-edged metal scraper called 'khunti' to prevent caramelization. The light brown mass is finally shaped into a large ball or small pats. Though naturally sweet, khoa is sometimes further sweetened with sugar (one-fourth of its weight) to yield burfi and flavoured with cardamom to make pedas. Khoa from batch sizes of 200-500 kg milk is produced in the countryside where milk in plenty is available at relatively low cost. It is then shipped to urban centres for use in making sweets.

Using cereals, wheat flour, sugar, flavours and other additives, depending upon the local preferences, a wide range of milk sweets/ confections/delicacies are made from khoa on small-to-large scale. These include burfi, kalakand, peda, milk cake, gulabjamun, pantua, malai ke laddoo, gujia and carrot halwa. Concentrated milk and khoa form the base of kulfi, a frozen dessert.

The 'batch-wise' method of khoa production and lack of standardization cause wide variations in the physico-chemical and micro-biological quality of the marketed product. For commercial trade, three main types of khoa are recognized—Dhap, Pindi and Danedar, each type having preferred end uses (Table 2.1). The Bureau of Indian Standards specifications for three types of khoa are given in Table 2.3.

Table 2.2 : Types of khoa and their preferred end uses.

Type of khoa	TS(%)	Fat(%)	End uses
Dhap	56—63	20—23	Gulabjamun, pantua
Pindi	67—69	21—26	Burfi, peda
Danedar	60—65	20—25	Kalakand, milk-cake

Table 2.3 : BIS standards for three khoa varieties.

per cent

Khoa type	Total solids, minimum	Fat in dry matter, minimum	Ash in dry matter, maximum	Titratable acidity, as % lactic acid in mass, maximum
Dhap	55	37	6	0.6
Pindi	65	37	6	0.8
Danedar	60	37	6	0.9

The shelf-life of khoa is two to four days under ambient conditions and three weeks under refrigerated conditions. Traditionally, khoa-pats move from village to towns wrapped in leaves and put in bamboo baskets. The shelf-life can be enhanced by using vegetable parchment paper wrappers, plastic (polyethylene) film bags/pouches, laminated (preferably aluminium coated) pouches, tin plates, or cans, in pack sizes varying from 0.5 (or even less) to 1 kg.

Size of Industry: The annual production of khoa is estimated at more than one million tonnes, utilizing about 6 million tonnes of milk, equivalent to 7 per cent of total milk production. Khoa production is mainly confined to the non-organized sector. However, now some 20 plants have undertaken mechanized production of high quality khoa on an industrial scale, including a few on continuous production basis.

Technology: The traditional method of preparing khoa utilizes simple utensils and direct smoke-free fire for desiccation. The fat level is usually adjusted at 4 per cent for cow milk and 5 per cent for buffalo milk. Typically, 4 to 6 litre lots of milk are taken in a shallow, iron/mild steel pan and simmered over direct non-smoky fire with constant and vigorous stirring and occasional scraping of the heating surface to avoid building of scale/scorching. Milk thickens with progressive heating and coagulated solidified portion is seen on the heating surface, while liquid milk and air begin to appear on the upper peripheral sections of the heating pan. These are constantly scraped and brought back into the thickened milk. After about 10 to 12 minutes of rapid evaporation, when concentration of about 2.5 to 3 times has been attained, coagulated particles are brought together with the stirrer and compacted as a semi-solid mass.

As heating continues further with constant agitation and scraping of the heating surface, free fat oozes out. From this stage, subsequent heating has a pronounced effect on the development of typical khoa flavour and texture. Since colour tends to change rapidly at this stage, heating is slowed down. Gradually, the solid mass tends to leave the heating surface cleanly, and a pat is formed.

The Pindi type khoa is prepared by heating for a longer period in the pan to achieve lower moisture content than that of the Dhap type. If citric acid (about 0.1% of khoa) is added towards the last stages of desiccation, Danedar khoa is obtained. The end-product is then removed from the pan, spread uniformly over trays and allowed to cool under atmospheric conditions.

Table 2.4 : Defects in khoa, their causes and prevention.

Defects	Causes	Prevention
Flavour		
Smoky	• Smoky fire used for boiling and dehydration of milk.	• Using non-smoky fire for boiling and dehydration of milk.
Sour/Acid	• Excessively high acidity in milk used.	• Using fresh sweet milk.
Rancid	• Fat hydrolysis due to lipase action in khoa during storage (at room temperature and above).	• Early disposal/marketing of khoa.
Stale	• Excessively long period of storage of khoa at low temperature (5—10°C).	• Early disposal/marketing of khoa.
Body & Texture		
Hard body	• Excessively low fat content of milk used.	• Using milk of optimum fat content.
	• Excessively low moisture content of khoa due to faulty production technique.	• Optimum moisture content of khoa by adopting correct production technique.
	• Adulteration of milk with starch.	• Using unadulterated milk.
Coarse texture	• Excessively high acidity in milk used.	• Using fresh sweet milk.
	• Excessively low fat content of milk used.	• Using milk of optimum fat content.
	• Excessively high temperature of dehydration, especially in the last stages.	• Optimum temperature of dehydration, especially in the last stages.
	• Excessively low speed when stirring milk/pan contents.	• Optimum speed when stirring milk/pan contents.
Grittytexture	• Presence of sand-like particles due to incorrect straining of milk.	• Correct straining of milk.
	• Presence of large crystals of lactose due to incorrect method of manufacture.	• Correct method of manufacture.
Colour & Appearance		
Dry surface	• Excessively low fat content of milk used.	• Using milk of optimum fat content.
Visible dirt/foreign matter	• Incorrect or no straining of milk used.	• Correct straining of milk.
	• Heating-pan and/or stirrer not cleaned.	• Heating-pan and/or stirrer well cleaned.
	• Dirty/windy surroundings during manufacture and/or handling of khoa.	• Clean surroundings during manufacture and/or handling of khoa.
	• Transport of unpacked khoa.	• Transport of properly packed khoa.

Browning and/or presence of burnt particles	• Excessively high heating temperature, especially in the last stages. • Excessively low speed when stirring cum-scraping pan contents.	• Optimum heating temperature, especially in the last stages. • Optimum speed when stirring-cum-scraping pan contents.
Mouldy surface	• Excessively high moisture content of khoa in storage. • Excessively high humidity of storage room.	• Optimum moisture content of khoa in storage. • Optimum humidity of storage room.
Fat and/or water leakage	• Air-leaky packaging of khoa. • Incorrect method of manufacture of khoa.	• Air-tight packaging of khoa. • Correct method of manufacture of khoa.

The yield of khoa depends upon the type of milk used. When milk is standardized to 4.5 per cent fat and 8.5 per cent SNF, its yield is about 20 per cent. It is about 18 per cent for cow milk and about 20 per cent for buffalo milk. Khoa from buffalo milk is considered distinctly superior, being whiter in colour and having soft smooth body and granular texture. These characteristics are considered desirable for making high quality sweets. Common defects in khoa, along with their causes and prevention, are given in Table 2.4.

Process Mechanization: The traditional process for khoa-making was meant for domestic or cottage-scale operations. This method is labour and energy-intensive and the end-product varies in quality from batch to batch. Since desiccation is done under open atmospheric conditions, the micro-biological quality of the product is open to environmental influences.

Engineering a design for mechanized production and packaging of khoa presents many challenges. There is a lack of information on the thermodynamics of the various physico-chemical changes taking place during the process of manufacture. Such changes are critical determinants of the sensory and rheological characteristics of khoa. Nevertheless, several successful attempts have been made to mechanize the process for the large-scale manufacture of khoa in the organized sector.

A prototype for mechanized production of khoa was developed in the 1960s at the National Dairy Research Institute (NDRI), Karnal. The process involved pre-concentration of milk in a scraped surface heat exchanger (SSHE), followed by final concentration in an open cascading open steam-jacketed pan with mechanical scraper agitators. A vat of conical design has also been developed for the mechanized production of khoa. The final product is removed from the bottom of the cone by a screw type positive pump. This equipment is quite suitable to replace traditional appliances for cottage scale operations. A roller dryer has also been used for the manufacture of khoa.

Innovations: The Alfa-Laval group has developed a Contherm-Convap SSHE system that has been successfully employed for the large-scale production of khoa. Concentrated mass emerging from Convap at about 90°C is pumped through a holding tube to impart characteristic flavour and body. However, removal of the residual mass from the holding tube presents certain operational problems at the end of the process. This equipment is being used in commercial khoa production.

The NDRI process for mechanized production of khoa employs two SSHEs arranged in a cascade fashion. During khoa manufacture, milk is concentrated to 65—69 per cent TS levels. During initial stages of concentration (up to 45 per cent TS level), the capacity of the system (kg of milk processed per hour per unit heat transfer area) depends upon the mass-flow rate of milk, steam pressure, rotor speed and number of blades. The product comes out from the end of the second SSHE, and is cooled by spreading thinly over tray under atmospheric conditions. The product displays free fat content, averaging 73.6 per cent as against 69.3 per cent observed in the conventionally produced khoa. The product compared favourably with the traditional khoa in the sensory and rheological profile.

Continuous Khoa Machine: An Inclined Scraped Surface Heat Exchanger (ISSHE) was developed at the National Dairy Development Board (NDDB), Anand, for continuous production of khoa. The plant comprises a balance tank, a positive displacement pump and an ISSHE. Milk concentrate is used as feed. The input of feed in this equipment is in the form of vacuum concentrated milk of about 42—45 per cent TS. The inclined design of the heat exchanger permits formation of a pool of vigorously boiling milk, which constantly moves forward and gets applied on the heated surfaces as a thin film by the scraper agitator. It is here at the interface of the heating surface, liquid film and air in the middle section of the heat exchanger barrel that concentrated milk is coagulated to form semi-solid khoa.

The portion of concentrated milk constantly keeps coming back to the boiling mass of milk at the bottom of the heat exchanger barrel, while the coagulated particles keep moving with the forward motion of the Archimedes screw type scraper agitator. The barrel of the heat exchanger is jacketed into segments, in which steam pressure can be critically controlled to permit maintaining a temperature gradient, being higher at the lower end of the barrel, where concentrated milk continuously boils. The temperature gradient gradually lowers as the concentrated milk is progressively converted into the semi-solid mass.

The product emerges from the top of the barrel, and needs to be cooled by spreading uniformly in shallow trays by a manual process under atmospheric conditions. This process has been successfully employed at the Sugam Dairy, Vadodara, for commercial production of khoa for use in a wide range of sweets such as different types of burfi and peda. A complete khoa-making line was installed at the Sabar Dairy, Himatnagar, Gujarat, based on NDDB-developed technology. Although both these designs involving SSHEs are being successfully used for commercial production of khoa, further improvement on immediate cooling of the product as it emerges from the SSHE is required. The texture of khoa needs to be smoothened by appropriate working by hand or by use of mechanical devices such as colloid mill to facilitate its conversion into products like burfi and peda. In some cases, uniformly smooth khoa is required to impart the desirable texture to the finished product.

In industrial production of khoa, energy conservation is an important consideration (Table 2.5). Concentration of milk in an open pan is energy intensive. Double effect evaporators or pressure driven membrane separation process of Reverse Osmosis (RO) presents prospects for process upgradation. Energy can be conserved by partial concentration of milk either in an open pan, or vacuum evaporator or RO unit. After

Table 2.5 : Energy requirement for khoa manufacture (per 100 kg of product).

(a) *Mechanized (Continuous) process*	
Steam consumption	405 kg
Electrical energy consumption	8 kWh
Total energy consumption (as steam equivalent)	448 kg
(b) *Batch process*	
Jacketed kettle: Steam consumption	514 kg
Saving of steam through continuous process	66 kg

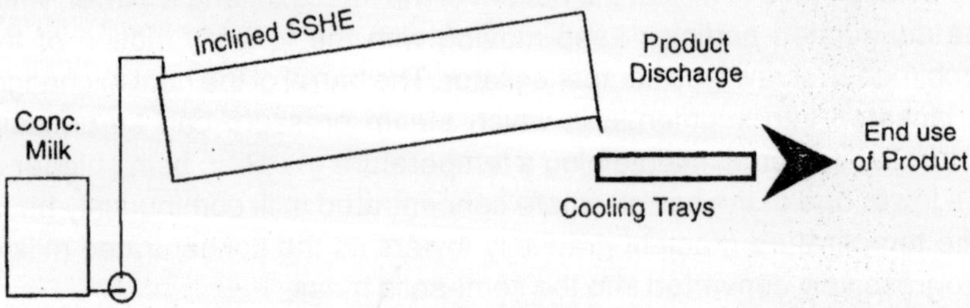

Figure 2.1 : Inclined SSHE khoa-making commercial plant at Sugam Dairy, Vadodara (Dr. J.S. Punjrath, et al.).

this, the finishing can be done in an open pan for effecting heat-induced chemical changes required to produce typical khoa flavour, body and texture.

R and D work on the pre-concentration of milk has demonstrated that good quality khoa can be obtained by integrating unit operations involving vacuum evaporators or RO equipment in an open pan for energy conservation. The relative thermal performance economies of these alternatives have been evaluated. Energy requirement for open pan is 455 Kcal/kg of milk; a double-effect evaporator requires about half of this energy; and a single-effect evaporator with mechanical vapour recompression system needs only one-third of the energy. The first commercial low-cost milk condensing unit for continuous khoa manufacture was installed at the Sugam Dairy, Vadodara, based on NDDB developed technology.

Advantages of the continuous khoa-making machine are:

- High heat transfer coefficient, principally due to a thin layer of product and the turbulence imparted by the rotor and hence compact design;
- Total absence of fouling on the heat transfer surface;
- Short residence time and consequently less heat damage to the product;
- Product is confined as a thin film on the heating surface, consequently the hold-up volume is extremely small thereby minimum loss due to spoilage inside the heat exchanger, unlike in batch process where the loss would be total;
- Improved flow characteristics of the product inside the equipment. The system can handle products even in semi-solid form without causing heat damage. Outlet to inlet viscosity ratio can be 1000 or more;
- Adaptable to automation and cleaning in place (CIP);
- Sanitary operation, as process takes place in a completely closed environment;
- Low physical strain on operators. Only small valves have to be closed or opened by them; and
- Uniform product quality, because the process is continuous.

Packaging of Khoa: Parchment paper, aluminium foil, polyethylene films and tin cans are used for packaging of khoa. Khoa samples packed in polyethylene bags remain acceptable for five days at 37°G and for 25 days at 7 ± 1°C, while the unpacked product starts deteriorating in two days. Khoa samples packed in aluminium foil and low-density polyethylene are found acceptable for consumption up to fourteen days at 13-15°C and for six days at 30-32°C. Among all packaging modes, tins offer maximum protection to khoa. If packed hot in tins, khoa has a shelf life of fifteen days at room temperature with minimal bacterial growth during storage.

For increasing the efficacy of tin packaging, it would be advantageous to presterilize the containers. Tin cans can be heat sterilized, whereas flexible packages need to be treated with chemicals.

Aseptic packaging of khoa in radiation sterilized laminated pouches extended its shelf-life to 7—22 days as against 13 days for unpacked samples when stored at 37°C. The use of radiation-sterilized packages did not impart any additional shelf-stability to khoa. Similar results were also observed with the use of unsterilized pouches, indicating insignificant microbial contamination of the product from the packaging material. The shelf-life of the product remains unaffected in vacuum packaging. It may be concluded that thermophiles surviving heat processing of the product and/or air contamination affect its quality.

Packaging Study: A study investigated the effect of less costly and easily available laminated packages, polyethylene and parchment paper on the keeping quality of khoa. The pre-irradiated laminates consisted of: (i) cellophane/low density polyethylene; (ii) poster paper/low-density polyethylene/0.15 mm aluminium foil/lowdensity polyethylene; and, (iii) poster paper/ lowdensity polyethylene/0.02 mm aluminium foil/low-density polyethylene. The changes occurring in khoa packs during storage at 37°C, 8 ± 1°C and 20°C were studied in respect of organoleptic properties, moisture, lactic acidity, peroxide value, free fat acidity and tyrosine content.

Micro-biological changes in terms of differential count, spores, yeast and moulds and lipolytic counts at 37°C and 8 ± 1°C were also recorded. Khoa samples packed in parchment paper and polyethylene remained acceptable up to five days at 37°C and up to 14 days at 8 ± 1°C. Laminate packed samples were acceptable for more than five days at 37°C, 30 days at 8 ± 1°C and more than 75 days at 20°C. Fourply aluminium coated laminates proved to be the best for packaging of khoa followed by two-ply packs, high-density polyethylene and parchment paper. Ionizing radiation was employed for sterilization of packaging materials before packing khoa. A dose of 2.5 mRad from a gamma radiation source was found to be quite effective for sterilization of flexible packages.

Recommended Packaging: Films capable of forming a good barrier against moisture loss and oxygen permeation are recommended for khoa

Table 2.6 Physico-chemical/sensory characteristics of khoa prepared by different mechanized systems.

Physicochemical characteristics	ISSHE	Conical vat	Contherm-Convap	Roller
Total Solids (%)	65. 63	63. 14	63. 76	70. 96
Fat (%)	21. 97	21. 51	21. 50	27. 75
Free fat (% of total fat)	35. 00	43. 53	58. 37	51. 15
Acidity (%)	0. 53	0. 54	0. 61	0. 58
pH	6. 35	6. 38	6. 35	6. 22
Colour (Lovibond tintometer readings)	1. 61Y (1. 4Y to 2. 5Y)*	1. 68 + 0.3R (1. 3Yto 2. 6Y+1R)*	2. 03Y + 0.5R (1. 5to3Y+1R)* 1. 6Y)*	1. 5Y (1. 4Y to
Sensory characteristics	*Mean Sensory Scores*			
Flavour (50)	48	40	38	45
Body and Texture (35)	32	22	24	29
Colour and appearance (15)	14	10	9	12
Total score	94	72	71	86
Comments	No comments	Lacks typical khoa flavour, sticky, lumpy, pasty, burnt particles, slicing characteristics, lacks grainy texture, uneven colour	Lacks typical khoa flavour, sticky, lumpy, pasty, burnt particles, slicing characteristics, lacks grainy texture, uneven colour but no lumps	Milk khoa flavour, lacks grains, presence of hard flakes (nodules)

*Under laboratory conditions.

packaging. The objective is to exclude oxygen in the package to control mould and yeast growth as well as oxidation of fat. Saran coated films, coextruded films of multiple layers, and laminations with aluminium foil or metalised films composed of polyester/polypropylene constitute some of the effective packaging materials. Storage and distribution temperature should be 2—4°C to avoid separation of free fat in khoa and to maximize shelf-life. Vacuum packaging or modified atmospheric packaging with a flush of nitrogen/carbon dioxide would enhance marketing areas. There is a potential of achieving a 120 days refrigerated shelf-life by using modern techniques.

Physico-chemical Aspects: Researchers have analysed the composition of khoa and studied its physicochemical characteristics, presented in Tables 2.2 and 2.6. Changes in thermal conductivity during concentration process of khoa-making and that of the end-product have been evaluated. At 80°C, the thermal ' conductivity changed from 0.473 to 0.439, and 0.398 as the moisture content varied from 68 to 57 and 49 per cent, respectively. The thermal conductivity of khoa at 32 per cent moisture changes from 0.259 to 0.327 as the temperature increases from 16°C to 83°C.

Table 2.7 : Typical composition of khoa.

per cent

Type of milk	Total solids	Fat	Protein	Lactose	Ash
Buffalo milk*	78.40	30.50	17.70	23.90	5.90
Cow milk*	80.70	25.20	15.80	33.50	4.10
Mixed milk*	79.80	29.00	16.70	30.10	5.20
Market sample	71.60	24.60	19.00	25.20	3.60

*Prepared under laboratory conditions.

Preparation of khoa involves intensive heat treatment during the desiccation process, as a result of which heat coagulation of milk occurs towards finishing stages of the process. The physico-chemical changes that occur during khoa-making are not fully understood. However, several studies on the effect of heat on buffalo milk may be extrapolated to the khoa-making process. The heat-induced acidification is the single most important change leading to coagulation of milk and its neutralization can over-ride all other modifications.

Heat coagulation of milk observed during the final stages of khoa-making may be attributed to the destabilization of caseinates in colloidal suspension under the combined influence of progressively higher total solids concentration, altered salt balance, decreased pH, and high temperature. The exact mechanism of heat coagulation involved in khoa making is yet to be elucidated on a scientific basis.

Casein and whey proteins undergo constant changes as the heat desiccation of milk progresses at near boiling temperatures under atmospheric conditions. Heating of milk results in changes in the Zeta-potential of Kcasein, while a and Pcaseins remain relatively less affected. Following heat treatment, caseins display decreased amounts of phosphorus and sialic acid per unit weight of caseins. Interaction between heat denatured β–lactoglobulin and K-casein is a major factor affecting the complex heat coagulation behaviour of milk. Heat coagulation is determined by the amount of K-casein present on the surface of casein micelle.

Severe heating during desiccation of milk under atmospheric conditions also increases substantially the size of casein micelles. This is accompanied by about 50 to 60 per cent increase in the level of soluble K-casein. This release of K-casein from the micelle, particularly from the surface, probably results in a loss of stability, and contributes to coagulation of milk. Finally, a rapid increase in the size of casein micelles occurs just prior to visible coagulation.

The highly ordered structure of whey proteins is quite susceptible to heat treatment. The main whey protein components, viz., β–lactoglobulin and α–lactalbumin, tend to undergo varying degrees of self-aggregation, denaturation/coagulation and interaction with the K-casein as the heating temperatures rise. Whey proteins of buffalo milk are somewhat more resistant to heat denaturation than those of cow milk. Heating of buffalo milk above 90°C results in denaturation of almost all the whey proteins. The amount of β–lactoglobulin present in milk is inversely related to the heat coagulation time.

Interaction between heat denatured β–lactoglobulin and K-casein via disulfide bonding is partly responsible for the pH sensitive coagulation behaviour of milk. The α–lactalbumin component of milk has an almost similar effect on heat coagulation. All these changes may be important in the heat coagulation during the final stages of khoa-making process. That coagulation of milk first occurs at the air-milk interphase and not in the underlying layers, when milk is being desiccated either by the batch process or the continuous process of khoa-making is an interesting observation.

Vigorous agitation at elevated temperatures during desiccation of milk disrupts the fat globule membrane, releasing free-fat. Formation of free fat during transition from the liquid phase to the semi-solid phase is very significant for development of typical flavour, body and texture of khoa. This may be comparable to the frying effect towards the finishing stages of the khoa-making process. Proteins and carbohydrates that undergo controlled caramelization are significant in imparting typical flavour and desirable sensory characteristics to, the end product, khoa.

Water Activity of Khoa: Elucidation of water activity in a given food system permits a better understanding of its storage and packaging-related behaviour. The equilibrium relationship between the amount of water absorbed and the shelf-life of khoa at different temperatures (15° to 45°C) has been established. The desorption isotherm of khoa is a classic sigmoid shape of Type-II. Water activity of khoa at its normal moisture content is observed to be 0.96. There is a steep fall in equilibrium moisture content of khoa with the decrease in relative humidity up to 85 per cent. Between the water activity values of 0.25 to 0.60, the equilibrium moisture content of khoa remains almost constant. Further, with the rise in temperature from 15° to 45°C, the monolayer moisture content decreases from 3.89 to 2.46 g water/g solids. This relative effect of temperature on monolayer moisture content is important in dehydration, shelf-life and storage behaviour of khoa.

Rheology of Khoa: Texture profile analysis of khoa— measurement of various properties making-up the sensorily perceived texture—has been conducted using Instron Universal Testing Machine. The total solids content of khoa seems to be the single most important variable affecting its texture profile hardness ($r = 0.89$), cohesiveness ($r = 0.71$), gumminess ($r = 0.83$) and chewiness ($r = 0.75$), whereas water dispersible protein has a smaller but significant effect ($r = 0.58$). These instrumental data were correlated with sensory data, which enabled development of a mathematical model aimed at predicting the textural quality on the basis of instrumental cohesiveness, gumminess and chewiness.

Microbiological Quality: Considering the severity of heat treatment during the manufacturing process of khoa, survival of the original micro-flora (except spores) present in milk used is a rare possibility. Presence of micro-organisms in khoa is invariably the result of the post-manufacturing contamination. Results of analysis of micro-biological quality of the market samples of khoa are summed up in Tables 2.8 and 2.9.

Preservation of Khoa: Addition of any preservative in khoa is prohibited under the PFA Rules (1955). However, some research has been carried out to improve the shelf-life of khoa using preservatives, like nisin, potassium sorbate and sodium and potassium metasulphites. Their effect on the khoa shelf-life is presented in Table 2.9. Addition of potassium sorbate to khoa in doses of 0.2 to 0.4 per cent by weight of the product increased the shelf-life to 14 days at room temperature. It has been found effective in inhibiting yeast and moulds in khoa during storage.

The shelf life of khoa was improved by incorporating sodium and potassium metabisulphites at the rate of 1,000 ppm on milk basis during final stages of manufacture. These preservatives suppressed development of acidity, free fatty acid level, proteolysis, oxidation and browning, and microbial growth. They could also eliminate the growth of

Table 2.8 : Typical micro-flora of market khoa.

Group	Genera
Yeasts	*Saccharomyces, Candida, Rhodotorula*
Moulds	*Aspergillus, Geotricum, Mucor, Syncephalostrum, Fusarium, Rhizopus, Cladosporium*
Bacteria	*Streptococci, Micrococci, Bacillus*
Pathogenic bacteria	*Staphylococci*

Table 2.9 : Typical micro-biological profile of khoa samples.

Microbial count cfu in thousands/g

Parameters	Lab sample	Market sample
Total plate count	521	17.02
Acid producers	211	2.54
Proteolytic	25	2.50
Chromogenic	23	2.42
Lipolytic	0.91	0.43
Spore count	0.050.3	0.30
Yeast & mould count	0.010.03	0.04

Table 2.10 : Effect of common chemical preservatives on shelf-life of khoa.

Preservative	Level	Shelf-life
Potassium sorbate	0.2—0.4 per cent	14 days (ambient)
Sodium metabisulphite	1000 ppm	14 days (ambient)
Nisin	0.02 per cent	21 days (ambient)

yeasts and moulds for a maximum period of 14—15 days. Addition of nisin at 0.02 per cent level helped to maintain flavour, body and texture of khoa up to three weeks.

Partial hydrolysis of lactose prior to khoa-making enhances the shelf-life. Mould growth on the surface of control samples of khoa was observed after 3-4 days while khoa made from lactose-hydrolyzed milk remained mould-free for one month. This improvement in shelf-life was caused by increased amounts of browning intermediates. Reduced water activity may be another controlling factor in the growth of moulds due to extra molecules of glucose and galactose produced from hydrolysis of lactose.

Nutritive Value of Khoa: Khoa is a concentrated form of milk solids. It is a rich source of energy, about 458 kcals/100 gram of product. During khoa production, heat desiccation of milk under atmospheric conditions brings about minor changes in the nutritional value of milk proteins (Table 2.11). Heat treatment also results in condensing of the amino acid group of lysine and aldehyde group of lactose, accounting for 2.59 per cent reduction of the available lysine. The vitamin content of milk is considerably reduced during the khoa manufacturing process (Table 2.12).

Table 2.11 : Effect of heat-treatment during khoa preparation on the nutritional quality of its proteins.

Nutritional quality parameter	Milk	Dhap khoa	Pindi khoa
Biological value (per cent)	98.88	99.22	99.20
Net protein utilization (per cent)	82.03	84.98	85.93
Digestibility coefficient (per cent)	99.12	97.70	96.34
Modified protein efficiency ratio	3.61	3.83	3.61
Net protein ratio	2.33	3.96	4.12
Available lysine (gm/gm of nitrogen)	0.48	0.48	0.47

Table 2.11 : Vitamin losses during khoa preparation

Vitamin	Per cent loss
Vitamin A	18.78
Riboflavin	28.76
Vitamin B_6	19.39
Folic acid	18.47
Vitamin C	25.05

KHOA POWDER

Dehydration is a universal method used for extended preservation of foods. Khoa powder, a desiccated product, potentially offers an economically attractive, long-life product that can supplement the traditional, perishable khoa. The drying process results in the reduction of water. It preserves the product and facilitates its marketing over long distances. Dried khoa process technology is still at the experimental stage. The technical challenge is to reproduce the functional properties in khoa, reconstituted from its powder and water, for the end point user in the production of various sweets like gulabjamun, burfi, peda and kalakand. Gulabjamuns of satisfactory quality have been prepared from khoa powder made from cow milk, but not so that from the buffalo milk. The product was found to possess an undesirable after-taste. More research is needed to produce an acceptable, high quality khoa powder. Various processes tried for making khoa powder include reverse osmosis, tray drying, spray drying, fluidized bed drying and roller drying.

Reverse Osmosis (RO): The feasibility of using RO-concentrated milk for making khoa powder has been demonstrated. In this process, skim milk was first concentrated to 28 per cent TS. The concentrate was then standardized by mixing 20 per cent cream to obtain 6 per cent fat in the final mix. The standardized concentrate was subsequently passed through a scraped surface heat exchanger to heat it to 126—130°C to impart the typical khoa colour and flavour. The heat-treated concentrate was then cooled down to about 65.6°C and finally dried over a steamheated roller drier to obtain khoa powder.

Tray Drying at Atmospheric Pressure: A flow diagram for the preparation of khoa powder by tray drying process is given in Figure 2.2. The khoa particles in trays can be dried at 70°C for four hours. Alternatively, the drying can be accomplished in three hours under vacuum (25 inches of mercury).

Spray Drying Process: It involves concentration of milk to 35 per cent solids in a vacuum evaporator, then heating it to develop cooked flavour, followed by spray drying. Inlet air temperature of 190°C and outlet air temperature of 88°C in the spray dryer is recommended.

Fluidized Bed Drying: In this process, khoa with 20 per cent moisture is finely ground and dried in a fluidizing chamber at inlet air temperature of 92°C and outlet air temperature of 80°C.

Table 2.13 : Physico-chemical and sensory characteristics of khoa powder.

Characteristics	Patel and De (1977)	Thompkinson and De (1981)	Rizvi et al. (1987)	
	Buffalo	Cow	Buffalo	Cow
Moisture (%)	2.9	3.0	2.9	2.5
Fat(%)	33.9	31.3	33.9	29.0
Protein (%)	27.0	31.3	33.9	29.0
Lactose (%)	30.9	26.8	30.9	38.0
Ash (%)	5.3	4.8	5.3	4,0
Solubility Index (g/ml)	—	13.0	14.5	—
Loose	0.26	0.33	0.27	—
Packed	0.35	0.43	0.35	—
Free fat (as % of total fat)	64.5	58.7	64.2	—
Colour	Light brownish white	Creamy yellow	White greenish tinge	—
Flavour	Pronounced cooked sweetish taste	Mild khoa-like	Slight cooked	—

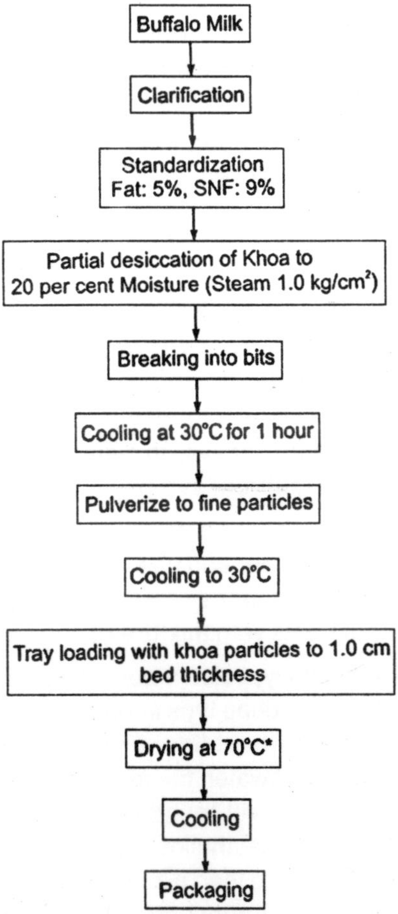

* Drying is done for 4 hours under atmospheric pressure and for 3 hours under vacuum (25 inches of mercury).

Fig. : 2.2 : Khoa powder production from buffalo milk by tray drying (atmospheric pressure/ vacuum).

Roller Drying Process: It involves pumping heated/cooked milk to steam-heated rollers and scraping the dried khoa. After grinding, the khoa powder is obtained.

The chemical, physical and sensory properties of khoa powder prepared by different methods have been investigated. When made from cow and buffalo milk, it did not show much difference in the moisture content, though wide variation was observed in the fat and lactose content. Free-fat content of buffalo khoa powder was comparatively higher than that of cow khoa powder. The water activity of khoa powder ranged between 0.15 and 0.20. Physico-chemical characteristics of khoa powder have been highlighted in Table 2.3.

Khoa powder can be packaged in tins in a way similar to that for whole milk powder. The tin-packed khoa powder is expected to have a shelf-life of about six months.

GULABJAMUN

Gulabjamun is a nationally popular khoa-based sweet. Originally, it was made with khoa and maida (flour). As it looked like the monsoon fruit, jamun, and was flavoured with rose water, it got its name of gulabjamun. It is usually consumed hot. The gourmet version of gulabjamun has centre-cored honey with pistachio and cardamom seeds and is preserved in kesar (saffron) syrup.

Product Description: Shaped both round and cylindrical, gulabjamun is golden to dark brown in colour and has a soft to firm body and smooth texture. It is soaked in thick sugar syrup. Variations include pantua and lalmohan, both Bengali treats with mixture of chhana and khoa.

Technology: Traditionally, gulabjamun is prepared on a small scale. In this process, 300 grams of dhap type khoa of 40—50 per cent moisture is mixed with 100 grams of wheat flour (maida) and 3 grams of baking powder. After adding sufficient water, the mixture is kneaded into a uniform dough and then rolled into small round or cylindrical shape. They are then deep-fried in edible oil in a shallow pan until they acquire a golden brown colour. The fried balls are then put into 62.5 per cent sugar solution and allowed to soak for a few hours before being served hot.

New technology for industrial production of gulabjamun has been developed using an assembly-line system and is in operation at the Sugam Unit of the Baroda District Cooperative Milk Producers' Union Ltd., Vadodara in Gujarat. A process flow diagram for the conversion of khoa into gulabjamun is shown in Figure 2.3. Canned gulabjamun is now being largely exported to the Gulf countries and America. Several dairy plants in India and abroad are producing gulabjamun on a large scale.

Khoa with 60—70 per cent total solids is mixed in a planetary mixer with 19—22 per cent of maida and leavening agent (baking powder). The dough is divided into 8 grams portions and transported to the ball forming machine. Then the balls are shaped like a cylinder and are carried to a frying system containing oil at a temperature of 140°C. After frying, the balls are soaked in 62.5 per cent sugar syrup solution. The gulabjamuns swell and weigh about 16 grams each. The gulabjamuns are then packaged in plastic containers and an appropriate amount of hot syrup is added. Lids are applied on the cups and subsequently sealed. Packaged gulabjamuns are stored under refrigerated conditions. Canned gulabjamuns are stored at room temperature.

Composition: The composition of gulabjamun on a drained weight basis is: fat (10%), protein (6%), sugar (42%) and other solids (14%). Acidity of the syrup for gulabjamun should not exceed 6 ml of 0.1N sodium hydroxide, needed to neutralize 100 ml of the syrup. Concentration of the syrup should be maintained at 62.4° Brix.

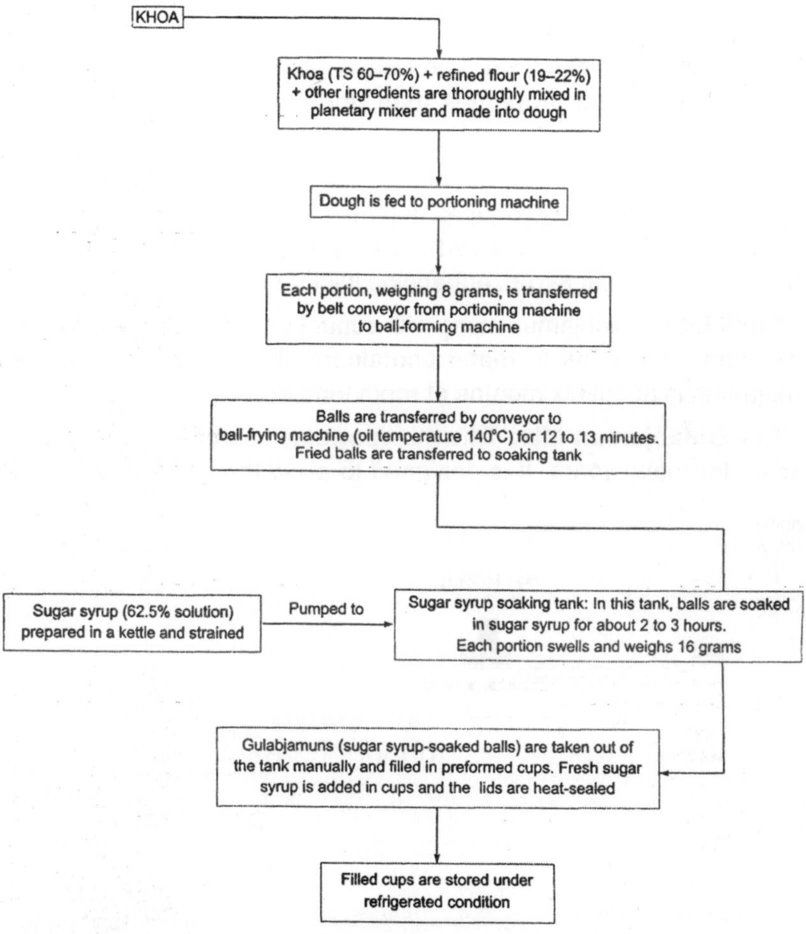

Fig. 2.3 : Flow chart of making gulabjamun.

Rheological Properties: Sponginess and other important sensory characteristics of gulabjamun have been studied using the Instron Universal Testing Machine. Their values are presented in Table 2.14. Instron hardness and deformation energy were highly correlated with sensory firmness. Also, correlations were apparent between instrumental fracturability and sensory crumbliness and chewiness.

Potential Process Modifications: The use of homogenized-milk khoa did not improve the quality of gulabjamun. However, when made with this khoa containing 0.08 per cent baking powder, gulabjamun exhibited good acceptability.

Various binders have been used and the most widely used is maida. Its recommended proportion is 10 per cent of weight of khoa. Wheat flour and suji have also been tried. The results showed that pre-soaked suji has better functional properties than dried suji, which improved the organoleptic attributes of gulabjamun.

Addition of trisodium citrate to the dough at a level of 0.5 to 0.8 per cent (w/w) of milk solids produced gulabjamuns of approved profile. The product was softer and showed more springiness and consequently absorbed more sugar syrup, enhancing juiciness.

Shelf Life: Gulabjamun along with sugar syrup is packaged in plastic containers as well as in metal containers. The shelf-life of canned gulabjamun is about six months at room temperature.

Dry Gulabjamun Mix: This mix (powder) has been a commercial product for many years. It is designed to allow the housewife to make

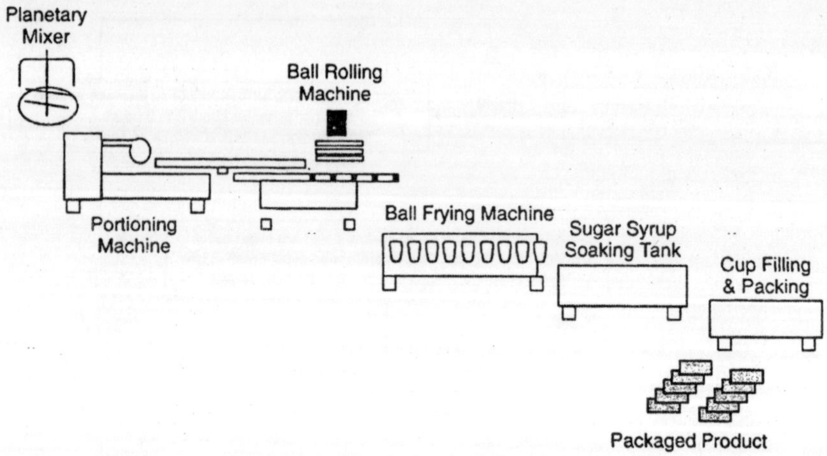

Fig. 2.4 : Process for industrial production of gulabjamun at Sugam Dairy, Vadodara.

gulabjamun at home. Traditionally, gulabjamun is made from khoa but the gulabjamun mixes are made from skim milk powder. Khoa is a perishable product and to impart long shelf-life to the gulabjamun powder, skim milk powder substitutes khoa. In some cases, roller-dried whole milk powder may be used. The chemical composition of the gulabjamun mix is given in Table 2.15. The Godhra Dairy in Gujarat is producing gulabjamun mix, based on technology from NDDB.

Table 2.14 : Texture profile of gulabjamun.

Texture profile	Most acceptable sample
Instron parameters	
Hardness, N	14.09
Deformation energy, N.mm	139.95
Cohesiveness	0.123
Springiness, mm	7.88
Fracturability, N	9.74
Gumminess, N	1.75
Chewiness, N.mm	14.21
Adhesive force, N	0.53
Sensory parameters*	
Firmness	51.4
Crumbliness	48.8
Sponginess	56.3
Gumminess	39.8
Chewiness	56.6
Juiciness	49.4
Overall texture quality	74.3

*Scored on a 100-point linear rating scale with the lower parametric extreme at one end (score, 0) and the higher extreme at the other end (score, 100).

Table 2.15 : Composition of gulabjamun mix.

Characteristics	Percentage
Moisture	8.44
Fat ' '	15.03
Total protein	19.45
Total ash	3.89
Carbohydrate (by difference)	53.19

Skim Milk Powder-based Gulabjamun Mix: This formulation consists of rollerdried skim milk powder (43.4%), maida (25%), semolina (suji) (15%), butter-fat/vanaspati (15%), baking powder (1.5%) and powdered cardamom (0.1%). All the ingredients are mixed uniformly in a power-driven mixer. Fat, after melting, is incorporated slowly to ensure thorough mixing. The mix is packaged into printed polyethylene bags or laminated pouches and stored in a dry place. Its shelf-life is more than six months at room temperature. To make gulabjamuns, 100 grams of the mix powder is mixed with 50—55 ml of water or milk to make the dough, and the rest of the procedure is the same as for traditional gulabjamun.

Whole Milk Powder-based Gulabjamun Mix: In this formulation, both skim milk powder and fat are replaced with whole milk powder. It consists of roller-dried whole milk powder (58.4%), maida (35%) and semolina (suji) (15%), baking powder (1.5%) and cardamom powder (0.1%). The packaging and other conditions are the same as in the skim milk powder-based gulabjamun mix.

Gulabjamuns made from dry mixes lack typical khoa taste. There is a potential of formulating gulabjamun mix with khoa powder in place of milk powder. The reformulated mix is likely to yield better tasting product with distinct khoa flavour.

KALAJAMUN

Kalajamun is similar to gulabjamun, but darker in colour—almost blackish (kala). Hence, its name. It is prepared from either khoa or chhana or a mixture thereof. It is also called kalajam in certain parts of north India. It has a hard crust outside and soft inside, with stuffing.

Technology: Khoa and chhana is mixed with small amounts of wheat flour (56%) and baking powder (0.5%) and kneaded into a smooth dough. It is then portioned into balls which are deep-fried in ghee till the surface is almost black in colour. Frying at temperature higher than that for gulabjamun imparts a black colour to the ball crust, but its inside remains white and soft. The balls are removed from the oil and soaked in sugar syrup (60%) for a few hours to permit the sugar syrup to permeate inside them. Finally, kalajamuns are removed from the syrup and stored till consumption.

The mechanized system developed for industrial production of gulabjamun could be adapted for kalajamun manufacture with minor modifications.

PANTUA

Pantua has its origin in the eastern region of India. It is similar to gulabjamun, except that its dough is made of a mixture of khoa and chhana, along with other ingredients such as cereals. As Lady Canning, the Vicereine of British India, patronized pantua during her time, its one variety has since been named after her as "Ledikeni", a Calcutta speciality. It is round in shape and also has stuffing inside. It has a higher proportion of khoa.

Product Description: Though very similar to gulabjamun in colour and appearance, pantua differs essentially in the ingredients used in its manufacture. It is cylindrical in shape and has stuffings of nuts and at times, saffron. The proportion of chhana is high compared to that of khoa. Starch is reported to be a common additive used.

Technology: The production of pantua is confined to the non-organized sector, which uses the traditional energy-intensive production process. The product-profile varies from producer to producer. Standardization of the traditional process in terms of manufacturing techniques, sensory profiles, and compositional and physico-chemical attributes has been attempted. Technology is now available for attaining a product of uniform standard and assured quality. It can be adapted to modify the existing method of continuous gulabjamun manufacture for pantua production in the organized dairy sector. In the traditional method, chhana is mixed with about 1 per cent baking powder and 12 per cent wheat flour. The mass is kneaded into a uniform dough, portioned and rolled into balls between the palms. The balls are deep-fried in ghee in a shallow pan till they are deep brown in colour. The fried balls are dipped in 60 per cent sugar solution for a few hours before serving.

A method for the manufacture of pantua has been standardized, wherein cow milk chhana (58% moisture) and dhap type khoa (40% moisture) were used. The final formulation contained chhana (50%), khoa (40%), maida (3%), arrow-root (3%), suji (3%), ground sugar (0.7%) and baking powder (0.3%). The ingredients were kneaded together to form a dough with 40 per cent moisture. The spherical balls (2.5 cm diameter and 12 grams weight) were fried in hydrogenated oil at 120°C and then dipped in 55 per cent sugar syrup at 60°C for 4 hours.

Physico-chemical Aspects: Wide variations have been found in the chemical composition of market samples of pantua. Table 2.6 compares the proximate chemical composition of the standard product with market samples.

Table 2.16 : Comparative composition of pantua.

per cent

Parameter	Standard product	Market samples
Total solids	59.7	57.7—68.3
Fat	15.5	8—11
Protein	8.7	6.7—7.9
Ash	0.67	0.32—0.53
Sucrose	27.1	37.8—43.6
Other carbohydrates	7.7	—

LALMOHAN

Though similar to gulabjamun, lalmohan is made from chhana and is lighter in colour than gulabjamun. It is similar to pantua, but round in shape. It has no stuffing inside.

Technology: Chhana is mixed with 23 per cent of wheat flour and kneaded into a uniform dough. The dough is then rolled into small balls and deep-fried in ghee until light brown in colour. The fried balls are transferred to 60 per cent sugar syrup and allowed to soak for a few hours before serving.

The mechanized system developed for the industrial manufacture of gulabjamun has the potential of being adapted for the mechanized production of lalmohan.

BURFI

Burfi has been favoured as one of the most popular khoa-based sweets all over India. The unique adaptability of khoa in terms of its flavour, body and texture to blend with a wide range of food adjuncts has permitted development of an impressive array of burfi varieties. Among these, fruit, nut, chocolate, coconut, saffron and rawa burfi are popular. These food adjuncts may be artfully used singly or in innovative combinations to delight a gourmet. The artful ingenuity of the sweet-maker in creating special qualities in burfi fetches higher consumer prices. The myriad combinations include burfi prepared with cashewnut as katli (a wafer-thin slice), almond, pistachio, coconut, mango, orange, mud apple, bottle gourd and potato. The sublime manifestation of burfi is launj, made with pistachios. It is soft and chewy, resembling halwa-burfi.

Technology. Preparation of burfi is mainly confined to the non-organized sector, although during the past decade a promising endeavour has been made to produce burfi through mechanized systems. On the cottage scale, burfi is prepared in small batches, employing mild steel shallow pans. When prepared directly from milk, buffalo milk with a fat: SNF ratio of 1:1.5 is preferred. Depending upon the type of burfi desired, specially prepared quality of khoa may be selected. Khoa is thoroughly worked by hand to produce as smooth texture as possible. Heat from direct fire is applied for blending khoa with sugar at 30 per cent of khoa (either in crystalline or syrup form), and other adjuncts. Contents of pan are skillfully handled to produce desired attributes of flavour (mild or strongly cooked, caramel, nutty), body (moist, soft, semi-hard or hard) and texture (smooth, coarse, chewy, grainy). Flavouring materials are judiciously added in the pan at a suitable stage, but mostly towards the end of the cooking process. When desirable organoleptic attributes have been developed, the product is poured in trays or moulds in a uniform layer, thickness of which is consistent with the final form of burfi. The product is allowed to set, as it cools under atmospheric conditions. Once properly set, burfi is cut into required shape and size and finally packed in paper or corrugated cardboard boxes or high impact polystyrene tubs.

Industrial Manufacture: Investigations carried out at the National Dairy Research Institute (NDRI), Karnal, indicate that in the manufacture of burfi of acceptable quality, a Thin-film Scraped Surface Heat Exchanger (TSSHE) can be utilized for initial concentration of milk, followed by finishing operations in a processing kettle. Alternatively, a two-stage TSSHE assembly coupled with a conical double-jacketed vat or even a three-stage TSSHE assembly may be used. Cardamom and potassium sorbate are added at the rate of 0.1 per cent of khoa (w/w) as preservatives followed by hot packaging of the product into multilayer coextruded nylon barrier pouches under vacuum. This method permitted a shelf-life of about 45 days at 30°C.

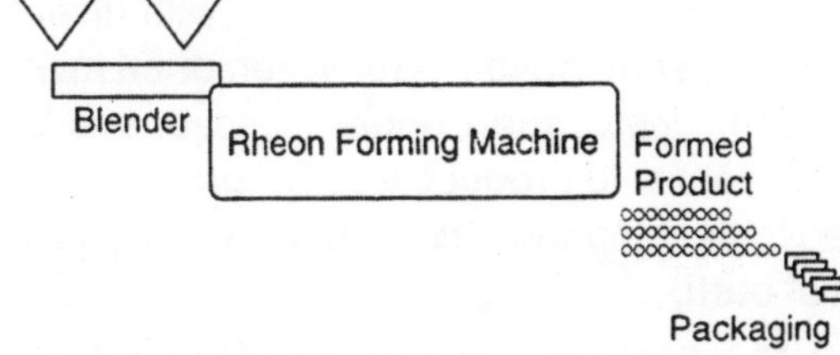

Fig. 2.5 : Mechanized process for production of burfi.

A mechanized process for commercial production of burfi was successfully developed by the NDDB and installed at the Sugam Dairy, Baroda (Fig 2.5), although no longer in use currently. The process line was conceptually linked with the continuous khoa-making unit. In this process for the production of plain burfi, all the ingredients, viz., khoa, sugar and additives, such as cardamom, nuts, etc., are first heat processed to blend uniformly in a planetary mixer. The processed ingredients are then fed to a Rheon-shaping and forming machine. A die at the end of the encrusting machine permits imaginative choice of a wide range of designs that may be imparted to shape the burfi emerging from the machine in a continuous uninterrupted flow. Burfi is then packed in corrugated cardboard boxes. For packaging, multi-layer coextruded nylon barrier film having structure PE/bonded layer and nylon/bonded layer have also been successfully tried.

For preparation of the layered form of burfi, another 'premix' is simultaneously formulated in another planetary mixer in addition to the basic khoa-based formulation as described above. The layered coating could be of chocolate, saffron, nuts or a suitable fruit pulp, such as mango. A dough of the coating is prepared in the second planetary mix, the consistency of which is crucial to permit passage through a encrusting machine as well as its application as a smooth and uniform layer on the khoa-based portion of the burfi. The two premixes are then led to a encrusting machine. The thickness of the coating layer can be controlled through the operating parameters of the encrusting machine. Selecting variable extruding dies at the end of the layering barrel can help develop an imaginative range of product shapes and designs.

Quality Factors: In commercial practices, burfi may be prepared directly through concentration of buffalo milk or alternatively by use of khoa. Due to regional or seasonal scarcity of either milk or khoa, plain concentrated milk or spray dried/roller dried skim milk powder/whole milk powder may also be used. When concentrated milk or dried milk is used as the source of milk solids, a slurry is made with desiccated milk in a shallow pan to form a semi-solid mass. When dried milk is used for the preparation of burfi, desiccation under atmospheric conditions after reconstitution is essential to produce free SH groups from whey proteins that are required to develop the desirable cooked/pleasant caramelized flavour, typical of burfi.

Fat Content: The final product must have at least 20 per cent fat for imparting optimum mouthfeel to it. During the heat desiccation of milk accompanied by constant/ vigorous agitation, fat globule is ruptured resulting in the liberation of free fat. The presence of free fat during the final stages of desiccation is essential to impart desirable flavour, mouthfeel, body and texture characteristics to the product. A good sample of burfi should contain 67—69 per cent free fat.

Stage of Sugar Addition: Finely ground sugar is preferable especially when the starting material is khoa or concentrated milk to ensure uniformity of mixing. Presence of large crystals of sugar leads to the development of a gritty texture in the finished product. Sugar should be mixed at not less than 50°C and sufficiently processed with khoa using brisk mixing motion to ensure smooth texture in burfi.

Effect of Additives: A number of ingredients such as nuts, chocolates, fruits, saffron, etc., may also be incorporated in burfi during the manufacturing process. The nature of additives affects the flavour, body, texture and shelf life of burfi. Recent R and D work has shown that addition of 0.015 per cent saffron to burfi improves the shelf-life of the product by acting as a deterrent to microbiological activity during storage.

Corn Syrup Addition: Further Rand D work has shown that up to 50 per cent of the cane sugar may be replaced advantageously with corn syrup (42 DE). Burfi samples prepared with a mixture of cane sugar and corn syrup displayed superior gloss on the surface, body and texture. Corn syrup also tends to inhibit the growth of bacteria and imparts a longer shelf-life of the product.

Desiccation Temperature: Temperature of about 80°C for heat desiccation is considered ideal. A temperature lower than 80°C is inadequate to impart pleasant caramel flavour in the product. On the other hand, temperature of 90°C tends to impart brown colouration as well as an objectionable cooked flavour.

Physico-chemical Characteristics: The generic nomenclature "burfi" covers a wide range of product variations that include plain burfi, danedar burfi, dudh burfi, chocolate burfi, fruit burfi and coconut burfi. Their flavour, colour, body and texture vary.

Flavour: Typically, burfi has a mildly caramelised and pleasant flavour. When additives like cardamom, chocolate, coconut, fruit, etc., are added, the mild pleasant flavour is further complemented to enhance both product appeal and value.

Colour: The colour of burfi may range from off-white to creamy or light caramel, depending mainly upon the type of milk solids used as base material and also the extent of heat desiccation during the preparation of burfi.

Body: The body characteristics of burfi and its flavour vary considerably among product varieties. It may range from very loosely compacted to a closely-knit body. The texture could also vary from smooth to granular and crisp to chewy. A microscopic thin layer of free fat separates granules in the closely-knit mass.

Texture: Light and scanning electron microscopy has been employed to study the structure of burfi. The main structure consists of thread-like particles consisting of protein-protein bonding in which fat globules and sugar solutions are dispersed. Minute crystals of sugar may also be observed depending upon the type of burfi. A sheet structure covers the space occupied by sugar solutions. Values of the rheological properties of burfi have been recorded: hardness 35.2 mN, cohesiveness 0.15, springiness 5.25 mN, gumminess 5.49 mN, chewiness 28.80 mN, penetration value 79—90 (0.1 mm), and viscosity 30,000—33,500 cp. The sensory texture descriptors of soft and hard types of burfi are given in Table 2.17.

Table 2.17 Sensory texture descriptors of burfi.

Descriptor	Soft burfi	Hard burfi
Firmness	53.0	79.4
Elasticity	24.7	15.1
Crumbliness	61.0	71.8
Chewiness	30.0	24.9
Stickiness	33.8	11.3
Smoothness	36.2	27.0

Equilibrium Relative Humidity (ERH) of Burfi: The shelf-life of burfi is related to the ERH value. Lower the ERH value, longer the shelf-life. The ERH value of a plain burfi sample has been reported as 70 per cent at 30°C. The sample contained 15.15 per cent moisture (the corresponding equilibrium moisture content being 14.86%).

Free Fatty Acids: The level of free fatty acids has a significant effect on the shelf-life of burfi. Fresh samples of burfi may contain traces of free fatty acids, depending upon the severity of heat desiccation as well as the quality of khoa used. Under laboratory conditions, about 0.21 per cent free fatty acid (as oleic acid) was present in burfi.

Hydroxy Methyl Furfural (HMF) Content: The HMF content of burfi reflects the intensity of heat treatment imparted during manufacturing, leading to degradation of the eamino acid group of lysine with the aldehyde group of lactose. The initial HMF content of the burfi sample is also indicative of the extent of browning that may take place during storage period. Freshly prepared samples of burfi under laboratory conditions may contain 10.6 mmole of HMF per 100 grams, and market samples 16.2 to 20.7 mmole per 100 grams, of the TS content.

Microbiological Quality: It is mainly governed by the initial quality of milk, quality of additives and the microflora of the environment. Despite desiccation of milk at near boiling temperature, the product is susceptible to atmospheric contamination.

The standard plate count (SPC) of burfi has been reported to vary in the range of 240 to 1,100 cfu/g, when burfi is prepared under controlled conditions. Freshly prepared market samples are reported to contain 1,000—350,000 cfu organisms/g. Various bacterial species found in samples of burfi belong to the thermophillic and mesophillic species, including spores. Proteolytic and acid-forming bacteria tend to predominate in the normal microflora of burfi. Among the moulds, the Mucor and Rhizopus spp., and among yeasts, Saccharomyces and Candida spp. are predominant. Chromogenic yeasts and moulds may be also found in the stored samples of burfi. However, a mechanized and enclosed system for burfi manufacture followed by mechanized packaging obviates the possibility of undesirable microbial contamination of the product.

Several studies have been carried out to profile the microbiological changes during storage of burfi. Under controlled conditions of preparation, the total viable count was found to increase from 2.50 to 4.47 (log 10 per g) during storage at 30°C for 20 days. When 0.1 per cent potassium sorbate was used as a preservative, the rate of microbial growth was slower, reaching a level of 4.70 (log 10 per g) at the end of 60 days storage at the same temperature. The yeast and mould counts under identical conditions were found to be 3.09 and 2.70 (log 10 per g), respectively.

Shelf-life: Both moisture content and free fat have a major influence on the shelf-life of burfi, and both vary widely. Further, the manufacturing conditions and packaging as well as type of package also influence the shelf life of the product.

Rancidity: The high percentage of free fat in burfi makes it susceptible to oxidative rancidity. Due to the denaturation of milk lipase during the heat desiccation stage of khoa-making, hydrolytic rancidity does not develop on storage of burfi unless the product has been contaminated in the subsequent stages of handling. Under controlled conditions of product preparation, the free fatty acid content (as oleic acid) of burfi may increase from 0.21 to 0.31 per cent. During its storage, keto-glycerides may also be formed.

Studies have been carried out to extend the shelf-life of burfi by incorporating antioxidants like propyl gallate and dodecyl gallate. Samples of burfi containing 5—9 per cent moisture content with added antioxidants can be stored for a period of 12 months at 20—30°C without development of rancid flavour. On the other hand, untreated control samples develop rancidity within six months. Packaging of burfi in metalized polyester film under vacuum further retards rancidity development.

Acid Development: Due to recontamination during post-desiccation process of khoa production, a large number of lactic acid-forming bacteria may be present in khoa. These make burfi vulnerable to microbial growth during storage. Under controlled conditions of preparation and storage, the pH of burfi may drop from an initial value of 6.40 to 6.21 during the 20 days storage at 30°C. Storage at 57°C is recommended for prolonging the shelf-life of burfi.

Browning: During storage of burfi, carbonyl compounds are converted into DNP-hydrazones. Methyl ketones, also associated with the pleasant flavour of the freshly prepared product, tend to be converted into the saturated aldehydes, which exhibit off-flavour upon prolonged storage, especially at higher temperatures. During storage of burfi samples at 30°C for 20 days, the HMF content has been observed to increase from an initial value of 10.57 to 12.30 mmole per 100 TS of the product. The use of antioxidants as preservatives tends to reduce the rate of browning only marginally. The rate of browning proceeds at a faster rate as SH groups liberated during the heat processing are converted into SS groups. Samples of burfi prepared from roller-dried milk powder tend to undergo brown discolouration and flavour deterioration faster during storage as compared to samples prepared directly from liquid milk.

Packaging: The current commercial practice of cutting burfi into pieces and packing them in paper cartons/corrugated cardboard boxes is inadequate to guard against atmospheric and manual contamination. The product tends to pick up odours from the surrounding atmosphere and lose its typical pleasant aroma. At the same time, it is also prone to oxidative rancidity.

Vacuum packaging of burfi has been attempted under laboratory conditions with favourable results. Among packaging materials used are LDPE, aluminium foil, LDPE-metal laminate, cryovac film and metalized polyester. Metal container permits shelf-life of 30 days at 30°C. The use of film for packaging of burfi is useful in preventing the surface growth of microflora and also for reducing the development of oxidative rancidity. The surface of packaging film may be treated with hydrogen peroxide (0.5%).

Cryovac pouches prove to be superior for packaging than polystyrene tubs, both in efficiency of storage and economy. Burfi packaged in pre-sterilized pouches was acceptable up to 30 days at 30°C, while in Cryovac it could be stored for 180 days at 5°C. Incorporation of 0.1 per cent sorbic acid further improves the shelf-life to 190 days at 5°C. An equilibrium relative humidity (ERH) of 70 per cent (having moisture content of 15%) was optimum for storage at 30°C. Higher ERH encouraged the mould growth and lower ERH impaired the textural quality of burfi. Loss of moisture from the product during storage at 3037°C also influences the Theological properties of burfi. The hardness was found to increase from an initial value of 30.2 to 38.6 mN, cohesiveness from 0.16 to 0.20, springiness from 5.25 to 7.32 mN, gumminess from 4.98 to 7.76 mN, and chewiness from 26.15 to 56.80 mN when burfi samples were stored at 30°C for a period of 60 days.

KALAKAND

The granular texture of kalakand represents an ingenious innovation (probably of more recent origin) over other forms of khoa-based sweets. It has been achieved through deliberate texturization of the concentrated mass of milk solids during the concentration process. This delicacy has been described in Annaji's Soundara Vilasa (17 AD) as 'milk thickened by boiling till it fell in flakes'. There are also references elsewhere of kene-payasa, a sweet concoction of cream. Presently, kalakand is popular all over the country, particularly in the northern, eastern and central parts.

Product Description: Kalakand is prepared by blending sugar with 'danedar' khoa. It is typified by a pleasant caramel flavour and granular texture. The granular mass is fused, and holds together a loosely compacted body. The colour of kalakand varies from off-white to light caramel. So far, no compositional standards for kalakand have been laid down under either the PFA Act or the Bureau of Indian Standards (BIS). Variations in proximate composition of laboratory made kalakand are given in Table 2.18.

Table 2.18 : Approximate composition of kalakand.

per cent

Composition	Arora etal., (1991)*	Suresh & Jha (1994)**
Total solids	63.59—84.75	70.0—80.1
Fat	4.75—26.46	19.1—22.2
Proteins	9.40—17.91	13.2—15.7
Sugar	15.38—42.14	34.5—39.9
Lactose	11.96—21.90	(Total carboyd rates)
Ash	1.78—3.48	2.1—2.3
Acidity	0.26—0.70	0.5—0.7

* Samples taken from all over India including Mumbai, Hyderabad, Anand and various towns in the State of Haryana.

** Samples taken from different markets in the State of Uttar Pradesh.

Size of Industry: Despite its wide popularity across the country, the manufacture of kalakand is confined to the non-organized sector to meet the local demand. Lack of suitable technology and packaging systems for large scale industrial production severely limits the task of maintaining its keeping quality over a long period. This impedes production and marketing of the product by the organized sector. Due to the batch-wise nature of production as well as absence of a scientific approach, variations in the chemical and microbiological quality of product are wide.

Technology: Buffalo milk, standardized to about 6 per cent fat and 9.09.5 per cent SNF, is generally preferred for the preparation of kalakand. Standardized milk is boiled in an iron karahi placed over a brisk and non-smoky fire with continuous stirring by a khunti (ladle) in a circular motion with occasional scraping of the heating surface. Alternatively, a double jacketed kettle may be used with steam at 1—1.2 kg/cm pressure. After 10—15 minutes of boiling, 0.02 per cent of citric acid (of the volume of milk, in the form of 12% solution) is added to permit the formation of well-defined granules. At this stage, vigorous stirring is required to obtain a product of good quality. When a semi-solid state is reached, intensity of heating is reduced and sugar (67% by weight of milk) is added and stirred well. If desired, flavourings and chopped nuts may be added at this stage. Heating is continued for another five minutes to permit uniform mixing of additives with the semi-solid mass of milk. The finished product is transferred to a tray greased with ghee for cooling and setting. After cooling to room temperature, the firmly set product is cut into required shape and size, packaged and stored.

Kalakand is also manufactured from Danedar khoa by mixing various ingredients such as sugar, aromatic spices, etc., over the fire in a shallow pan. The entire mass is potted in a thin layer and slabs of desired size are cut after cooling for final serving once the product forms a compact mass.

Sensory Quality: The sensory attributes of kalakand such as colour, body and texture and the overall acceptability of the finished product are influenced by the fat level of milk, amount of sugar and strength and type of coagulant.

Fat: Cohesiveness, the most desirable characteristic of kalakand, is optimum in the samples made with 6 per cent milk fat. Fat level in buffalo milk lower than 6 per cent yields less acceptable product.

Sugar: Good quality kalakand in terms of colour, flavour and body and texture is obtained by using sugar at 7 per cent level. Although the product prepared with higher level is acceptable, it possesses an inferior colour due to browning. A sugar content of 11 per cent results in cooked flavour, syrupy body and excessive browning in the final product.

Strength and Type of Coagulant: Citric acid at 0.02—0.05 per cent levels is commonly used to induce good granule formation during kalakand preparation. Use of 0.02 per cent citric acid results in kalakand possessing optimum chewiness, gumminess and hardness values. Use of tartaric acid leads to a pasty product. Aged whey (3%) yields a product exhibiting loose texture and slight bitterness, whereas the product made with alum is sticky, irregular in granule size and inferior in colour.

Table 2.19 : Microbiological quality of kalakand.

Cfu/g

Microbial counts	Market samples			Lab samples	
	Magadum (1990)	Arora etal. (1991)	Suresh & Jha (1994)	Rao (1992)	Suresh & Jha(1994)
Total counts	1836—41160	1000—123000	29500—92000	4033	1000
Conforms	0—228	0—4000	660—1500	0	40
Yeasts & moulds	2—154	0—9250	440—1200	10.33	10

Microbiological Quality: Microbial counts of laboratory and market samples of kalakand are presented in Table 2.19. Besides micro-organisms found in milk/khoa, kalakand may also contain those found in sugar and other flavourings and nuts used in its manufacture. The post-manufacturing contamination occurs in the product due to the environmental conditions of manufacturing, handling, packing and storage.

Biochemical Quality: Market as well as laboratory samples of kalakand were analysed for various biochemical characteristics. The market samples constantly exhibited inferior quality attributes as compared to the laboratory samples (Table 2.20).

Table 2.19 Biochemical characteristics of kalakand.

Characteristics	Laboratory sample	Market sample
Tyrosine value (mg/100 g)	58.70	3.8
Peroxide value (meq/kg fat)	0.3—0.4	0.1
Sulphydryl groups (mg cystine HCl/g)	2.6—7.7	1.00
Hydroxymethyl groups (μ moles/100g total solids)	18.0	26.6
Free fatty acid (per cent oleic acid)	0.2—0.4	0.2

Sensory Quality: Commercial samples of kalakand vary from a slightly cooked, sweet pleasant to cooked caramelized flavour, are whitish yellow to brownish colour, which may be attributed to the amount of sugar and the extent of heat treatment. The body and texture of the market samples is observed to be less chewy and having bigger granules.

Packaging and Storage: Due to its high water activity level, kalakand is highly susceptible to microbial and enzymic spoilage. The packaging system should be so improved as to provide sufficient protection to the product against microbial and oxidation spoilage.

Attempts have been made to prolong the shelf-life of kalakand up to 21 days by wrapping it in parchment paper and storing under refrigeration temperature (8—10°C). The use of flexible films and laminates has been suggested for packaging with or without vacuum. Kalakand packaged under vacuum in metalized polyester and saran-coated cellophane/LDPE and stored in cartons remains acceptable for 50 days and 21 days at 6—10°C and 30°C, respectively.

Laboratory studies for extending the shelf-life of kalakand indicate beneficial effect of employing ultraviolet (UV) radiation on the surface of packaging material as well as use of potassium sorbate as a preservative. Kalakand samples with 0.2 per cent potassium sorbate had been added and were then packaged in polyethylene bags pre-exposed to UV irradiation for 20 minutes at 30° ± 1°C and stored at 30° ± 1°C and 37° ± 1°C remained acceptable up to 24 and 15 days, respectively. However, the control samples without potassium sorbate became unacceptable after the sixth and third day at the respective temperatures.

The prevalent practice of packaging kalakand in parchment paper and cardboard boxes does not provide sufficient protection against environmental contamination, and the product becomes unacceptable for consumption after a short period of time. Even the use of flexible laminates may not be suitable for distant outstation retail sale of the product as they would not be able to counter transportation hazards, making the product unacceptable to consumers. Therefore, a suitable system for its packaging needs to be developed conforming to the requirements of the nutritional labelling and quality assurance consistent with international norms.

MILK CAKE

Milk cake resembles kalakand except for its colour and flavour. It has typical grainy texture and distinct caramelized flavour, with layers of white to light brown colour from top to bottom. This value-added product offers entrepreneurs a new avenue to add to their profits, provided its traditional method of preparation is adapted in modern technology.

Technology: Milk cake is produced in the non-organized sector of the industry. Currently, its production entails energy and labour intensive inputs. Standardization of production process and product quality would enhance its popularity and profitability. Based on the traditional process of milk cake production, the following method can be adopted for its commercial production.

Milk is standardized to 6 per cent fat and 9 per cent solids-not-fat (SNF). It is boiled in a karahi for three minutes and citric acid is added at the rate of 0.02 per cent (w/volume of milk). Desiccation is continued. When the volume is reduced to 50 per cent of the original milk, sugar is added at the level of 6 per cent (w/v). Further desiccation is continued with fast stirring to obtain dough-like consistency. The hot dough is transferred to greased tray, and it is slowly cooled in an insulated box for five to six hours. Alternatively, the bottom of the tray can be cooled in chilled water to enhance colour differential in top and bottom layers.

After the product is cooled, it is cut into desired shapes and packaged in parchment paper. To achieve longer shelf-life, milk cake may be cooled in sealed moulds placed in an insulated box to slow down cooling and to produce desirable flavour and colour. Storage and distribution of milk cake should be at 5°C. This formulation and processing regime can be further optimized to develop attributes as per regional preferences of consumers.

In the traditional method, hot dough of milk cake is poured into trays. The bottom of the tray is cooled in iced water while the top of the tray is cooled slowly at room temperature exposing of this portion to high heat. It causes a differential in caramelization of top and bottom layers. The top layer gets a darker colour and stronger flavour. The rapidly cooled bottom layer retains white colour. To effect softness in the product, some milk cake producers add a pinch of sodium metabisulfite to the mixture prior to the removal of its heating vessel from fire.

The R and D Group at NDDB, Anand, has undertaken the development of continuous line for the manufacture of milk cake for the Alwar Milk Union in Rajasthan. It is also working on the design of a packaging system to increase the product's shelf-life to about four to five weeks under ambient temperature.

PEDA

Peda is a khoa-based indigenous milk product, popular all over India. According to industry estimates, the production of pedas exceeds that of any other indigenous milk-based sweet. It is prepared by mixing khoa with copious quantities of sugar. During production process, the stirfrying dries out the moisture, and sugar provides the preservative, giving peda a long shelf-life, making it an ideal prasad. Peda is the sandesh (a Bengali delicacy) of North India. Peda is as popular in the north as sandesh is in the east. The best peda in the land comes from Brindavan in Mathura (Uttar Pradesh) and from Rajkot in Gujarat. Two finest purveyors of the art of peda making in Brindavan, the janambhoomi (birth place) of Lord Krishna, are Shankar and Brijwasi.

The manufacture of peda is mostly restricted to halwais. Since peda has lower moisture content than burfi, it has a better keeping quality. Pedas are mostly offered as prasad during religious worship in temples, as well as on various ceremonial celebrations. In some parts of Punjab, crushed peda is added to lassi to sweeten and enrich this delicious drink. During certain fasting festivals, the devotees are required to refrain from eating grain or cereal products. Peda is recognized as a pure food (prasad), suitable for consumption during the festival period and for breaking the fast on religious occasions.

Product Description: Peda or doodh peda is prepared using khoa as base material. Khoa is mixed with sugar and then heated in a karahi made of food-grade metal. After heating, desired flavourings and nuts are added to the peda mass. The heat process removes some of the moisture of khoa. Sugar provides sweetness and exerts a preservative effect. It is nearly half as sweet as Western style fudge, but is rich and satisfying.

Technology: Peda is generally prepared by mixing khoa and sugar in the ratio 3:1. The khoa-sugar mixture is heated on a gentle fire till the mixture turns relatively firm. Then, the pan is removed from the fire. If desired, nuts and flavouring substances are added. The contents are mixed thoroughly and made into balls of 15 to 20 grams size by rolling between the palms after applying a little ghee to avoid sticking. The balls are flattened to give them disc shape. The product may also be formed into different shapes, using dies or moulds. Cardamom is commonly added for flavouring the peda. Some manufacturers also use permitted colours to prepare pedas of different colours. Incorporating 12 per cent cocoa makes chocolate pedas. For kesar or saffron peda, a preferred variety, saffron is mixed for added flavour and colour.

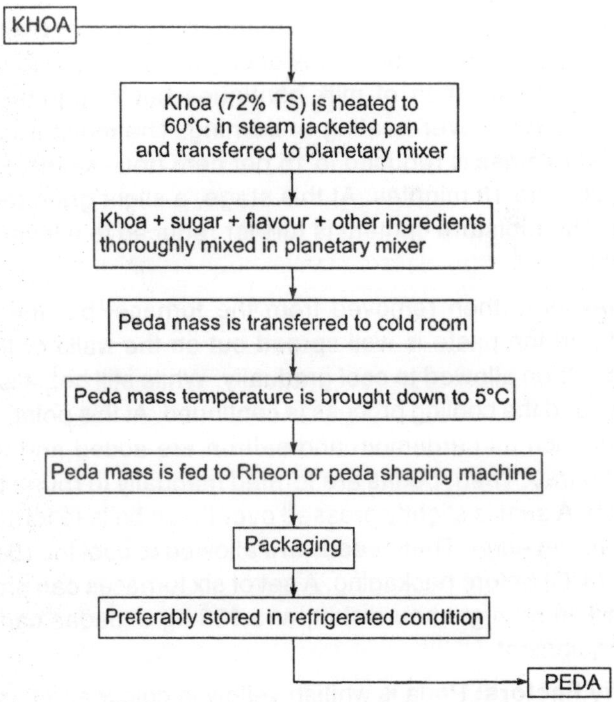

Fig. 2.6 : Flow-chart of Peda making.

Current Status: Recently, some plants have undertaken peda production using mechanized equipment and Rheon extruder. They use a planetary mixer for effecting uniformity from batch to batch. The R and D Group of NDDB, Anand, has recently developed a peda-moulding machine and a continuous peda line.

Figure 2.6 shows a flow diagram for the conversion of khoa into peda. Khoa is concentrated to 72 per cent total solids and heated to 60°C in a steam-jacketed pan. After transferring khoa to a planetary mixing vessel, sugar and flavourings are added and mixed thoroughly. The peda mass is then stored at 0—4°C for about 10 hours to bring the temperature down to 4—5°C and then fed into the peda-shaping machine. The pedas are shaped, packaged and then stored under refrigeration.

The Rajkot District Cooperative Milk Producers' Union Ltd., Rajkot, Gujarat, has developed special equipment for making peda. Five litres of chilled buffalo raw milk containing 6 per cent fat and 9 per cent SNF is poured into a specially designed clean vessel, which is then placed on a heating furnace. Stirring is done manually right from the beginning. When milk comes to boil, 450 grams of sugar is added, and the stirring is continued. Desiccation of milk continues but it requires skill and experience to avoid over-heating or burning. The moisture content of the desiccated mass is reduced to 15 per cent (total solids: 85%). This takes about 15 to 18 minutes. At this stage, a slight grain formation is observed. The moisture content is further reduced to a level of 13.5 to 14 per cent.

The vessel is then removed from the furnace, but the stirring is continued and the paste is well spread out on the walls of the vessel. The paste is then allowed to cool gradually. While still hot, it is placed in a large tray and the cooling process is continued. At this point, flavouring ingredients such as cardamom and saffron are added and thoroughly mixed in the tray. Then, pedas are formed manually to round balls of 20 grams each. A seal is slightly pressed over these balls to form a circular peda with round edge. Then, pedas are allowed to cool for 16 hours in a cold room (4°C) before packaging. A set of six furnaces can process 600 litres of milk in an eight hours shift, and 168 kg of pedas can be made with this equipment.

Quality Factors: Peda is whitish yellow in colour and has a coarse grainy texture. Its quality is determined by the quantity of sugar added, heating parameters and storage conditions. Typical chemical composition of peda is shown in Table 2.21.

Table 2.21 : Average composition of peda.

per cent

Constituent	Value
Moisture	14.36
Fat	19.31
Protein	15.34
Lactose	15.25
Ash	2.47
Sucrose	33.27

Packaging: Traditionally, peda is packaged in paperboard cartons with a parchment paper liner or grease-proof paper liner and sold through confectionery shops.

Shelf-life: Shelf-life extension of peda, using different packaging techniques has been studied. Peda has been packaged in multi-layer transparent laminates under modified atmospheric packing (MAP) of nitrogen and carbon dioxide in proportion of 80:20 (N_2:CO_2:: 80:20) and also under normal atmospheric environment with oxygen scavenger. The control samples consisted of peda packaged in cardboard box without barrier film or MAP or oxygen scavenger. Irrespective of storage temperature, the control peda showed mould growth after seven days. Samples with MAP exhibited shelf-life of 15 days at 37°C and at ambient temperature, but at 20°C storage the shelf-life was extended to 30 days. Peda samples packaged with oxygen scavenger showed extended shelf-life of two months at 37°C, five months at ambient temperatures and 6 months at 20°C.

This MAP system has been introduced in the Surat District Cooperative Milk Producers' Union Ltd. (Sumul), Surat, Gujarat, to increase the shelf-life of peda at ambient temperature, based on the process and product innovation of the R and D Group of NDDB, Anand. Consequently, Sumul has launched the longlife peda, as also the Karnataka Cooperative Milk Producers' Federation Ltd. (KMF), Bangalore.

DHARWAD PEDA

Like other milk sweets, Dharwad peda was also introduced by migrants from North India in the southern region. Introduced by Sri Mohan Singh, a Thakur, about 150 years ago, it is essentially a variant of the earlier known Lucknow peda with certain adaptations. Typically, Dharward peda is dark brown in colour. It has a soft but firm, cohesive body and granular texture. It stands up well in rounded shape. The product is yet to be characterised through scientific studies.

Size of Industry: Dharwad peda is essentially produced on small scale by local sweetmeat makers in the non-organised sector. Everyday, an estimated 1,000 to 1,500 kg of it is sold in Dharwad (Karnataka).

Technology: Dharwad peda is essentially prepared from fresh buffalo milk. In the traditional production method, milk is first boiled in a large round pan to make khoa, which is then fried in ghee and mixed with sugar. The resulting thick paste is poured into small moulds and powdered sugar and some broken almonds are sprinkled over the surface and the product is allowed to solidify. Peda is then taken out from the moulds and arranged in shallow trays for display at the sale point.

THIRATTUPAL

Popular in Tamil Nadu and Kerala States, thirattupal is similar to peda, except that its texture is coarsely granular. It is obtained by partially coagulating the hot milk by addition of one or two spoons of sour curd prior to sugar and completion of desiccation. Largely prepared in homes for family consumption, thirattupal has fairly good keeping quality.

Technology: Buffalo milk is generally preferred for making this product. Milk is concentrated over direct fire in 56 litre lots in an open shallow vessel (karahi) with vigorous stirring/scraping of the heating surface by a flat surface iron scraper (kadhchi/khunti). When partial concentration has taken place, sour curd is added to it at the rate of about 0.1 per cent of the milk and heating is continued till semi-solid body is formed. A pleasant caramel flavour appears and coarse granular texture develops. Partial coagulation of milk in early stages helps in the separation of whey and production of a granular product. Separation of whey at the early stage of desiccation enables quicker evaporation of moisture during subsequent desiccation.

When the desired desiccation has taken place, ground sugar or powdered jaggery is added in the ratio about 3:1. The mixture is heated on a gentle fire till it turns relatively firm. Then the pan is removed from the fire. At this stage, powdered cardamom (0.01%) and traces of borneol (a type of edible camphor) are added to impart typical flavour. The contents are mixed thoroughly and made into balls of 15 to 20 grams size by rolling between the palms after applying little ghee to avoid sticking. The product may also be formed into different shapes, using dies or moulds.

Prospects of Mechanization: The mechanized system, which has been developed for the industrial manufacture of peda at the Sugam Dairy, Baroda, has the potential for its manufacture on an industrial scale.

RABRI

Rabri is a concentrated, sweetened whole milk delicacy, containing several layers of clotted cream, and skimmed off from slowly evaporating milk. Rabri is in demand during festivals and other celebrations, specially in the northern and eastern parts of India.

Product Description: Rabri is creamy white to caramelised in colour, possesses viscous body containing several layers of clotted cream with a chewy texture. It has a pleasant caramelised flavour.

Technology: Buffalo milk is normally used for preparingrabri, owing to its high total solids and superior taste in the final product. Rabri is traditionally prepared by heating small quantities of whole milk at simmering temperature in a shallow karahi over an open fire. The milk is slowly evaporated, without being stirred, with frequent scraping at the bottom. The surface of milk, simmering in karahi, is intermittently fanned to permit formation of skin. Pieces of skin, which form on the surface of the milk, are continuously broken up and moved to cooler parts of the vessel.

When the desired body and texture have been developed and the volume of milk has been considerably reduced, sugar is added. The layers of the clotted cream are immersed in the remainder of the concentrated milk. The whole mass is heated for a short period to mix the clotted mass uniformly into the concentrated milk. The end-product has a pleasant caramel flavour and a thick consistency. It is then suitably flavcured, garnished with nuts and/or saffron and usually served in chilled condition. Figure 2.7 shows the flow diagram of traditional method of preparation of rabri.

Physico-chemical Aspects: Rabri has a white to brownish colour with a pleasant caramelized flavour. It is of a creamy consistency and has a viscous body with several layers of clotted cream. Heating the product after immersing the layers of cream in the milk results in a honeycomb textured mass. Formation of clotted layer of milk solids on the surface of simmering milk seems to result from denaturation at the liquid-air interphase of milk protein, which entraps substantial amounts of milk fat globules. The product's chemical composition depends on the initial composition of the milk, the degree of concentration of the milk

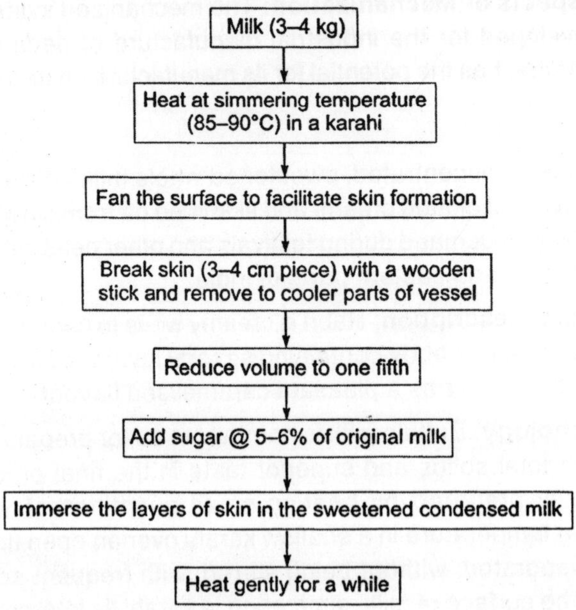

Fig. 2.7 : Flow-chart of traditional method of rabri making.

solids and the quantity of milk added. The approximate composition is as follows:

Moisture	30 per cent
Fat	20 per cent
Protein	10 per cent
Sugar	20 per cent
Lactose	17 per cent
Ash	3 per cent

Current Status: At present, rabri is a specialized product of halwais (traditional confectioners). Its manufacture is confined to the non-organized sector. Its traditional method of production is labour and energy-intensive. The product profile varies from region to region. Standardization of the traditional process in terms of manufacturing techniques, sensory profiles, and compositional and physico-chemical attributes is necessary for attaining a product of uniform standard and assured quality. Once the method of manufacture and the quality aspects of rabri are standardized, application of scraped surface heat exchanger for direct conversion of milk into rabri in a single pass and the integration of packaging systems are areas of promising commerical development. It may be possible to make rabri in a batch process, suitable for commerical conditions. The product can be packed and sold in any of the modern type of containers.

KHURCHAN

Khurchan is a concentrated, sweetened whole-milk product. A major delicacy in its own right, khurchan has had its origin in the town of Haathras, Uttar Pradesh, an important destination on India's sweets atlas. It is popular mainly in the rural and semiurban northern and central parts of the country. It is produced mainly on a cottage scale in the non-organized sector.

Product Description: Traditionally, khurchan is prepared from buffalo milk. It has white to light cream colour. Typical body of khurchan consists of firm layers of milk solids. It has a rich, smooth but somewhat chewy texture. This product has a distinctive pleasant caramel/ cooked flavour. Heat-clotted fraction of milk absorbs unclotted milk in the liquid phase, which imparts softness to the product. Table 2.22 presents composition of khurchan.

Table 2.22 : Composition of khurchan.

per cent

Constituent	Range
Moisture	22.8—27.2
Fat	22.6—24.4
Protein	14.6—16.2
Lactose	14.1—15.3
Sucrose	18.1—18.5
Ash	3.0 — 3.2
Total solids	72.8—77.2

Technology: Manufacturing of khurchan is a highly skilled technique and requires considerable experience and constant attention. Buffalo milk is preferred for its richness and the quality it imparts to khurchan. In a batchwise operation, a small quantity of milk, usually 500—700 ml at a time, is simmered over slow fire in a shallow pan (karahi). Milk is allowed to concentrate without excessive stirring. Temperature at which evaporation is done affects the colour of the finished product. Quicker evaporation at higher temperatures yields a whiter end-product, while slower evaporation at lower temperatures makes the endproduct somewhat brownish in colour. When almost 80 per cent water is evaporated, pan is kept for cooling. After cooling, thin layers of clotted milk are formed and are cut into layers with the help of khunti and then scraped. Its remaining concentrated liquid portion is poured over the solid layers. Then, powdered sugar (5% by weight of original milk) is sprinkled over it, which quickly dissolves into the liquid fraction of concentrated milk. If scraped before it is burnished and incorporated into the milk, it becomes the lachchedaar rabri.

BASUNDI

The exact origin of basundi is not known, but it has been prepared over several centuries in the western and southern parts of India. It is served during special festivities such as weddings and religious festivals. It is analogous to rabri and khurchan, which are popular in the northern and central parts of India.

Product Description: Basundi is a heat-desiccated, thickened milk dessert, having white to light caramel colour, creamy consistency with soft textured flakes that are uniformly suspended throughout the product matrix. Basundi has a sweetish caramel aroma. Consumed directly as a dessert, it contains all the solids of milk in an approximate twofold concentration plus additional sugar, with high food and nutritive value. Additives increase the calorific value of the product. Average composition range of the market samples of basundi is given in Table 2.23.

Table 2.23 : Composition of basundi.

per cent

Constituent	Range
Fat	12—15
Protein	7—9
Lactose	9—11
Ash	1.3—1.5
Sugar	20—22
Total solids	49—57

The manufacture of basundi is confined to the non-organized sector. Its traditional method of production is labour-intensive and energy-wise inefficient. There are variations in the product profile from region to region. Standardization of the traditional process in terms of manufacturing techniques, sensory profiles, and compositional and physico-chemical attributes is necessary for attaining a product of uniform standard and assured quality.

Size of Industry: The total production of basundi, estimated at 25,000 tonnes per annum, is mainly confined to the cottage scale in the non-organized sector. Basundi is a popular milk dessert in Andhra Pradesh, Gujarat, Karnataka, Kerala, Maharashtra and Tamil Nadu.

Technology: Buffalo milk is preferably used for basundi owing to its high content of total solids. Traditionally it is prepared by heating whole milk at simmering temperature in a shallow karahi over gentle fire. Milk is thickened through evaporative heating with occasional scraping at the bottom. As a thin skin forms on the surface of the hot milk, it is periodically removed by means of a khunti (a long handle flat-surface iron scraper) and set on the cooler sides at the top of the karahi. With progressive boiling, more and more of the skin is formed, which is removed and collected on the top sides of the karahi. When no more skin is formed and the milk is concentrated to the consistency of the condensed milk, sugar (about 15—17% of concentrated milk) is stirred into the milk until it is fully dissolved.

At this stage, the collected semi-dried skins from the top of the pan are scraped and mixed into the concentrated remnants of milk. The pan is removed from the fire, allowed to cool and the flavouring material added. Powdered cardamom (about 0.02% of concentrated milk) is added and mixed, along with saffron andborneol (edible camphor) (about 0.02% each of concentrated milk) and stirring continued till the desired plastic consistency is achieved. The end-product has a pleasant caramel flavour and a thick consistency. It is usually served chilled.

Physico-chemical Aspects: Basundi has a white to caramelized colour with a pleasant caramelized flavour. It is of a creamy consistency and has a viscous body. Its chemical composition depends on the initial composition of the milk, the degree of concentration of the milk solids and the quantity of milk added. Characteristic features of basundi are given in Table 2.24.

Table 2.24 : Characteristic features of basundi made under laboratory conditions.

Constituent		Physico-chemical properties	
Fat	11.6%	Acidity	0.47%
Protein	9.86%	pH	6.57%
Lactose	11.47%	Free Fatty Acids	1.35μeq ./ml
Ash	1.72%	HMF	15.51 umol./litre
SNF	23.05%	Browning Index	0.18 OD/g
Sucrose	12.69%	Aw	0.979
Total Solids	47.35%	Specific gravity	1.13
COB Test	Negative	Viscosity	52.96 mPas.
NPN	83.47 mg/100 g	Insolubility Index	0.3 ml
Soluble N	172.1 mg/100 g	Alcohol number	57.0

Innovations: It is recommended to standardise the fat content of basundi to about 5 per cent in case of buffalo milk and about 4 per cent in case of cow milk (fat:SNF ratio of about 0.5). Homogenization of milk at 75 kg/cm^2 at 65°C imparts a distinctively superior and rich body to the finished product. Milk may be concentrated by the Scraped Surface Heat Exchanger (thin film) when the product is made by the mechanized process. Alternatively, skim milk may be pre-heated to 90°C in a plate heat exchanger and concentrated by the Reverse Osmosis Process to 22 per cent TS level. Then, cream is mixed to this milk concentrate for adjustment of the fat content.

Conventional vacuum evaporator may also be employed for concentration of milk to a predetermined level. For consumerlevel marketing, the final product may be packaged in glass bottles, heat-sealable polypropylene cups with aluminium foil lids, metalised polylaminated pouches. Bulk packaging is used for institutional markets. For manufacture of long shelf-life basundi, the UHT processing may be employed for the milk concentrate, followed by aseptic packaging.

KULFI AND FROZEN DESSERTS

Kulfi is a popular frozen dessert (indigenous ice cream). A mass of partially desiccated milk containing chopped pistachio nuts and the essence of kesar (saffron) is frozen (in an ice-salt mixture) in a metal cone, sealed with a plaster of wheat dough.

Product Description: Kulfi is produced by freezing a mix obtained from concentrated milk (khoa-like) and sugar. It is a frozen blend of water, milk fat, milks-olids-not-fat, saffron and nuts. Kulfi differs from ice cream in that it contains practically no air. Kulfi products are formulated, processed and frozen in ice-salt mixture. Alternatively, they may be frozen and extruded through an ice cream freezer with very low overrun setting to deliver consumer-desired attributes of flavour and texture.

According to the PFA standards, kulfi is the frozen product obtained from cow or buffalo milk or a combination thereof or from cream, and/or other milk products, with or without the addition of cane sugar, dextrose, liquid glucose and dried liquid glucose, eggs, fruits, fruit juices, preserved fruits, nuts, chocolate, edible flavours and permitted food colours. It may contain permitted stabilizers and emulsifiers, not exceeding 0.5 per cent by weight. The mixture shall be suitably heated before freezing. The product shall contain not less than 10.0 per cent milk fat, 3.5 per cent protein and 36.0 per cent total solids except that when any of the aforesaid preparations contains fruits or nuts or both, the content of milk fat shall not be less than 8.0 per cent by weight. Starch may be added to a maximum extent of 5.0 per cent under a declaration on the label.

Technology: Halwais and small-scale manufacturers usually prepare kulfi. Lately, some organized dairies have also taken to its production and marketing. Cow, buffalo or mixed milk either as such or partially skimmed is concentrated in large open pan over a fire. Concentrated milk is cooled, sugar is added and the blend is thoroughly stirred. In some cases, a small quantity of khoa or non-fat dried milk is added during boiling of milk. After adding nuts and saffron, the mixture is filled into aluminium or plastic cones. The lids are put on and in some cases sealed with the cones with wheat flour dough. After sealing, the cones are immersed in salt-ice mixture in an earthenware pot (matka). Vigorous agitation is applied from time to time to effect heat transfer and expedite the freezing process. Agitation of cones apparently whips up some air, and kulfi develops a minor over-run.

The traditional method of making kulfi in ice-salt mixture by immersing kulfi cones gave the best sensory quality. If the mix is frozen and extruded from an ice cream freezer, the quality was quite acceptable. Direct hardening or hand whipping followed by hardening procedures did not produce good kulfi of desired quality.

The production of kulfi on a semi-industrial scale is being carried out in several metropolitan cities in India. In this process, standardized milk is concentrated to about half of the original volume. Alternatively, kulfi mix may be formulated to PFA standards, using permissible ingredients. After cooling, sugar is added. In some cases sugar is added before concentration. In that case, a caramelized brownish colour in the product is observed. The mix is cooled to 4°C and is aged for six hours. To the aged mix are added slivered pistachios or almond nuts, saffron colour and in some cases suitable flavourings. The mix is frozen in an ice cream freezer with a little overrun (10% or less) and filled into moulds. The moulds are chilled quickly in a brine tank at 20°C for 15—20 minutes. The frozen product is further hardened for 6 hours at 20°C. In some cases, single serve small earthenware kasora or matka may be used for freezing kulfi.

Innovations: Kulfi is very similar to ice cream in formulation and processing. For its production, it is possible to use the fully mechanized modern technologies associated with ice cream novelties. There is a lot of scope for adapting fully automated endless conveyor belt system,

Table 2.25 : Role and sources of various components of kulfi

Component	Role and functions	Limitations	Sources in order of preference
Milk-fat	Imparts desirable creamy rich flavour: Source of fat-soluble vitamins. Improves body texture. Improves melting resistance.	Calorifically dense. Too much fat (17%) gives too much viscosity to mix and hinders whippability. Source of oxidized, rancid, and fishy flavour defects	Fresh sweet cream Fresh milk Frozen cream Khoa
Milk-solids-not-fat	Improves texture. Imparts better body. Source of protein, minerals and vitamins.	Improper levels cause "sandiness" defect. Source of desirable cooked flavour.	Dry milk Fluid whole milk Fluid skim milk Condensed skim milk Skim milk powder Khoa
Sugar	Imparts sweet flavour.	Too much sugar impedes freezing process	Cane sugar

with slots to hold metal cones through freezing liquid/brine mixtures for kulfi production. Use of homogenization of the mix during processing is likely to improve the flavour.

Formulation of Kulfi: The standardization for kulfi production has shown that a mixture of equal parts of cow milk and buffalo milk produces good quality kulfi. Typical kulfi formulation constitutes 9 per cent milk fat, 17 per cent milk solids-not-fat and 13 per cent sugar and 12 per cent nuts. Dairy ingredients constitute approximately 65 per cent of total solids of kulfi and related frozen desserts. The choice of dairy ingredients and the formulation of a kulfi mix are determined by regulatory standards, the desired quality of the frozen dessert, marketing strategy, consumer demand, relative price, and availability of ingredients.

Milk and cream constitute the most important components of a good quality kulfi. Variables related to dairy ingredients exert a profound influence on the flavour, body and texture of the frozen product.

Optional dairy ingredients for kulfi and frozen desserts:

Cream

Milk (sweetened condensed skim or part-skim milk)

Condensed skim milk (sweetened or super-heated condensed milk).

Skim milk (dried milk, skim milk powder).

Concentrated milk.

The nature and intensity of kulfi flavour is a function of the flavour quality of the individual constituents and subsequent processing treatment of the kulfi-mix. Flavour defects in ingredients cannot be alleviated during kulfi making. Actually, flavour problems could be compounded as a consequence of negligent processing procedures.

The body or consistency of kulfi is related to the mechanical strength of the mix and its resistance to melting. Heat shock resistance is dependent on the nature and concentration of the stabilizer-emulsifier system used. The texture of kulfi depends upon the size, shape, number and arrangement of fat globules, ice crystals and the ratio of liquid and frozen water in kulfi.

Balancing quality and cost is a major challenge to the kulfi manufacturer. Factors responsible for overall quality are: raw material quality, sanitary care during mix preparation, processing parameters, flavouring used, freezing techniques, and storage conditions.

Formulation of kulfi-mix involves utilization of both the fat and solids-not-fat components of milk. The functions and preferred sources of major kulfi ingredients are summarized in Table 2.25.

Sweet Fresh Cream and Fresh Milk: Whole milk may be used primarily as a source of milk solids. There is no better source of fat than sweet cream because of its desirable flavour and convenience of handling. Fresh cream is judged by flavour, acidity and bacterial count. The titratable acidity should be low, and it should show no evidence of developed acidity. When fresh cream is not available at a favourable price, the alternative sources of fat should be considered.

Frozen Cream: The high price of sweet cream during certain seasons of the year makes storage of cream during the months of surplus economically attractive. All known precautions must be used to ensure prevention of the development of off-flavours in stored cream. Off-flavours likely to develop in frozen cream are rancid, fishy, oily, and tallowy. Only the best cream should be processed for storage, and it should contain no developed acidity.

Hydrolytic rancidity is due to certain bacteria and by the enzymes they produce. A proper heat treatment regime, an essential phase for the preparation of cream for freezing, consists of heating cream at 76.7°C for 20 minutes, or 82.2°C for 10 minutes, or 87.8°C for 5 minutes. This treatment not only inactivates the lipase enzyme naturally present in milk but also destroys 95—99 per cent of the bacteria present.

Following the heat processing, the cream is quickly frozen. Proper packaging and handling of frozen cream are also important. Preferred packages include stainless steel or plastic containers. Quick-frozen cream is held at 20°C. Disadvantages of frozen cream include the necessity for thawing before use, and the fact that it is messy to handle.

Fluid Whole and Skim Milk: Both are excellent sources of serum solids (SS) but their use is limited because their SS content is lower than that desired in kulf-imix. Skim milk should be purchased on the basis of a definite SNF content in order to guard against dilution with water.

Plain Condensed Skim Milk: Fresh condensed skim milk is easy and convenient to use, and has an excellent flavour. The concentrate may be paid for on the basis of the solids content, which is around 25—30 per cent. The keeping quality of condensed skim milk is better than that of cream. It should be stored at 0-1°C and used while fresh and sweet (usually for 7—10 days).

Plain Condensed Whole Milk: This is concentrated about two and a half times and contains 8 per cent fat and 20 per cent serum solids.

Super-heated Condensed Skim or Whole Milk: The super-heated condensed milk can substitute the heat-concentrated milk now used by halwais. The already-condensed product is slowly heated to a high temperature, usually in the range of 82.2°C. When properly done, a concentrate of much greater viscosity is obtained, which improves the whipping ability of the kulfi-mix and contributes a smooth texture, which then binds more free water. Accordingly, less water is available to form ice crystals during freezing, and the smooth texture of the kulfi is maintained throughout its shelf-life. Super-heating, therefore, functions like a stabilizer.

Sweetened Condensed Whole or Skim Milk: A sweetened condensed product may sometimes be used as a source of SNF. This ingredient provides 8.5 per cent fat and 28 per cent total milk solids. The added sugar (40-44%) imparts a better keeping quality to sweetened condensed milk than plain condensed milk. With this concentration of sugar, the osmotic pressure of the solution is high enough to suppress the growth of practically all micro-organisms. The product will keep at room temperature. The titratable acidity test should be applied to all condensed milk products. When diluted so as to contain the same SNF concentration as skim milk, the acidity should be approximately that of fresh skim milk (0.18%).

The optimum milk solids level in the kulfi-mix is found to be 26 per cent for desirable sensory quality. The fat percentage in the kulfi-mix is 9 per cent and the SNF 17 per cent. The cane sugar content is 13 per cent. The pH of the mix is 6.4 and surface tension 46.2 dynes/ cm.

Packaging: Traditional kulfi is packaged in plastic or aluminium moulds which are partially thawed by dipping in fresh water to remove the kulfi prior to serving. In certain areas, malai-kulfi is served as slices of kulfi. Here kulfi is frozen as a cylindrical block, which is covered by an insulating cloth, and then sliced for serving by vendors. Entrepreneurs may utilize packaging technology used in ice cream novelty packaging, using attractive shapes and colours. Kulfi may also be produced on stick.

Physico-chemical Aspects: Kulfi is a frozen product consisting of multiple phases. Its texture is dependent on the rate of freezing. For smooth texture, kulfi must be frozen as rapidly as possible to produce a very large number of small size crystals of ice. The butter-fat may be broken down into smaller globules by homogenization of the mix at pressures of 2000/500 psi. This treatment should lead to better flavour, distribution and improvement in the body and texture.

Shelf-life: Kulfi is frozen and normally used quickly after it is made. If a large scale manufacturing operation is undertaken, a shelf-life of 4—8 weeks can be achieved by using technology associated with ice cream production. By judicious selection of a stabilizer-emulsifier system, textural defects like coarseness due to ice crystals and grittiness due to lactose crystals can be avoided in stored kulfi. Storage and distribution at a temperature of 20°C (with minimum fluctuations) should maintain the sensory quality of kulfi.

MALAI-KA-BARAF

This term is loosely applied to a variety of frozen products in which sweetened milk or malai may form the chief ingredient. These products may also be prepared from diluted milk, thickened with some fruit pulp, etc., with a dash of colour and flavour. The latter kind is usually sold in the market.

FALOODA

Falooda is associated with Persian/Parsi festival called "Nawroze" (Navroz), meaning "new day" or "new year". To celebrate it, many delicacies are laid on the table and each item is symbolic. Among the drinks served for refreshment, falooda, an exotic milk-based flavoured drink, is popular. It has a refreshing and cooling effect and is available in sweet shops or traditional vendors especially during summer. It is popular in places, associated with the Muslim Rulers such as at Awadh, Hyderabad or Delhi, as well as in Mumbai that has a large Parsi population.

Product Description: Falooda is named for the strands of corn flour vermicelli that float in flavoured milk-based drink. Falooda appears quite similar to sevian and Chinese noodles. It is soft, gelatinous, thread-like and translucent. It can be coloured with natural colouring materials like saffron, rose etc. White strands glow like pearl and enhance the mouthfeel of the frozen products like kulfi, milk slush, etc. Typical falooda is a milk-based drink, flavoured with rose syrup and vermicelli strands floating in it. It is topped with ice cream or kulfi and decorated with dry cherries.

Technology: Starchy strands are called "mishashto", and these are prepared by the following procedure. In a pan, water is kept for boiling and in a separate pan, corn flour is mixed with small quantity of separate water to make a smooth pouring paste. When water starts boiling in the first pan, corn flour is poured into it with continuous stirring and cooked for about two minutes. Now, it is taken off from the fire and stirred. The hot-mix is passed through a colander that has been held at least six inches above the pan of iced water. It is poured slowly in small quantities through colander and stirred vigorously with wooden spoon so that when it passes through the holes of the colander into the icy water, it will instantly turn into pearl-like drops. These strands are kept under refrigeration and have a shelf-life of four days. Alternatives to corn flour for making threads are arrow-root and refined wheat flour.

To prepare falooda, essence (rose, kewara, sandal, saffron) and colouring material are mixed with sugar syrup. This sugar syrup is filled in half of a glass bowl or tumbler and milk. Falooda is added into it. Dry nuts are also added and topped with a scoop full of vanilla ice cream.

Innovations: In ice cream parlours and restaurants, falooda is prepared with slight modifications to suit the urban consumers. To make falooda, condensed milk and normal milk are mixed together and boiled on low medium flame. Custard powder is dissolved in small quantity of milk and poured into boiling milk. The whole mass is treated to gelatinize starch, and the process continued till the consistency becomes thick. It is divided into two different equal lots. In one lot vanilla essence and in another lot pistachio essence is mixed thoroughly and then kept in refrigerator. Commercially available jelly is also prepared and refrigerated. For serving in a glass, a layer of jelly is placed at the bottom followed by a layer of milk-based vanilla flavoured custard; to this pieces of fruits are added and topped with a layer with pistachio custard. Threads of falooda strands are placed on top and decorated with raisins, broken cashews and almonds.

KUNDA

Kunda as a traditional product is prepared in the Belgaum District of Karnataka and its neighbouring areas. Its origin is traced to the Joshi family, which had migrated to Belgaum from the Dehu area of Rajasthan and introduced khoa-based sweets in this region. Since then this product has become popular and has been commercialized since the beginning of the 20th century.

Product Description: This semi-solid delicacy is prepared by the concentration of milk, followed by desiccation with the addition of sugar. The desiccation with incorporated sugar gives a characteristic brown colour to kunda. It can be defined as a desiccated product, light brown to dark brown in colour, prepared by the continuous heating of milk or high moisture khoa, mixed with a calculated amount of sugar. The product has a characteristic rich taste with a pleasant caramel/nutty flavour. Addition of sugar (about 30%) and the low moisture content (about 25%) contribute to the relatively long shelf-life of the product, which should enable its wider marketing.

Technology: Traditionally, buffalo milk is used for the preparation of kunda. In commercial production, high-moisture khoa forms the base material and cane sugar is the sweetening agent. High-moisture khoa is mixed with crystalline sugar at the rate of 20—25 per cent (w/w) and desiccated over low flame in a shallow pan for 90—120 minutes to develop pleasant caramel flavour. Free-fat tends to ooze out towards the finishing stages and contributes towards a mild frying effect. A cohesive lumpy mass is formed, which tends to leave the bottom surface. Finally, when the proper body and texture has been achieved, the material is spread thinly over shallow trays and allowed to cool atmospherically. While studying the effect of incorporation of caramelized sugar during kunda making, about 10 per cent of total sugar to be added was caramelized and added at the khoa stage. The resultant kunda had a dark colour and a caramelized flavour, with slightly increased overall acceptability.

Physico-chemical Aspects: The colour of kunda varies from semi-brown to brown. In certain cases, solidified milk fat (white in colour) was observed all over the surface of the product. The darker product keeps for a longer time than the lighter product. Kunda has a soft body and grainy textural characteristics. When it is pressed with fingers, fat is observed to stick to the fingers. The mouthfeel of kunda is characterised by smooth body, granular texture and a typical after-taste in the mouth. Flakes of fat also gave positive sensation of the product on the tongue. Certain degree of cooked flavour was noticed in the product.

Shelf-life: The shelf-life studies on commercial samples indicated that light brown kunda kept well for about four days at ambient temperature (29°C) as compared to about twelve days for dark brown kunda. The spoilage was observed to begin with the visible growth of yeasts and moulds. Vacuum packaging of kunda using 65 micron film of LDPE was observed to increase the shelf-life to about twelve days for the light brown variety and to about twenty days for the dark brown product. At refrigerated temperature of 58°C, the vacuum packaged light brown product kept for nearly two months, while the vacuum packaged dark brown variety was observed to keep at least for three months.

BAL MITHAI

Bal Mithai, a heat desiccated product, has its origin in the hilly region of Kumaon. The region has its own unique culture and traditions as well as a wide range of exquisite, milk-based products (singari, singal, kumaoni, raita etc.). It is the most patronized form of milk sweet in the Almora District of Uttarakhand. It is a popular offering to gods.

Product Description: It is prepared from khoa, chocolate brown in colour and topped with small sugar granules, giving the surface a distinctive mosaic look. The product has a rubbery body and chewy texture.

Technology: To prepare bal mithai, khoa is cooked in a heavy-bottomed shallow pan on a slow fire with intermittent stirring till the colour turns dark brown. Sugar is then added and the mixture heated till a thick consistency is attained. Finally, the product is poured into a greased tray, and is allowed to cool and set. The product surface is finally garnished with granular sugar.

3

Raw Material, the Milk Used for Making Sweets

Milk is a unique biological secretion of the mammary gland, endowed by nature with nutrients to fulfil the nutritional needs of the off-spring. Milk is closely associated with reproduction among mammals, and its yield and composition vary among various species to meet the post-natal growth requirements of their off-spring (Table 3.1). Milk, therefore, contains all the chemicals essential for growth in the form of six major nutrients: water, fat, proteins, lactose (milk sugar), minerals (salts) and vitamins. In India, milk usually refers to that from cow or buffalo or a mixture of these two. However, milk sold without any qualification is taken to be buffalo milk according to the Prevention of Food Adulteration (PFA) Rules, 1955.

Definition of Milk: Milk, according to the PFA Rules, is the normal mammary secretion derived from the complete milking of healthy milch animal without either addition thereto or extraction therefrom. It shall be free from colostrum. Milk of different classes and of different designations shall conform to the standards laid down in Table 3.2. It shall conform to both the parameters for milk fat and milk solids-not-fat (SNF), independently, as prescribed in columns four and five of this Table. Milk shall include cow's or buffalo's, or sheep's or goat's or a mixture thereof.

From chemical point of view, milk is a complex fluid with more than 100 separate chemical entities in levels that vary with species. From physical point of view, milk is an opaque, white heterogeneous fluid, having various constituents in multi-dispersed phases of emulsion, colloidal suspension or solution.

The chemical make-up of milk and its physico-chemical behaviour provide scientific basis for processing of milk and manufacture of products. In India, milk from buffalo and cow (desi, cross-bred and exotic) is commercially important. Depending on its characteristics, each type of milk is eminently suitable for certain types of region-specific indigenous milk products.

Milk drawn from a healthy dairy animal is usually free from any bacteria. It is "sterile". However, it must be protected against infection as soon as it leaves the udder. Microbes, capable of spoiling the milk, are present in the environment. They multiply rapidly and render milk unsuitable for processing and/or unfit for human consumption. Therefore, unprotected milk is a potential carrier of disease-causing microbes. Outbreaks of food poisoning can be usually traced to consumption of contaminated milk and milk products.

Table 3.1 : Average composition of milk of different animal species.

per cent

Species	Water	Fat	Protein	Lactose	Ash
Friesian cow[1]	87.92	3.40	3.13	4.86	0.69
Sindhi cow[2]	86.07	4.90	3.42	4.91	0.70
Gir cow[2]	86.44	4.73	3.32	4.85	0.66
Tharparkar cow[2]	86.58	4.55	3.36	4.83	0.68
Sahiwal cow[2]	86.42	4.55	3.33	5.04	0.66
Crossbred cow	86.54	4.50	3.37	4.92	0.67
Buffalo[3]	82.76	7.38	3.60	5.48	0.78
Goat[4]	87.10	4.25	3.52	4.27	0.86
Sheep[5]	81.00	7.90	5.80	4.50	0.80
Camel[6]	86.50	3.10	4.00	5.60	0.80

[1] *Bos taurus;* [2]*Bos indicus;* [3]*Bubalus bubalis;* [4]*Capra hircus;* [5]*Ovis aries;* [6]*Camelus dromedarius.*

Bacterial growth in milk can be retarded by refrigeration, thereby slowing down the rate of its deterioration. Under certain conditions, refrigeration may not be feasible due to economical and/or technical reasons. In such situations, another method has been developed for retarding bacterial growth in raw milk during collection and transportation to dairy plants. Recent research has successfully demonstrated the utility of this method which is based on the lactoperoxidase/thiocyanate/ hydrogen peroxide system (LP-system). Its guidelines have been published by the FAO/ WHO Codex Alimentarius Commission. However, the use of LP-system is not permitted in India.

The traditional practice in India of boiling the raw milk within hours of production before its consumption provides a safety net for minimizing occurrence of microbes. However, pasteurization is designed to destroy

Table 3.2 : PFA standards for different classes and designations of milk in India.

Class of milk	Designations	State and Union Territories	Minimum percentage	
			Milk fat	*Milk solids-not-fat (SNF)*
Buffalo milk	Raw, pasteurized, boiled, flavoured and sterilized	Assam; Bihar; Chandigarh; Delhi, Gujarat; Maharashtra; Haryana; Meghalaya; Punjab; Sikkim; Uttar Pradesh; West Bengal; Andaman & Nicobar; Andhra Pradesh; Arunachal Pradesh; Dadra & Nagar Haveli; Goa; Daman & Diu; Kerala; Himachal Pradesh; Jammu & Kashmir; Karnataka.	6.0	9.0
	-do-	Kerala; Lakshadweep; Madhya Pradesh; Manipur; Mizoram; Nagaland; Orissa; Pondicherry; Rajasthan; Tripura; Tamil Nadu.	5.0	9.0
Cow milk	-do-	Chandigarh; Haryana; Punjab.	4.0	8.5
	-do-	Andaman & Nicobar; Andhra Pradesh; Arunachal Pradesh; Assam; Bihar; Dadra and Nagar Haveli; Delhi; Goa; Daman & Diu; Gujarat; Himachal Pradesh; Jammu & Kashmir; Karnataka; Kerala; Lakshadweep; Madhya Pradesh; Maharashtra; Manipur; Meghalaya; Nagaland, Pondicherry; Rajasthan; Sikkim; Tamil Nadu; Tripura; Uttar Pradesh; West Bengal.	3.5	8.5
	-do-	Mizoram; Orissa.	3.0	8.5

Goat or Sheep milk	-do-	Chandigarh; Haryana; Kerala; Madhya Pradesh; Maharashtra; Punjab; Uttar Pradesh.	3.5	9.0
	-do-	Andaman & Nicobar; Andhra Pradesh; Arunachal Pradesh; Assam; Bihar; Dadra & Nagar Haveli; Delhi; Goa; Daman & Diu; Gujarat; Himachal Pradesh; Jammu & Kashmir; Karnataka; Lakshadweep; Manipur; Meghalaya; Mizoram; Nagaland; Orissa; Pondicherry; Rajasthan; Sikkim; Tamil Nadu; Tripura; West Bengal.	3.0	9.0
Mixed milk	-do-	All India	4.5	8.5
Standardized milk	Pasteurized, flavoured and sterilized	All India	4.5	8.5
Recombined milk	-do-	All India	3.0	8.5
Toned milk	-do-	All India	3.0	8.5
Double toned milk	-do-	All India	1.5	9.0
Skimmed milk	-do-	All India	Not more than 0.5	8.7
Full cream milk	Pasteurized and sterilized	All India	6.0	9.0

Source: Prevention of Food Adulteration (PFA) Rules, 1995.

relatively more heat-resistant pathogens, namely, *Mycobacterium tuberculosis* and *Coxiella burnettii.*

Milk is valued commercially for its two important parameters: (i) Milk Fat (F), and (ii) Solids-not-Fat (SNF). The SNF largely consists of proteins, lactose and minerals. These solids are also referred to as 'serum solids'. These two parameters usually form the basis of payment to milk producers in India. The term 'Total Solids' (TS) refers to the quantity of SNF plus fat present in milk. It may range from 12 to 16 per cent depending on its source. For cow milk, TS is 12 per cent3.5% F and 8.5% SNF) while for buffalo milk it ranges between 15 and 16 per cent (6-7% F and 9% SNF).

Apart from breed-related differences, certain other factors also influence the gross composition of milk. They are:

- individuality of animal;
- stage of milking;
- intervals of milking;
- completeness of milking;
- frequency of milking;
- irregularity of milking;
- portion of milking;
- different quarters of udder;
- lactation period;
- yield of milk;
- season;
- feed;
- nutritional level;
- environmental temperature;
- health status;
- age;
- weather;
- oestrum or heat;
- gestation period;
- exercise;
- excitement; and
- administration of drugs and hormones.

In general, these variables tend to average out but show a seasonal pattern in the production of commercial milk used by dairy processors. This periodic fluctuation could have an important impact on properties of the finished products. In practice, dairy plants usually procure mixed milk of both buffaloes and cows, received from collection centres linked to a network of village milk producers' cooperative societies.

Suitability of Cow/Buffalo Milk for Products' Manufacture: In India, commercial milk is mostly a combination of buffalo and cow milk. Therefore, it is important to recognize both qualitative and quantitative differences in the major constituents of buffalo and cow milk (Table 3.3).

Table 3.3 : Composition of cow and buffalo milk.

per cent

Constituent	Cow milk	Buffalo milk
Water	86.50	83.18
Fat	4.39	6.71
Protein	3.30	4.52
Lactose	4.44	4.45
Total solids	13.50	16.82
Solids-not-fat	9.11	10.11
Ash	0.73	0.80
Calcium	0.12	0.18
Magnesium .	0.01	0.02
Sodium	0.05	0.04
Potassium	0.15	0.11
Phosphorus	0.10	0.10
Citrate	0.18	0.18
Chloride	0.10	0.07
Calcium/Phosphorus ratio	1.20	1.80

The intrinsic quality of chemical constituents through differences in species/breeds makes their milk eminently suitable for certain specialized products. For example, qualities such as high total solids content, superior whiteness and viscosity render buffalo milk eminently suitable for production of khoa, dahi, paneer, kheer, payasam, malai, kulfi, ghee and other traditional milk products. Cow milk, on the other hand, yields a soft coagulum, making it suitable for preparation of chhana and its products such as sandesh, rasogolla, chumchum and rasmalai. In certain regions, only cow's milk is available and is utilized for the manufacture of products specific to cow's milk.

Physical Equilibria: Milk has well-defined physical equilibria among its various constituents that exist mainly in three forms—as an emulsion, as colloids and in true solution. In milk, fat is present as an emulsion, protein and some mineral matters in colloidal suspension, and lactose together with some minerals and soluble proteins in true solution. Milk lipids, commonly known as milk fats, are present as an 'oil-in-water type' emulsion in the form of microscopic globules varying in diameter from 0.1 to 22 μm. The colloidal phase contains casein micelles, calcium phosphates and globular proteins. Whey proteins are in colloidal solution and casein in colloidal suspension. Lactose, vitamins, acids, enzymes and some inorganic salts are present as true solutions. Table 3.4 gives the relative sizes of these particles in milk.

Table 3.4 : Physical state and relative-size of particles in milk.

State	Size (mm)	Type of particle
Emulsion	10^{-2} to 10^{-3}	Fat globules
Colloidal suspension	10^{-4} to 10^{-5}	Casein-calcium phosphate
Colloidal solution	10^{-5} to 10^{-6}	Whey proteins
True solution	10^{-6} to 10^{-7}	Lactose, salts and other substances

Factors that tend to influence the physical equilibrium between colloidal dispersion and salts in milk are:

- addition of polyvalent ionizable salts;
- concentration of serum solids;
- changes in pH;
- heat-treatment (which may alter the surface charges or unfold proteins); and
- addition of alcohols (which reduces bound water associated with the colloidal constituents).

All these factors tend to disturb colloidal systems and thus influence the technological behaviour of milk during product manufacture.

TERMS RELATED TO MILK STRUCTURE

Milk Lipids: Commonly known as milk fat, they are present in milk in microscopic globular emulsion of fat.

Milk Plasma: The fluid portion of milk minus fat globules, almost similar to skim milk.

Milk Serum: Miik plasma minus milk fat and casein micelles.

Whey: Removal of casein micelles from skim milk by clotting with rennet or by acidification to pH 4.6 yields the liquid called whey. It is different from milk serum in that it contains some polypeptides cleaved from casein by rennet.

CONSTITUENTS OF MILK

Water: Water is the medium in which all the other components of milk (total solids) are dissolved or suspended. Water content varies from 83.18 per cent to 87.2 per cent in milk of different species of cows and buffaloes. In commercial milk, the range is 83.18 to 86.50 per cent. A small percentage of water in milk is hydrated to the lactose and salts, while some portion is bound with proteins.

Fat: Milk fat, though quite bland in taste, imparts richness/ smoothness to fat-containing dairy products. In freshly secreted milk, it occurs as a microscopic globular emulsion of liquid fat in an aqueous phase of milk plasma. Fat is the most variable component of milk. The average size of fat globules in buffalo milk is larger (4.15 to 4.60 μ,m) than that of cow milk (3.36 to 4.15 μm). Milk lipid globules fall into three overlapping size distributions (Table 3.5).

Table 3.5 : Size distribution of milk lipid globules.

Class	Diameter (μm) the	Proportion of total globule population (%)	Fraction of total milk lipid (%)
Small	Below 2	70—90	< 5
Intermediate	3—5	10—30	90
Large	8—10	0—01	1—4

The fat globules are stabilized by a very thin membrane of 5—10 μm thickness, closely resembling plasma membrane. The membrane consists of proteins, lipids, lipoproteins, phospholipids, cerebrosides, nucleic acids, enzymes, trace elements and bound water (Table 3.6). The membrane is important in keeping fat from separating as free oil when it is subjected to physical abrasion during handling/processing of milk. It also protects milk lipids against the action of enzymes, notably lipase, in development of rancidity. Certain enzymes such as alkaline phosphatase and xanthine oxidase, as well as certain important minerals like iron and copper, are preferentially attached to the fat globule membrane.

Table 3. 6 : Estimated average composition of membranes of milk fat globule.

per cent

Component	Buffalo	Western cow
Lipid content	38.5	35.7
Neutral lipids	74.4	65.7
Phospholipids	19.7	18.6
Triglycerides	52.7	45.5
Diglycerides	7.4	5.5
Sphingomyelin	4.3	3.2
Phosphatadyl serine	3.1	2.4
C 18:0 Stearic acid	34.4	24.1
$C^{16:0}$	22.4	23.8
$C^{18:1}$	14.5	14.5
$C^{14:0}$	12.6	14.4
Protein (g/100 g fat globule)	1.36	1.8

Fatty Acid Profile: Both buffalo and cowmilk fats consist chiefly of the triglycerides of fatty acids, which make up 95—99 per cent of milk fat. The remaining portion of milk fat is composed of diglycerides (about 4.1% in buffalo milk and 1.26—1.59% in cow milk), monoglycerides (about 0.7% in buffalo milk and 0.016—0.038% in cow milk). High, medium and low molecular weight triglycerides in buffalo milk occur in the proportion of 42.5, 17.1 and 40.5 per cent, respectively. Corresponding values for cow milk fat are 52.9,18.9 and 28.2 per cent, respectively. Free fatty acid content of buffalo milk fat is lower (0.22%) as compared to that in cow milk fat (0.33%).

The functional properties of milk fat are attributed to its fatty acid make-up. In general, milk fat consists of 65 per cent saturated, 32 per cent mono-unsaturated and 3 per cent poly-unsaturated fatty acids. It also contains 7 per cent short-chain fatty acids (C_4-C_9), 15—20 per cent medium-chain fatty acids (C_{10}-C_{14}) and 73—78 per cent long-chain fatty acids (C_{16} or higher). In all, milk fat contains 19 or more fatty acids (Table 3.7).

Buffalo milk fat contains appreciably higher butyric acid in its triglycerides in comparison to cow milk fat. However, other short-chain fatty acids (caproic, caprylic, capric and myristic) are lower in buffalo milk fat. The content of long-chain fatty acids (palmitic and stearic) is relatively higher in buffalo milk. The unsaturated fatty acid level of buffalo and cow milk is comparable. Milk fat also consists of varying quantities of other lipids such as phospholipids, sterols, carotenoids, vitamins A, D, E and K and some traces of free fatty acids.

Table 3.7 : Fatty acid profile of buffalo and cow milk fat

Fatty acids	Common name	Composition (wt/wt %)	
		Buffalo milk	Cow milk
$C_{4:0}$	Butryic	4.36	3.20
$C_{6:0}$	Caproic	1.51	2.11
$C_{8:0}$	Caprylic	0.78	1.16
$C_{10:0}$	Capric	1.28	2.57
$C_{10:1}$	—	—	0.31
$C_{12:0}$	Laurie	1.78	—
$C_{14:0}$	Myristic	10.81	11.93
$C_{14:1}$	Myristoleic	1.27	2.12
$C_{15:0}$	—	129	1.23
$C_{16:0 \text{ (branched)}}$	—	0.18	0.30
$C_{16:0}$	Palmitic	33.08	29.95
$C_{16:1}$	Palmitoleic	1.99	2.16
$C_{17:0}$	—	0.58	0.34
$C_{18:0 \text{ (branched)}}$	—	0.24	0.35
$C_{18:0}$	Stearic	11.97	10.07
$C_{18:1}$	Oleic	27.15	27.42
$C_{18:2}$	Linoleic	1.51	1.49
$C_{18:3}$	Linolenic	0.47	0.59

There are characteristic physico-chemical differences between fats of buffalo and cow milk. Table 3.8 summarizes some of these differences.

Cholesterol: The cholesterol content of milk is significantly affected by the species, breed, feed, stage of lactation and season of the year. Generally, the cholesterol content is higher in the western breeds of cattle (317—413 mg/100 g fat), followed by zebu (humped like desi) cow (303—385 mg/100 g fat). It is lowest for buffalo (235—248 mg/100 g fat). Significantly, crosses between Sahiwal and Holstein-Friesian showed progressively higher levels of cholesterol content as the inheritance of exotic levels increases, varying from 302—465 mg, 228—494 mg and 300-421 mg for ¾, 5/8 and ½ crossbred, respectively.

Table 3.8 : Some physico-chemical constants of buffalo and cow milk fat.

Physico-chemical constant	Buffalo milk fat	Cow milk fat
Softening point range	34.3—36.3°C	33.5—35.9°C
Melting point range	33.4—46.4°C	31.5—35.2°C
Acid value	0.17—0.352	0.26
Refractive index	1.4515—1.4533	1.4498—1.4530
BR reading	41.00—43.50	41.05—42.40
Saponification number	218.23—236.10	221.0—238.0
Iodine value	27.00—33.90	27.70—37.32
Reichert-Meissel value	27.83—35.50	24.60—29.70
Polenske value	0.70—1.60	1.30—1.80
Density	0.905—0.917g/ml	0.888—0.911 g/ml
Grain size	0.20—0.41 mm	0.098—0.190 mm
Fat globule size	4.15—4.60 µm	3.36—4.15 µm
Unsaponifiable matter	392—398 mg/100ml	414—50 mg/100ml

The cholesterol content, generally lowest at the beginning of the lactation period, progressively rises to reach its highest level towards the end. With the increase in oil ration from 40 ml to 140 ml, the cholesterol content of milk fat progressively declines from 420 to 380 mg per 100 g fat. It is quite high for colostrum, being 570 to 1950 mg per 100 g fat in the first milking after parturition, progressively declining to normal levels during subsequent milkings.

Phospholipids: The total phospholipid content of buffalo milk fat averages 21.04 mg/100 ml of milk, whereas for cow milk the corresponding value is 33.71 mg/100 ml. Table 3.9 shows the concentration of various fractions of phospholipids present in buffalo and cow milk.

Table 3.9 : Concentration of phospholipid fractions in buffalo and cow milk

mg/100 ml

Phospholipid fraction	Concentration	
	Buffalo milk	Zebu cow milk
Lecithin	7.29	10.01
Cephalin	9.12	15.57
Sphingomyelin	4.63	8.13

Proteins: Casein, the principal milk protein, makes up 80 per cent of the total protein content, and whey proteins the remaining 20 per cent. These fractions, shown to be heterogeneous, consist of many proteins (Table 3.10).

Table 3.10 : Concentration of various proteins in buffalo and cow milk

g/100ml

Polypeptide	Concentration in milk		
	Buffalo	Indian cow	Western cow
a_{s1}-casein	1.44—1.8	1.04—1.3	1.2—1.5
$O_{s\text{-}2}$-casein	0.22—0.28	0.26—0.34	0.3—0.4
β-casein	1.26—1.58	0.94	0.9—1.1
γ-casein	0.16	0.15	0.1—0.2
k-casein	0.43—0.54	0.3—0.37	0.3—0.4
β-lactoglobulins	0.39	0.31—0.38	0.2—0.4
α-lactalbumins	0.14	0.71—0.1	0.1—0.15
Proteose peptone	0.33	0.24	0.6—1.8
Serum albumins	0.029	—	0.1—0.4
Lactoferrin	0.032	0.005	

Caseins: Typical of milk proteins, caseins display a distinctive structure as well as physical, biological and nutritional properties. These exist in milk as particles called casein micelles, which are made up of calcium phosphate and casein compounds, A very small proportion of casein is also present in soluble form.

Caseins are heat stable. Heat has little or no effect on casein molecules since they exist naturally in an open and extended state (gain in water entropy) at higher temperatures. However, heating of milk at elevated temperatures for a long time may result in hydrolytic cleavage of peptide and phosphate bond, which affects the stability of the complex, contributing to coagulation of milk.

The £-amino group of lysine present in casein interacts with the aldehyde group of lactose at elevated temperature, leading to the formation of brown pigments (Maillard reaction). This explains browning of heat-desiccated products during storage.

As compared to cow milk, buffalo milk is richer in total proteins, particularly the casein and whey proteins. However, the proportion of various protein fractions is similar in milk of both species. Distinct differences exist in the physico-chemical make-up of casein in buffalo and cow milk. The proportion of micellar casein is nearly 100 per cent in buffalo milk, while that of soluble casein is very low whereas in cow milk, the micellar casein is of the order of 90—95 per cent. The voluminosity of the buffalo milk casein is 2.68—3.72 ml/g at 25—27°C, while that of the cow milk casein is 4.18 ml/g. The hydration (solvation) of the buffalo micelle is lower (2.60—2.90 g Water/g casein) as compared to 3.48 g water/g casein for cow micelle. The particle size of the buffalo casein micellar is larger in diameter (110—160 nm) than that of the cow casein micellar (70—110 nm). The buffalo casein micelle is more opaque (about three times, when suspended in a different medium) than the cow micelle. Buffalo casein has superior whitening as compared to that of cow casein due perhaps to a higher proportion of calcium present in it. The magnesium content of buffalo milk is also higher. However, the sialic acid and hexose content in buffalo milk is lower than that in cow milk.

Whey Proteins: Whey proteins consist of β-lactoglobulin and α-lactalbumin, bovine serum albumin, immunoglobulins (mainly IgGI, IgG2 and IgM), lactoferrin, proteose-peptone, serum transferrin, glycoprotein and enzymes.

The average range of whey proteins in buffalo milk is found to be between 0.70—0.74 per cent as compared to 0.50-0.53 per cent in cow milk. The average level of proteose-peptone in buffalo milk (330.5 mg/100 ml) is significantly higher than that in cow milk (240 mg/100 ml).

Milk proteins display significant functional characteristics (Table 3.11), due to which they have become important ingredients in various foods.

β-*lactoglobulin:* This is the major whey protein present in buffalo and cow milk. The buffalo milk β-lactoglobulin displays molecular weight of about 38,500 daltons, as compared to that of 37,600 daltons observed in the cow milk β-lactoglobulin. In milk of Indian cattle breeds, mainly two genetic variants (A and B) of β-lactoglobulin are found, whereas in the western breeds, C and D variants have also been reported. Milk of Murrah buffalo shows the pre-dominant presence of two genetic variants of β-lactoglobulin. Their electrophoretic mobility is similar to that of A and C variants of cow milk β-lactoglobulin. Buffalo milk also shows the presence of yet another variant of β-lactoglobulin, which has faster electrophoretic mobility than the A variant of cow milk β-lactoglobulin.

Table 3.11 : Functional characteristics of milk proteins.

Functionality	Casein or caseinates	Whey proteins
Water binding	Very high, minimum at pH 4.6	Water-binding capacity increases with denaturation of protein.
Solubility	Insoluble at pH 4.6	Soluble at all pH levels. If denatured, insoluble at pH 5.
Viscosity	High at or above pH 4.6	Low for native protein. Higher if denatured.
Gelation	No thermal gelation except in the presence of Ca^{+2} Micelles gel with rennin	Heat gelation at 70°C (158°F) or higher; influenced by pH and salts.
Emulsification	Excellent at neutral and basic pH	Good except at pH 4-5, if heat denatured.
Foaming	Good overrun. k-Casein best followed by β - and α_{s1}-caseins. Poor foam stability	Good over-runs. β-Lactoglobulin better than α-lactalbumin.
Flavour binding	Good	Retention varies with degree of denaturation.

α-lactalbumins: The α-lactalbumins present in buffalo and cow milks display almost similar attributes. The, molecular weight of buffalo α-lactalbumins has been observed to be 16,200 daltonsand that of cow α-lactalbumins 14,176 daltons. There are two genetic variants of α-lactalbumins — variants A and B — both in cow and buffalo milk. They have almost similar electrophoretic mobility.

Immunoglobulins (Ig): They are antibodies synthesized in response to stimulation by specific antigens. These offer non-specific humoral response to Gram-negative enteric and respiratory bacteria. There are five major classes of immunologlobulins, viz., IgA, IgD, IgE, IgG and IgM. The basic structure of all Igs is similar. These are composed of two identical light chains (23,000 daltons) and two identical heavy chains (53,000 daltons). Of the five-immunoglobulin classes, IgG is the predominant fraction in buffalo and cow milk, comprising about 90 per cent of the total colostral immunoglobulins. The average immunoglobulin content of buffalo milk is appreciably higher as compared to cow milk, being 76.2 µg/100 gm whey proteins in first milking post-partum. It decreases to 43.4 µg/100 gm on the sixth day milking post-partum. The total concentration of immunoglobulins in Zebu cattle averages about 40.1 (µg/ml immediately after calving and it declines to 0.45 µg/m on the eighth day post-partum.

Lactoferrin: This glycoprotein displays a strong inhibitory effect towards Gram-negative enteropathogenic bacteria by virtue of its ability to bind free ionic iron, which is essentially required for the growth of enteropathogenic micro-organisms. Apart from the antibacterial effect, a nutritional role in iron metabolism has also been ascribed to lactoferrin. The average lactoferrin content of buffalo milk is relatively higher at 0.32—0.5 mg/ml than the average of 0.15—0.32 mg/ml for cow milk.

Proteose-Peptone: The average level of proteose-peptone in buffalo milk at about 330.5 mg/100 ml is significantly higher when compared to 240 mg/100 ml in cow milk.

Lactose: Also called milk sugar, lactose is the major carbohydrate of milk. It is a disaccharide of one residue each of D-glucose and D-galactose. Buffalo milk usually contains lactose in the range of 4.7—5.0 per cent, while cow milk has slightly lower amounts of lactose in the range of 4.5—4.8 per cent. Crystallization of lactose, when milk is concentrated, is of importance in regard to the texture of end-products. Lactose has only 16—33 per cent of the sweetening power of sucrose. This makes lactose uniquely suitable for certain food applications. Its use as icing toppings and various types of fillings can improve the quality of food formulations. Being a reducing sugar, it reacts with proteins to form a highly flavoured golden brown substance, commonly found on the crust of baked foods. Lactose contributes significantly to the flavour, texture, appearance, shelf-life and toasting qualities of baked foods. The pharmaceutical industry has used lactose for many years for making tablets or pills. A compound formed from lactose in heated milk products is lactulose. It stimulates the growth of *Bifidobacterium bifidum* and is thus beneficial for producing useful microflora in the gut.

Minerals: Average normal milk contains 0.70 per cent ash, and this amount represents a salt content of about 0.90 per cent. The percentage of salt and ash in milk varies with the breed, feed, season, and stage of lactation /and disease. The white residue after incineration of a given weight of milk is used as a measure of the mineral content of milk.

The mineral make-up of milk is crucial to the stability of the physico-chemical equilibrium. Minerals in milk are present in complex equilibria such as colloidal, soluble: ionic and non-ionic. Although their concentration is less than 1 per cent in milk, minerals significantly affect the technological behaviour of milk thus:

- Heat stability and alcohol coagulation of raw milk;
- Preparation quality and storage stability of products like concentrated/heat desiccated milk products;

- Clumping of fat globules upon homogenization of cream; and
- The calcium content of milk influences the firmness of curd during paneer and chhana making.

Table 3.12 : Concentration of major minerals and trace elements in buffalo and cow milk.

Elements	Concentration (mg/100 ml)		
	Buffalo	Indian cow	Exotic cow
Major minerals			
Calcium	183.9	114.2	123
Magnesium	49.02	11.0	12
Sodium	44.75	50.0	58
Potassium	101.6	148	141
Phosphate	88.74	84.8	95
Citrate	177.6	166	160
Chloride	63.82	106	119
	Concentration in (xg/100 ml of milk		
Trace elements			
Boron	52—145		27
Cobalt	0.69—1.61		0.6
Copper	7—21		13
Iron	42—152		45
Manganese	38.2—65.8		22
Sulphur	15700—31400		30000
Fluoride (ppm)	12.3—18.5		20-180
Iodine (ppm)	8.5—19.4		5—50
Zinc	147—728		390

Sodium, potassium and chloride are to a large extent (95-96%) pre sent in true solution and in ionic form and therefore diffuse freely across the membrane during ultrafiltration, reverse osmosis and electrodialysis of milk and whey.

Buffalo milk contains more calcium and phosphorus (0.22% and 0.13% respectively) than cow milk (0.12% and 0.09% respectively). Moreover, the calcium/phosphorus ratio is higher in buffalo milk (2.26) than cow milk (1.96). Buffalo milk has low heat stability in concentrated form (2:1). Heat stability, expressed as heat coagulation time at 130°C, is 31.82 minutes for buffalo milk, while it is 32.28 minutes for cow milk. However, when milk is concentrated 2 to 1, their corresponding heat coagulation times are 2.89 and 6.58 minutes, respectively. The soluble forms of calcium, magnesium and citrate are lower in buffalo milk than in cow milk.

MINOR CONSTITUENTS

Vitamins: Minor constituents of buffalo and cow milk and concentrations of some vitamins are given in Tables 3.13 and 3.14.

Table 3.13 : Concentration of certain vitamins in buffalo and cow milk.

Vitamins	Concentration in milk		
	Buffalo	Indian cow	Exotic cow
Vitamin A (μg/ml)	340	230	136—157
Thiamine (μg/ml)	0.2—0.5	0.2	0.2—0.8
Riboflavin (μg/ml)	1.59	2.33	1.7
Nicotinic acid(μg/ml)	2.60		
Biotin (μg/ml)	26.75		
Pantothenic acid (μg/ml)	1.5		3.1
p-aminobenzoic acid (μg/ml)	26.75		
Pyridoxine (μg/ml)	3.25	2.6—3.0	0.4
Choline (mg/ml)	0.114	0.091	0.107
Ascorbic acid (mg/100 g)	6.72	1.94	1.65—2.75
Vitamin D(IU)			1.1356—2.8056
Tocopherol (μg/g)	25.9	312.2	34.8
Vitamin K (μg/ml)			0.0—0.0160

Enzymes: Milk is a repository of a variety of enzymes. Over 20 enzymes have been isolated and characterized in cow milk. However, information on enzymes in buffalo milk is very limited. Several enzymes in milk are utilized for quality testing and control. Some important enzymes from the processing point of view are listed below:

Alkaline Phosphatase: This enzyme has assumed significance because of the relationship between the temperature at which it is inactivated and the temperature employed for pasteurization of milk. Buffalo milk on an average contains about two-thirds the activity of alkaline phosphatase as that of cow milk. Alkaline phosphatase is distributed through milk although its concentration is higher in the cream fraction.

Lipoprotein Lipase: Residual activity of lipase remaining in processed milk or milk products tends to reduce their shelf-life.

Table 3.14 : Concentration of some minor constituents in buffalo and cow milk.

Constituent	Concentration in milk		
	Buffalo	Indian cow	Exotic cow
Choline (μg/100 ml)			13.7
Folacin (μg/100 ml)			0.0059
Myo-Inositol (μg/100 ml)			11.0
Non-protein nitrogen (mg/100 ml)			22.9—30.8
Urea N (mg/100 ml)			8.4—13.4
Creatine N (mg/100 ml)	2.5	1.6	0.6—2
Uric acid N (mg/100 ml)	24	37	0.5—0.8
Taurin (moles/100 ml)	5.9	4.1	4.1
Orotic acid N(μg/100 ml)	19.5	52.6	1.2—1.3
N-acetylneuraminic acid (mg/100 ml)			12—-27
Lactic acid (mg/100 ml)			3.4—10.4
Acetic acid (mg/100 ml)			0.3—5
Formic acid (mg/100 ml)			1—8.5

Protease/Plasmin: Residual proteolytic activity in processed milk and milk products reduces their shelf-life.

Lactoperoxidase (LP): This enzyme is naturally present in milk. One of its unique biological functions is an antibacterial effect in the presence of hydrogen peroxide and thiocyanate. Both these substances are naturally present in milk in varying concentrations. This enzyme has gained significance in view of its supportive role in preserving raw milk under ambient conditions through the LP-system. Lactoperoxidase activity in buffalo milk ranges between 5.2—9.8 units/ml, which is on average higher than the corresponding value of 4.4—7.2 units/ml for cow milk.

To activate LPs in milk, add about 10 PPM (parts per million) of thiocyanate (preferably in powder form) to the raw milk. It increases the overall thiocyanate level to 15 PPM from the natural level of 5 PPM. The resultant solution is thoroughly mixed for 30 seconds and then an equimolar amount (8.5 PPM) of hydrogen peroxide is added (generally in the form of a granulated sodium carbonate peroxyhydrate). The LPs activation has a bacteriostatic effect on the raw milk, extending its shelf-life by 7-8 hours under tropical conditions. This means that milk can be transported from the collection point to the processing plant without affecting its quality, thereby significantly increasing the income generated at the producer group level.

Lysozyme: This is a relatively small, single peptide chain protein. Its content in cow milk is about 13 (μ/100 ml. Recently emphasis has been focussed on the antibacterial role of lysozyme as a natural defence in milk. During mastitis, lysozyme levels in milk tend to increase considerably, being in the range of 100 to 200 μg/100ml.

Pigments: In cow milk, carotene is the major pigment and it is derived from feed. It gives cow milk a pale yellow appearance. However, buffalo has the ability to convert carotene into Vitamin A before passing it into milk and so it appears white. Milk also contains bile pigments. Among them, biliverdin predominates. Its concentration is 50.4 mg/ml of milk. It binds to caseins. In the course of souring of milk, biliverdin is detached from casein and it undergoes a rapid chemical reduction to a fat-soluble yellow pigment called bilirubin. Butter fat from soured buffalo milk develops a greenish yellow colour, reaching its maximum in two hours. This is attributed to the presence of two pigments, non-carotenoid in nature. Of them, the predominant pigment is green and the minor component is blue.

PHYSICAL PROPERTIES OF MILK

Appearance: The opacity of milk is due to its contents of suspended particles of fat, proteins and certain minerals. Milk colour varies from white to yellow according to the colouration (carotene content) of the fat. Skim milk is more transparent with a slightly bluish tint. Colour of buffalo milk is richer than that of cow milk due to larger number of fat particles in it. Homogenization increases the number and total volume of fat globules. This results in whiter colour of homogenized products than their unhomogenized counterparts. Lack of fat globules and water-soluble pigment riboflavin produces a yellowish or bluish green tint in skim milk. After removal of casein particles from skim milk, the resultant whey has a distinct green fluorescence. Yellow colour of cow milk fat—both butter and ghee—is due to the presence of fat-soluble pigments carotene and xanthophyll. The dense white colour of buffalo milk is due to absence of these pigments as well as larger size of casein micelles/colloidal calcium phosphate complex.

Flavour: The flavour of milk is a property difficult to define, but there is no doubt that taste and aroma are critical to the assessment of milk. Milk flavour constitutes a critical criterion of judging its quality by the consumer. It is a sensory property in which odour and taste interact. The sweet taste of lactose is balanced by the salty taste of chloride, and both are somewhat moderated by proteins. This balance is maintained over a fairly wide range of milk composition even when the chloride ion level varies from 0.06 to 0.12 per cent. Saltiness can be detected by sensory tests in samples containing 0.12 per cent or more of chloride ions and it becomes marked in samples containing 0.15 per cent chloride ions. The characteristic rich flavour of dairy products is due to the lactones, methylketones, certain aldehydes, dimethyl sulfide and certain short-chain fatty acids. Milk has a clean, pleasantly sweet flavour, but any off-flavours are readily discernible. They develop when the balance of flavour compounds is disturbed due to the microbiological activity or processing treatments, or chemical or biochemical reactions during milk production, processing and storage. A common cause of off-flavour development is tainted feed.

Acidity and pH: Freshly drawn milk is amphoteric to litmus, i.e. it turns red litmus blue and blue litmus red. The pH of normal, fresh, sweet milk usually varies from 6.6 to 6.8. Buffalo milk tends to have a slightly higher pH than cow milk. Higher pH values for fresh milk indicate udder infection (mastitis) and lower values, bacterial action. Skimming and dilution with water raise the pH of milk while sterilization usually lowers it. Milk displays an innate ability to resist the changes in the pH, mainly due to the presence of caseins, colloidal salts (calcium phosphate complex, citrates etc.) and whey proteins.

Oxidation-reduction Potential: The oxidation-reduction (E_h) potential of milk is due to the presence of several soluble constituents, capable of yielding or accepting electrons. Heating of milk above 70°C also causes a noticeable decrease in the E_h due to liberation of -SH groups from whey proteins.

Thermal Expansion: When warmed, the volume of milk increases which affects the design considerations for storage and flow rates through processing treatments. The volume of buffalo milk increases steadily by 1.26 per cent when heated from 4 to 40°C. Upon further heating, it increases by 6 per cent up to a temperature of 95°C. The coefficients of thermal expansion for cow milk are slightly lower due to its lower fat content.

Density and Specific Gravity: Density of milk is the resultant of the densities of its constituents, their concentration and state of being at a particular temperature. The density of milk with 3-5 per cent fat averages 1.032 g/cm^3. Accordingly, the weight of one litre of milk is 1.03 kg. The density of milk decreases from a maximum at 5.2°C to a minimum at 40°C. Above 40°C, change in density is erratic. Specific gravity of milk, which is the ratio of density of milk to that of water at that temperature, is reported at 15.5°C (60°F). The specific gravity of fresh whole milk lies in the range 1.030—1.035, with an average of 1.032. Milk fat, milk SNF, skim milk and evaporated whole milk at 15.5°C have specific gravity of 0.93, 1.614, 1.036 and 1.066, respectively. Although buffalo milk contains more fat than cow milk, it has higher specific gravity because it contains more SNF as well.

The percentage of total solids or SNF in milk is calculated using the following formula:

$$\%TS = 0.25D + 1.22F + 0.72$$

$$\%SNF = 0.25D + 0.22F + 0.72$$

where,

D = 1000(d-1)

d = density of sample of milk at 20°C

F = fat percentage of sample.

Viscosity: The viscosity of milk and cream gives an impression of "richness" to the consumer. From an organoleptic standpoint, viscosity contributes to mouth feel and flavour. Viscosity of milk and dairy products depends on temperature, concentration and state of casein micelles and fat globules. As the percentage of total solids is more in buffalo whole milk, its viscosity is also more.

Surface Tension: Surface properties are relevant to creaming, fat globule membrane function, foaming, and emulsifier use in dairy products. Normal cow milk has an inherent surface activity. Surface tension decreases as milk temperature rises. Processing treatments such as heating, sterilization, homogenization and shear tend to increase surface tension. However, homogenization of imperfectly pasteurized milk or contamination of homogenized pasteurized milk with raw milk causes partial hydrolysis of milk fat, resulting in low surface tension, bitter flavour and rancidity of milk.

Curd Tension: This property is considered important in relation to the cheese making characteristics as well as digestibility of milk. The curd tension of buffalo milk is significantly higher at 32.85 g than that of cow milk, which is 28.54 g. Heat treatment of buffalo milk causes reduction of curd tension, so also does the homogenization treatment. Addition of some salts such as sodium citrate and sodium hexametaphosphate tend to reduce the curd tension of milk.

Foaming: Milk and milk products rich in milk fat and/or milk proteins interact frequently with air and foam. This process is desirable as in whipping of cream, and at times it also creates a nuisance, as in handling of skim milk. Fat globules make foam less stable. Foaming properties affect handling of milk products and the manner in which dairy-based ingredients are incorporated into other products. Heating of milk to such an extent that whey proteins are denatured yields more voluminous and more stable foam on heating. However, sterilization diminishes its foaming capacity. A concentrate of 30 per cent dry matter that has been vigorously homogenized forms very stable foam.

Foaming of milk is minimum at 30—35°C. At 60°C, the foam volume is independent of the fat content. Below 20°C and above 30°C, the foaming tendency appears to increase. Fat tends to stabilize the foam formed below 20°C, for instance, during churning. Skim milk produces slightly more stable foam above 30°C than whole milk or light cream.

Freezing Point: Milk freezes at a temperature slightly lower than water due to the presence of soluble constituents such as lactose, soluble salts, etc., which lower the freezing point. The average freezing point of cow milk is —0.547°C (31.02°F) and buffalo milk, 0.549°C (31.01°F). The freezing point of milk is used for detecting water adulteration in milk. Addition of water lowers the concentration of lactose and salts, thus increasing the freezing point.

The Association of Official Analytical Chemists (AOAC) has specified that milk with a freezing point of —0.525°C or below may be presumed to be water free. But readings above this support a strong suspicion of water addition to milk. As little as 3 per cent water added to milk can be detected by this method. The freezing points of cream, skim milk and whey are identical with that of the milk from which they are prepared. Therefore, the freezing point test does not detect addition of skim milk or removal of fat from milk samples. Moreover, watered milk, which has soured, may pass the test because souring results in a lowering of the freezing point due to an increase in the amount of soluble molecules. Hence, the freezing point should be determined in fresh samples (having no developed acidity) for greatest accuracy.

Boiling Point: The milk constituents in true solution are mainly responsible for the elevation of the boiling point above 100°C. The boiling point of buffalo milk is marginally higher than that of cow milk. Their respective boiling points are: 100.55°C and 100.17°C. For detecting added water in milk, the freezing point method is far superior on the grounds of accuracy and convenience.

Specific Heat: Specific heat is the ratio between the amount of heat necessary to raise a given weight of a substance to a specified temperature and the amount of heat necessary to raise an equal weight of water to the same temperature. For processing, it is important to determine the quantity of heat either to be added or removed from milk to reach the desired temperature. For cow milk, heat capacity of whole milk, skim milk, whey, milk fat, 40 per cent cream and dried skim milk powder, between 15—20°C, is 0.93, 0.95, 0.97, 0.52,0.68, and 0.30 (cal/gm/C), respectively. The heat capacity of milk and cream depends upon the fat content. The heat capacity of buffalo milk ranges between 0.84 to 0.86 cal/g/C at 30°C.

Thermal Conductivity: It determines the rate of cooling and heating of milk. It changes with variation in temperature, level of concentration and fat content. For example, thermal conductivity decreases at higher concentration and higher fat content in milk for a given temperature.

Electrical Conductivity: Current passes through milk by virtue of the activity of its ionic mineral constituents, of which chloride ions carry 60—68 per cent of the current. The average value of current for buffalo milk ranges between 0.003 to 0.007 mho/cm. Higher values usually represent mastitic infections. Electrical conductivity of milk may be used to detect added neutralizers. The development of acidity by bacterial action during fermentation of milk increases its conductance because of conversion of calcium and magnesium to ionic forms. Thus, by measuring their electrical conductance, the progress of fermentation can be followed during the manufacture of yogurt and other fermented dairy products. Electrical conductance can also be used to follow demineralization of whey during manufacture of whey protein concentrates.

Refractive Index: The components of milk contributing to its refractive index in descending order of importance are: water, proteins, lactose and minor constituents. The refractive index of milk fat varies from 1.4537 to 1.4552 at 50°C and it is used to indicate its purity.

Osmotic Pressure: Milk is formed from blood, the two being separated by a permeable membrane. Hence, they have the same osmotic pressure. The osmotic pressure of blood is remarkably constant although the composition, as far as pigment, protein, etc., is concerned, may vary.

Salt Balance: During thermal processing of milk, its heat stability plays a very important role. The heat stability of milk is mainly determined by the make-up of proteins as well as the relative concentration of various salts present in colloidal and ionic states. Because of the inherent differences in the concentration of various minerals in milk, buffalo and cow milks display distinctive differences in their heat stability. Added to this complexity is also the inherent difference in the genetic and chemical make-up of caseins of the milk of the two species.

Heat Stability: In the manufacture of certain high heat-treated/concentrated milk products, the heat stability of milk plays a significant role. A number of factors interact in a complex manner, which ultimately determine the heat coagulation of milk. On the basis of findings the role of various interacting factors may be summarized as follows:

- *Protein Make-up:* The larger the amount of β-lactoglobulin, the higher the maximum heat coagulation temperature.
- *Salt Balance:* Heat stability is maximum at the optimum salt equilibrium, defined by the relative concentration of calcium, magnesium, citrate and phosphates in ionic form.
- *pH:* The pH affects both the molecular disassociation of casein components and formation of aggregated protein complexes through protein-protein interactions. Further, pH strongly affects the salt equilibrium between the colloidal and ionic states of the minerals of milk. Maximum heat stability is observed between pH 6.6 and 6.8.
- *Concentration of Milk Solids:* The heat stability of milk decreases progressively as milk is concentrated to higher levels of total solids.
- *Homogenization:* Although fat itself does not affect heat stability of milk, homogenization of milk brings about certain significant changes in the physical equilibrium of milk. During homogenization of milk, the original fat globule is disrupted and surface area increases by many folds. It marginally reduces the heat stability.

The differences in physico-chemical properties of buffalo and cow milk are of significance in their characteristic functional and processing properties. Table 3.15 gives some important properties.

Table 3.15 Physical properties of buffalo and cow milk.

Physical property	Buffalo milk	Cow milk
Specific gravity at 20°C	1.0323	1.0317
Viscosity at 27°C in Centipoises	2.245	1.450
Curd tension, g	32.85	28.54
Surface tension, dynes/cm at 20°C	45.50	42.50
Freezing point, °C	—0.5454	—0.530
Titratable acidity, as % lactic acid	0.16	0.15
pH, 20°C	6.7	6.6
Redox potential, volts	+ 0.310	+ 0.258
Electrical conductivity, m mho/cm	3.22-6.67	4.00—5.50
Thermal conductivity, Kcal/h m°C at 37°C	0.569	0.46
Heat capacity, Cal/g/°C at 30°C	0.852	0.93—0.95
Colour	White	Creamy yellow

4

Technology of Bengali Sweets

RASOGOLLA

Rasogolla is undoubtedly the undisputed king not only of Bengali sweets, but of all Indian sweets. This soft, succulent ball of chhana (cottage cheese) soaked in sugar syrup has delighted the taste buds of millions of connoisseurs for more than hundred years. Its popularity has spread beyond the Indian shores to captivate epicureans the world over. Rasogolla was "created" in 1868 by Nobin Chandra Das, a scion of Bengal's famed sweet-maker family of K.C. Das.

Product Description: Rasogolla is a delicacy, stored and served in sugar syrup. In size and shape, it resembles a ping-pong ball. Snow-white in colour, it possesses a spongy, chewy body, and smooth texture. Innovations and experimentations have led to the evolution of rasogolla into a multitude of forms and flavours—flattened into patties and blended with rabri floating in a fragrant milk bulk created rasomalai, an all-time favourite. Rajbhog is another "incarnation" of rasogolla that is ballooned, and saffron added to fashion a golden-hued delight. There are also variations such as cardamom-centred and orange-flavoured. And, the latest from the house of K.C. Das is the nolen "gur"-flavoured rasogolla, with a faint tint of pink, popular during winter months when khajur gur is available. Those with poetic inclination call it "blushogolla". The Bureau of Indian Standards (BIS) has laid down the standards for rasogolla (Table 4.1).

Size of Industry: The rasogolla production is largely confined to the cottage and small-scale industry. In recent years, its marketing in cans has become a flourishing business, with a number of brands jostling for shelf-space in retail stores. Bikaner in Rajasthan has emerged as a leading centre for the production of canned rasogollas and their marketing all over India as well as exports. Its annual production is estimated at 60,000 tonnes. The shelf-life of canned rasogollas is three months. The development of canning in lacquered tins has helped in rapid expansion of the rasogolla market. The tins come in sizes from 400, 800 gm consumer packs to 15 kg packs for supply to wholesalers.

Table 4.1 : BIS standards for rasogolla.

Characteristics	Specifications
Moisture	45—55%
Milk fat	5%
Sucrose	45%
Protein	5%
Requirements for syrup	
Acidity of syrup (ml of N/10 NaOH required to neutralize 100 ml of the syrup), max.	6.0
Concentration of syrup, max.	55° Brix
Bacterial count, per gram, max	500
Coliform count, per gram	Nil

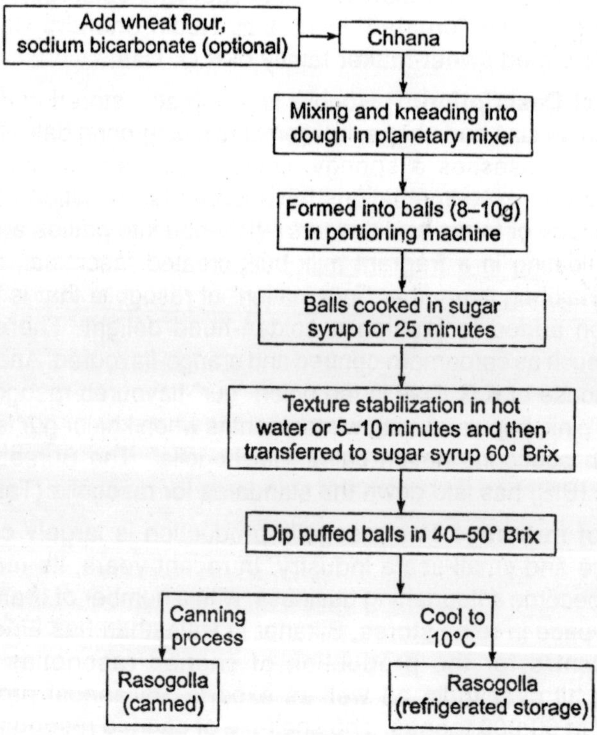

Figure 4.1 : Flow chart for manufacture of rasogolla.

Technology: Rasogolla is prepared by texturization of milk protein under controlled cooking conditions in boiling syrup. This gives rasogolla an interwoven fibre-like structure. The controlled cooking in sugar syrup imparts spongy characteristics to rasogolla balls and improves their sugar holding capacity (Figure 4.1).

Rasogolla is prepared from soft, freshly-made cow milk chhana. Use of chhana made from buffalo or mixed milk is avoided because of its somewhat inferior body (less chewy) and texture (grainier).

For rasogolla production, chhana is manually kneaded to a smooth paste. Then, the paste is portioned and rolled between palms to form balls of about 15 mm diameter and around 8—10 grams in weight. Each ball should have a smooth surface with no cracks. In case of buffalo milk, chhana needs to be modified by mixing it with flour (6% arrowroot, 2% semolina, 0.6% baking powder of the chhana weight) and subsequently kneaded manually to a smooth paste. One kg of chhana yields 90—100 rasogollas.

To prepare cooking medium, three parts of sugar are mixed with one part of whey and two parts of water. In case of the buffalo milk chhana, three parts of water are necessary for making the sugar syrup. The pH is adjusted to about 6.8 with the addition of calcium hydroxide. The solution is boiled, and the scum that forms at the top is scooped off before it is ready for cooking.

Rasogolla balls are dipped in the cooking medium. The heating is regulated to impart a stable form to balls that are cooked for about 15 minutes. During cooking, a small amount of water and whey solution is continuously added to maintain its concentration. This makes up for the loss of water due to evaporation. The ratio of whey and water is so adjusted as to maintain the pH of the medium at about 6.8 during cooking. After cooking, the balls are transferred to a container with water at 30—35°C for their texture stabilization and colour improvement. About 10 per cent of the cooking solution is replaced by fresh one, every time it is reused to cook another batch of rasogollas.

Sugar Syrup: After 5—10 minutes of texture stabilization in water, the balls are transferred to sugar syrup. The desired sugar syrup concentration in the final product is 45—50 per cent. This is achieved by dipping the texture-stabilized balls first in 50—60 Brix sugar syrup for 1-2 hours, followed by second dipping in 40—50 Brix sugar syrup. Finally, the product acquires the desired sugar concentration after a balance is reached between the sugar syrup inside the balls and outside them. To exercise better control over the sugar syrup concentration in the finished product, dipping of the texturized balls may be done in three stages—first stage dipping in 50-60 per cent concentration, second stage dipping in 40—50 per cent concentration, and final dipping in 50 per cent concentration. Rasogollas are stored at or below 10°C to obtain a more precise sugar concentration of 45—50 per cent in them.

Mechanized Production: R & D studies have been undertaken to develop a mechanized process for manufacture of rasogollas. The mechanized production would help maintain consistent quality standards under better hygienic conditions and provide an attractive packaging system and increased shelf-life. A mechanical disc grinder has been designed for kneading chhana. Its overall sensory score on rasogolla has been reported to be comparable with hand-kneaded channa.

A properly designed screw conveyor with a kneading section and a cutter provided at the exit can simultaneously perform the operation of kneading and portioning channa into lumps of about 10 grams each. They can be made to fall on a spinning disc, while a stationary disc above it can form the lumps of channa into spherical balls. Thereafter, they can be made to fall directly into a tank containing sugar syrup for cooking. Development of a continuous rasogolla cooker will help in completing the mechanization of the rasogolla production process. A mechanism can move channa balls through the cooker for the required time. Another device can maintain the concentration of the cooking mixture by adding the required quantity of water to compensate for the water evaporated from the sugar syrup during cooking.

Use of Milk Powder: The problems posed by shortage of milk during the lean season and short shelf-life of chhana can be overcome by using milk powder. The suggested process involves dissolving the whole milk powder to 17 per cent total solids, heating the reconstituted milk to boiling, its filtration and cooling to 70°C. Coagulation is done with either 1.0 per cent citric acid or lactic acid solution at 70°C at pH of 5.5 followed by delayed straining (15 minutes). The coagulum, contained in muslin cloth, is cooled to room temperature by immersing it in running tap water, and then kept for draining for three and half hours. Later, chhana is kneaded to a smooth consistency and rolled into balls. These are cooked in boiling sugar syrup of 50—60 per cent concentration for 20 minutes and finally transferred to hot (60°C) sugar syrup (40-50%) and cooled to ambient temperature before keeping them in refrigerated storage.

Dried Rasogolla Mix: A process has been developed for production of dried rasogolla mix. Skim milk is concentrated to required total solids level by using ultra- and dia-filtration process. A calculated amount of fat is added to the retentate before spray drying it. Certain additives and binders are dry blended in the retentate powder to yield dried rasogolla mix. Rasogolla prepared with dried mix is reported to have balanced flavour and spongy texture.

Yield: The yield of finished rasagolla (drained) is 254 grams per 100 grams of cow milk chhana. In case of buffalo milk, the yield is 342 g/100 g chhana. About 90—100 rasagollas of diameter 30 mm can be made from one kg of chhana.

Packaging: Rasogollas are usually packed in lacquered tin cans of one kg capacity, containing 14 pieces. The empty containers are first sterilized in hot air inside a closed chamber. Rasogolla balls with hot sugar syrup and permissible preservatives are filled in containers, and seaming tightly seals the lid. Sodium metabisulphite is used to maintain white colour of tinned rasogollas. Containers are kept in a tub containing chilled water to create partial vacuum by quick condensation of vapours inside the container. The shelf-life of rasogollas in tin containers is around three months.

RASOMALAI

Rasomalai was created by mingling the flattened rasogolla with North Indian Rabri. The credit for its creation goes to Krishna Chandra Das in the early 20th century, some 50 years after his father Nobin Chandra Das had "invented" the spongy rasogolla. Marwaris of Kolkata acquired a taste for it and made it their own. The Bikaneri halwai also became adept at its making. Thus, rasomalai is now popular all over India, particularly in eastern and northern parts.

Product Description: Rasomalai is marketed as flattened chhana patties floating in thickened sweet milk. It is a very delicate, chewy/ spongy sweet that has a delectable taste. In essence, rasomalai is rasogolla that has been flattened and blended with rabri. It is refrigerated and served chilled.

Technology: Chhana is kneaded into a smooth dough along with 1 to 4 per cent wheat flour. The dough is portioned and rolled into balls having a smooth texture without cracks. The balls are processed like rasogolla and subsequently stored in sweetened (5-6% sugar) milk thickened to one fourth of its volume. Light rabri is at times used instead of thickened milk to soak the chhana balls.

RAJBHOG

Rajbhog is a variety of rasogolla that is ballooned and so larger in size than rasogolla, being about 50—60 mm in diameter. It is blended with saffron that imparts an attractive golden yellow shade to it. A variation of rajbhog is kamalbhog that is blended with orange for flavour and colour.

Technology: Chhana is kneaded into a uniform dough, mixed with a small amount of saffron and portioned and shaped into balls with hands. While shaping, a raisin or a nut is placed at the centre of the ball which is larger in size (almost twice) than rasogolla. The balls are cooked in a 50 per cent solution of boiling sugar syrup. Cooking is continued until a desirable body and texture is achieved. Thereafter, the balls are removed from the syrup and may be wrapped in silver foil.

KHIRMOHAN

Khirmohan is a variation of rasogolla popular in the eastern region of the country. To prepare khirmohan, chhana is kneaded into a smooth dough along with 1 to 4% wheat flour. The dough is portioned and rolled into balls having a smooth texture without cracks. The balls are flattened into a round shape and processed like rasogolla. After cooking, the balls are dipped in concentrated milk, removed and sprinkled with grated khoa.

SANDESH

Sandesh is the most popular chhana-based sweet delicacy of the eastern parts of India, especially West Bengal. In the traditional custom of West Bengal, a good news "message" to friends and relatives is sent along with some "sandesh" (Bengali/Hindi word for "message"). Sandesh has been known for centuries and may even have been a khoa-based product till the evolution of chhana-based sweets. Literary works of the sixteenth century mention about Bengali feasts where sandesh was served. Utilization of chhana for sandesh production is greater than for all other Bengali sweets, including rasogolla. It is claimed that about 80 per cent of chhana produced in Kolkata is converted into sandesh. Chhana obtained with citric acid is usually preferred for the manufacture of sandesh. Traditionally, sandesh is sold by number of pieces rather than by weight.

Sandesh started as a simple, sweetened chhana known as "kachagolla". Soon, it began to be cast in various shapes to resemble flowers, fruits, shells and fish, using appropriate moulds. To enhance its looks and flavours, various sweeteners were used like palm jaggery, sugarcane, jaggery and sugar. It was flavoured with jackfruit, orange peel and rose essence. The use of palm jaggery gives a distinctive flavour and sweetness to sandesh.

Product Description: Sandesh is known for its palatability, aroma and as a rich source of milk proteins, fat, sucrose and fat-soluble vitamins. It has a firm body and smooth texture. Three distinct varieties of sandesh are popular: soft grade (naram-pak), hard grade (kara-pak), and raw grade (kachagolla). The most common variety is the soft grade sandesh. It has a soft body and smooth texture with fine grains uniformly distributed. It contains a relatively smaller amount of sugar and has

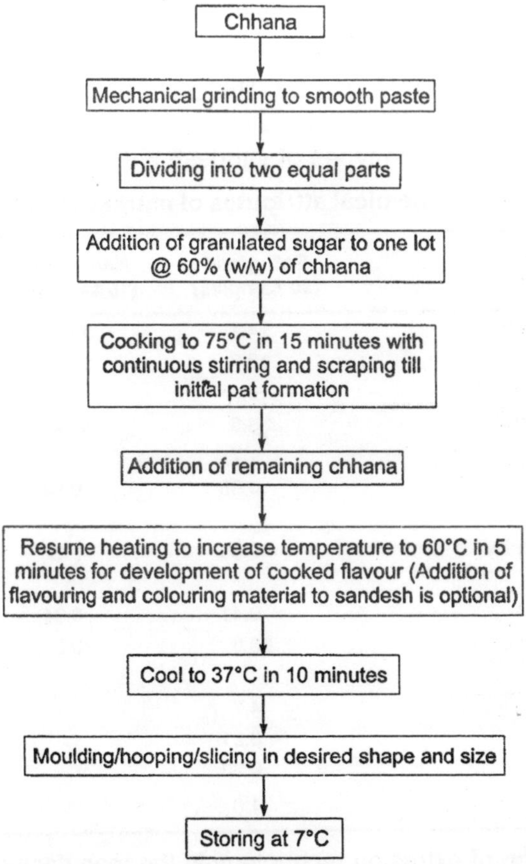

Figure 4.2 : Flow chart for the production of soft grade sandesh.

higher moisture content than the hard grade. Kara-pak has a firm body and dry appearance. Kachagolla is known for its raw chhana-like flavour, moist appearance, soft body and coarse, grainy texture. Another variety, known as nolen gurer sandesh, is prepared from khajur gur (date jaggery) during winter months when dates are available in plenty. It is considered a delicacy and fetches a much higher price. Sandesh is conventionally packaged in paperboard cartons or in tree leaves.

Technology: Cow-milk chhana (30—45%) and sugar are mixed and kneaded together and heated in a shallow vessel after addition of colour and flavour. Although sandesh is largely manufactured in the non-organized sector, a process has been standardized for its industrial production. It is labour-intensive and energy-inefficient. Mechanization of the existing technology with concomitant standardization of sensory profiles and compositional and physico-chemical attributes will help to attain a product of uniform standard and assured quality.

Physico-chemical Aspects: The physico-chemical attributes of sandesh vary widely with the type of product. The chemical profile of market samples of three types of sandesh is listed in Table 4.2.

Table 4.2 : Physico-chemical attributes of market samples of sandesh.

Attribute	Soft grade (30 samples)	Hard grade (15 samples)	Kachagolla (15 samples)
Moisture (per cent)	24.1	13.4	33.9
Fat (per cent)	18.7	20.5	15.5
Protein (per cent)	16.1	16.7	12.8
Sucrose (per cent)	38.6	46.4	35.8
Ash (per cent)	1.7	1.7	1.4
Titratable acidity (per cent LA)	0.88	0.82	0.7
Water-soluble acidity (per cent LA)	0.35	0.22	0.19
FFA (per cent OA)	0.41	0.34	0.46
Free fat (per cent of total fat)	68.6	80.8	56.9
Hardness (kg)	4.7		
Cohesiveness	0.21		
Springiness	0.30		
Gumminess	1.0		

Application of extrusion technology in the manufacture of sandesh has been attempted. A vented extruder with vent ports in the barrel for the volatiles and moisture to escape during the process is promising. A screw type kneader was used for mixing chhana and sugar to achieve homogeneity of the mixture critical for sandesh manufacture. Sandesh obtained from this continuous production method was superior in quality to the market product. The shelf-life of this product packed in polyethylene bags was 16 days at 10 ± 5°C.

CHHANA-MURKI

This product is very popular in the northern and eastern regions of India. In the northern parts of the country, it is served during weddings and feasts.

Product Description: Chhana-murki is a sweet prepared from a chhana base. It has the shape of small cubes, coated with sugar and has a firm body and close-knit texture. A similar sweet is chhana-pulao, in which chhana is shaped into rice-like grains and coloured golden.

Technology: Chhana is kneaded and formed into a 10 mm thick flat slab. It is then cut into small cubes of about 10 mm. The cubes are cooked in boiling sugar syrup (of three-string consistency) in karahi for five minutes with gentle stirring. The karahi is removed from the fire and stirring is continued till the sugar is coated uniformly around the cubes. The cooked cubes are then removed from syrup. After cooling, the cubes are sprinkled with flavours and colour and decorated with dry nut flakes.

Prospects for Mechanization: Potential exists for adapting suitably designed extrusion machine for forming chhana-murki cubes, spray coating them with sugar syrup and tumble drying them in a tunnel drier.

CHAM-CHAM

Cham-cham originated in eastern parts of India. It is a sweet prepared from chhana with a firm body and close-knit texture. It is coated with sugar or khoa.

Technology: Chhana is kneaded into a uniform dough, portioned and shaped by hand into balls. The balls are cooked in a 50 per cent solution of boiling sugar syrup. Cooking is continued until a desirable body and texture have formed. Thereafter, the balls are removed from the syrup and cut into half. A layer of khoa is sandwiched between the two halves and its surface coated with sugar or khoa powder before wrapping it in silver foil.

Prospects for Mechanization: The mechanized process for khoa production has potential for integration with encrusting machine for forming and layering of cham-cham.

CHHANA PODO

This baked sweet, resembling milk cake, is immensely popular in Cuttack District of Orissa in Eastern India. Its surface has a directly caramelised colour and flavour. Buffalo milk chhana is preferred for this sweet.

Chhana podo is prepared by mixing chhana and suji. A paste is prepared and filled in a shallow container. Its surface is coated with ground sugar and covered with sal leaves. Burning coal is placed on the sal leaves and the tray placed near the furnace to provide warmth for cooking that is accomplished through the steam formed by the burning coal on the surface. It makes the surface directly caramelised and imparts a sweetish fragrance to the product.

The process know-how and the design of equipment for the large-scale production of chhana podo is in operation in Orissa, based on technology developed and standardized by the NDDB, Anand.

SURTI PANEER

Among the few best varieties of paneer in India, Surti paneer is a soft cheese prepared with crude rennet, salted and kept steeped in acid whey for 2-3 days. Its name is derived from the Surat town in Gujarat in Western India where it was probably first prepared and marketed. Once a popular product, not much of it is marketed today.

Technology: Fresh buffalo milk, containing 6 per cent fat, is pasteurized and cooled to room temperature (35°C). About 0.5 to 2 kg of this milk is placed in a coagulating vessel whose temperature is maintained at 35°C. Good quality lactic starter at 0.5 per cent of milk is added and thoroughly mixed with milk. This is followed by addition of rennet (6-7 ml/100 litres milk). The strength of the added rennet should be such that it gives a clean cut in the curd at the end of about 60 minutes. After mixing adequately, the renneted milk is allowed to set till a firm coagulum fit for basketing is obtained. The temperature during this process is maintained at 35°C.

The curd is then ladled out with a vertical slant in thin slices, and filled into specially made bamboo/wicker baskets. These baskets are kept ready by cleaning them with scalding water and soaking them in a

10 per cent lukewarm salt solution for about 10 minutes, and then thinly dressing them with salt. Each successive layer of curd put into the baskets is uniformly sprinkled with salt. Salting is done at 4-5 per cent of the raw cheese.

After filling, the baskets are placed on a draining rack to allow the drainage of whey. Generally, at the end of 50 to 60 minutes, individual pieces of cheese are firm enough to be handled without breaking. These are then carefully turned upside down in their respective baskets. After draining for a further 30—40 minutes, the cheese pieces, on attaining the desired firmness and consistency, are turned a second time.

The collected whey is strained and kept in a vessel. The cheese pieces are removed from the baskets and put into the whey. These are left steeped in whey for 12—36 hours for increased acceptability. When kept steeped in the whey, Surti cheese has a fairly firm body and smooth texture with no internal cracks. It has a slightly salted, mild acid, curd flavour.

BANDEL CHEESE

An indigenous variety of soft cottage cheese from cow milk, Bandel cheese derives its name from its place of origin—Bandel, a Portuguese colony in Eastern India.

Product Description: Bandel cheese is an indigenous, unripened variety of salted soft cheese. Similar in characteristics to Surti cheese, it is made in perforated pots. It resembles directly acidified cheeses of South America.

Technology: Cow milk is heated to 80°C and salt is added at 1—1.5 per cent of the milk taken. Milk is cooled to about 45°C and coagulated, using either a lactic culture or whey. The coagulum is transferred to small perforated pots covered with muslin cloth to facilitate whey drainage. After a while the containers are turned upside down to impart a spherical shape to the cheese. After whey removal, the content is removed and pressed between the palms to flatten it to a circular shape. The product is consumed in this form. Another variety of this cheese exists in the form of Dacca cheese, where the product formed after removal from the perforated pots is smoked in a fire to impart a characteristic smoky flavour to it.

REGIONAL PRODUCTS

Ksheer Sagar: Buffalo milk is concentrated to the consistency of evaporated milk with a distinct caramelized flavour and colour, after which sugar is added. Chhana is kneaded and formed into either rectangular blocks or small balls, and allowed to soak in the concentrate milk before serving.

Sita Bhog: It is prepared by mixing maida with chhana and grinding the mixture to a pasty form. Noodle-like strands are prepared by pressing the mixture through a sieve. These are deep-fried in refined oil and immersed in sugar syrup. Buffalo milk chhana is preferred for the preparation of this product.

Chhana Gaja: This sweet is prepared by kneading chhana with 50 per cent sugar mixed with suji and maida. The kneaded chhana paste is given a ball shape and cooked in concentrated boiling sugar syrup till dark brown in appearance.

Chhana Jhele: This is a chhana-based product popular in the Neempara region near Bhubaneswar in Orissa. It is very similar to the pantua of West Bengal. Chhana jhele is prepared by kneading a paste of chhana, maida and suji in pre-determined proportions. Balls of approximately 30 mm diameter are made out of the kneaded material and deep-fried in oil. The extent of surface browning during frying varies from light golden brown to deep brown. The fried balls are placed in sugar syrup to permit formation of sugar granules so that a crunchy texture is imparted to the product.

Chhana Kheer: It is prepared by concentrating milk over an open fire to a thick consistency, resembling evaporated milk with distinct caramelisation. Immediately prior to serving, raw granular chhana is sprinkled over the sugar-caramelised milk.

Chhana Pakora: Its preparation involves mixing of chhana with maida, gram flour and sugar and kneading the mixture to a paste. The paste is sprinkled over hot oil for frying. The fried pieces are soaked in sugar syrup till they become quite hard.

Rasaballi: Its preparation involves kneading chhana, maida and sugar and rolling the mixture flat. Rectangular pieces are cut and fried in palmolein oil till they turn brown in colour. They are then soaked in a light sugar syrup. No sugar granulation is permitted in this sweet. Buffalomilk chhana is preferred for this product.

Shosim: Also known as somar, it is a product of Nepalese origin and is obtained by the anaerobic fermentation of sherghum, the Nepalese cottage cheese. The fermentation is done in previously used, airtight, wooden or earthen vessels, containing non-descriptive type of micro-organisms. It is used in Nepalese diet in the form of soups.

Kalari: It is a dairy product quite popular in the Dogra community of Jammu region in North India. It is mostly used as a fried snack with a

Table 4.3 : Typical composition of kalari.

Characteristics	Percentage
Fat	29.7
Protein	24.9
Moisture	43.2
Ash	1.7
Lactose	0.4

dash of salt, pepper or red chilly. After frying, the product gets a golden yellow and crisp outer layer with a soft interior with cheesy flavour. It is prepared from fresh cow or buffalo or mixed milk. Milk is first standardised to 4-5 per cent fat and about 8.8 per cent SNF. Milk is boiled in a suitable vessel and tempered to 70°—75°C. At this stage self-soured lassi is added with constant stirring till coagulation occurs and clear whey forms. The coagulum is collected and made into balls of about 2-3 cm diameter. These balls are then flattened manually. The flattened pieces are allowed to dry first in shade kept over cloth in a wooden basket. Finally these are sun-dried over a period of three days, during which a cheesy flavour develops. The Jammu Cooperative Milk Federation has been manufacturing and marketing this product. Table 4.3 presents the composition of kalari.

5

Technology of Dahi and Yogurt

Dahi and yogurt have many things in common. Both have live cultures that nurture therapeutic and health-promoting properties, along with proven nutritional benefits. In both, a part of the milk lactose is converted into lactic acid by the action of starter culture. The presence of lactic acid has a preservative effect on milk. Both have low pH value that inhibits the growth of putrefactive bacteria and other harmful micro-organisms, thereby prolonging their shelf-life.

The therapeutic significance of dahi and yogurt is considered to be more important than their nutritional value. It is believed that concentration of lactic acid bacteria in the intestines, obtained through the ingestion of these products, prevents decaying processes and arrests digestive disorders. Further, during fermentation, partial splitting of proteins and greater availability of calcium, present in milk, enhances the nutritional value of dahi and yogurt.

Different Flavours: Dahi and yogurt have different flavour profiles. Dahi uses mixed cultures of *Lactococcus lactis, Lactococcus diacetylactis, Lactococcus cremoris,* along with *Leuconostoc* species, a combination of acid-producing and flavour-producing bacteria. They help in the production of a firm body and a sweet, mildly acidic flavour in dahi that is relished by consumers. *Leuconostoc* generates diacetyl that imparts buttery flavour to dahi.

On the other hand, yogurt is highly acidic in taste and has a harsh acidic flavour. So, it is rarely consumed plain. It comes with a variety of added flavours, including fruits. It is produced by the activity of specific, well-defined cultures (called "thermophillic") at a higher temperature (42°C) as against use of 'mesophillic' cultures in dahi (curds) at lower temperature (20°—28°C).

Dahi, largely made at home, is a product of undefined culture mix, so its flavour and texture vary from day to day. Lately, dahi production has been standardised with a controlled culture composition and is manufactured under well-defined conditions of time and temperature. It results in a consistent flavour and texture. Industrial production of dahi by the standardised method has commenced in metro cities. Dahi culture may include secondary organisms, namely *Streptococcus thermophilus* and *Lact. acidophilus,* which impart health-sustaining probiotic properties to dahi.

Yogurt has been clinically studied thoroughly and its benefits established scientifically. It is usually classified as follows: Set type (like dahi), stirred/ drinking type similar to lassi and chhach (butter-milk) and frozen type (frogurt) like ice cream. Yogurt is served with various fruits, flavourings and aroma additives.

The popularity of yogurt in countries outside India has been propelled by sophisticated production and marketing techniques that helped in creating and fulfilling the consumer demand. Since dahi and yogurt are closely related in production and use, a study of factors which make yogurt a marketing success abroad would be useful for industrial production and marketing of dahi by the organized sector. The key factors are:

(a) Scientific evidence points to consumer perception of yogurt's good-for-you image. Indeed, clinical studies have established that yogurt is well-tolerated by individuals who suffer from distressing symptoms of flatulence and diarrhoea associated with the maldigestion of milk sugar (lactose) present in most dairy products. All consumers can thus benefit from the milk nutrients like protein, calcium, and B-vitamins through the consumption of yogurt. The live and active cultures present in yogurt may provide immuno-stimulatory effects. Studies indicate that yogurt bacteria may provide protection against pathogenic and undesirable bacteria introduced through food intake into the gastrointestinal tract. Similar to yogurt's image in the West, the Indian consumer has a healthy perception about dahi, which would facilitate its industrial production and marketing.

(b) Use of sweeteners such as cane sugar in dahi formulation would add a desirable dimension to the product taste and tend to moderate its acidic flavour. Further, synthetic sweeteners like aspartame or sucralose can impart desirable sweetness at a significant reduction of calories in the product.

(c) Addition of fruit preparations, fruit flavours and fruit purees in yogurt further enhances its versatility of taste, colour and texture. Fruits are generally perceived as healthy by the consumer. Their association with dahi would further endorse its health image.

(d) Incorporation of nuts and grains give yogurt multiple textures and flavours, thus providing a packaged, convenient and wholesome snack, dessert or breakfast food.

(e) Development and availability of fat-free, low-fat and reduced-fat yogurt has encouraged consumers to benefit from its current health-driven image.

(f) Marketing and merchandising practices have accelerated consumer acceptance and desirability of yogurt.

(g) Proliferation of allied products like hard-frozen and soft-serve yogurt have provided alternatives that are perceived healthier than their counterpart ice cream products.

Product Description: The PFA Act defines dahi or curd as a semi-solid product, obtained from pasteurized or boiled milk by souring (natural or otherwise), using a harmless lactic acid or other bacterial cultures. t)ahi may contain additional cane sugar. It should have the same minimum percentage of fat and solids-not-fat (SNF) as the milk from which it is prepared. Where dahi or curd, other than skimmed milk dahi, is sold or offered for sale without any indication of the class of milk, the standards prescribed for dahi prepared from buffalo milk shall apply.

The Bureau of Indian Standards (BIS) specifications for fermented milk products are based on the type of culture used in their preparation. Mild dahi is made from mesophillic lactococci. Leuconostocs may be adjunct organisms for added buttery odour and flavour. Sour dahi contains additional cultures belonging to the thermophillic group, which are generally employed in the manufacture of yogurt. These thermophillic organisms grow rapidly at 37—45°C, producing dahi in less than 4 hours.

Like dahi, yogurt is a semi-solid fermented product made from a standardized milk mix by the activity of a symbiotic blend of *Streptococcus thermophilus* and *Lactobacillus delbruekii subsp. bulgaricus* cultures. For brevity we shall term the yogurt culture organisms as ST and LB and typical dahi organisms as LL. The body and texture of yogurt depends largely on the composition of milk employed in its manufacture. Although milk of various mammals can be used for making cultured dairy products, their industrialised production is mainly based on milk of cows and buffaloes. The composition of various milks used in their manufacture is given in Table 5.1.

Table 5.1 : Composition of milk used in the preparation of cultured dairy foods.

Per cent

Mammals	Fat	Caseins	Whey proteins	Lactose	Ash	Total solids
Cow	3.7	2.8	0.6	4.8	0.7	12.7
Buffalo	7.4	3.2	0.6	4.8	0.8	17.2
Goat	4.5	2.5	0.4	4.1	0.8	13.2
Sheep	7.4	4.6	0.9	4.8	1.0	19.3
Mare	1.9	1.3	1.2	6.2	0.5	11.2
Sow	6.8	2.8	2.0	5.5	-	18.8

Dahi made from buffalo milk produces a thick-bodied product because of its higher SNF content. In the traditional method of dahi making, the intensive heat treatment given to milk prior to fermentation and subsequent cooling in open kettle results in evaporation of moisture and concentration of solids. In most cases, an increase of 10—15 per cent in solids is observed leading to a thick body and desirable texture. It is recommended to make yogurt/dahi from a mix containing 11—13 per cent SNF. It is common to boost the SNF fraction of the milk to about 12 per cent with addition of skim milk powder or condensed skim milk. The increased protein content in the mix results in a custard-like consistency following the required fermentation. Higher milk solids also keep the product from wheying off.

In general, dahi/yogurt contains more protein, calcium and other nutrients than milk, reflecting extra SNF contents. Bacterial mass content and products of the lactic fermentation further distinguish dahi/yogurt from milk. Fat content can be standardised as per the consumer demand for foods ranging from low-fat to fat-free. Post-fermentation heat treatment of dahi, lassi or yogurt results in extension of their shelf-life. However, it also destroys the culture micro organisms that give to the product its health-giving character. The Codex standards differentiate through labelling the live and heat-treated products. The latter should be labelled to reflect heat-treatment effect such as "contains no active cultures" for the consumer to make informed choices.

Table 5.2 : Starter cultures used in manufacture of fermented milk products.

Product	Primary micro-organism(s)	Secondary/optional micro-organism(s)	Incubation temperatures and time	Major functions of culture
Dahi, shrikhand, mishti doi, lassi, butter-milk	*Lactococcus lactis subsp. lactis* *Lactococcus lactis subsp. cremoris* *Lactococcus lactis subsp. lactis var. diacetylactis*	*Leuconostoc lactis* *Leuconostoc mesenteroides subsp. cremoris*	22°C for 12—14 hours or 37°C for 5—8 hours	Acidity, flavour, aroma
Yogurt	*Lactobacillus delbrueckii subsp. bulgaricus* *Streptococcus thermophilus*	*Lactobacillus acidophilus* *Bifidobacterium longum/bifidum/infantis* *Lactobacillus casei/lactis/jugurti/helveticus*	43—45°C/2.5 hours	Acidity, texture, aroma, flavour, probiotic

Criteria for the live and active product should include a number of colony forming units of the culture and activity tests. For example, the activity test is carried out by pasteurizing 12 per cent skim milk powder at 92°C for 7 minutes, cooling to 45°C, adding 3 per cent inoculum of the material under test and fermenting at 45°C for 4 hours. The total yogurt organisms are enumerated in the test material both before and after fermentation using the International Dairy Federation (IDF) method. The activity test is successful if there is an increase of one log during fermentation. Regarding the culture count, it has been proposed that the total population of organisms in live and active culture yogurt must be at least 10^8/g at the time of manufacture.

Starter Cultures: Milk is the normal habitat of a number of lactic acid bacteria, which cause spontaneous souring of milk, held at bacterial growth temperatures for appropriate length of time. Depending on the type of lactic acid bacteria gaining entry from the environmental sources (air, utensils, milking equipment, milkers, cows, feed etc.), the soured milk attains uncontrollable flavour and texture characteristics. Contamination of the product by extraneous organisms before or after fermentation may lead to a serious public health hazard. However, in the commerical manufacture of fermented products, starters containing specific genera, species and strains of cultures are used to generate desired flavour, body and texture characteristics.

A starter culture consists of food-grade micro-organism) that on culturing in milk produce predictable attributes. Table 5.2 lists lactic acid bacteria used as starters in the industrial production of dahi, shrikhand, mishti doi, lassi, butter-milk and yogurt.

In general, organisms that grow at ambient temperatures are termed mesophillic cultures and those growing at higher temperatures are called thermophillic cultures. Dahi and other Indian fermented milks use mesophillic cultures, whereas yogurt uses thermophillic cultures. Tables 5.3 and 5.4 show characteristics of mesophillic and thermophillic cultures, respectively.

The criteria essential for commercial success of a starter are: (a) Strain selection; (b) Maintenance of desirable ratios of component organisms; and, (c) Survival and viability during manufacture of starter, preservation, storage and distribution.

A starter's performance is judged by the following factors: (a) Rapid acid development; (b) Typical dahi/yogurt flavour, body and texture; (c) Exopolysaccharide secreting strains to enhance viscosity of product; (d) Scale-up possibilities in various production conditions, including

Table 5.3 : Attributes of typical mesophillic starters (lactic acid bacteria) used in dahi, lassi, shrikhand, mishti doi and buttermilk.

Characteristic	*Lactococcus lactis subsp. lactis*	*Lactococcus lactis subsp. cremoris*	*Lactococcus lactis subsp. lactis biovar diacetylactis*	*Leuconostoc mesenteroides subsp. cremoris*	*Leuconostoc mesenteroides subsp. dextranicum*
Cell-shape and configuration	Cocci, pairs, short chains	Cocci, pairs, short/long chains	Cocci, pairs, short chains	Cocci, pairs, short/long chains	Cocci, pairs, chains
Catalase reaction	-	-	-	-	-
Growth temperature (°C)					
Optimum	28—31	22	28	20—25	20—25
Minimum	8—10	8-10	8—10	4—10	4—10
Maximum	40	37-39	40	37	37
Incubation temperature (°C)	21—30	22-30	22—28	22	22
Heat tolerance (60°C/30 minutes)	±	±	±	-	
Lactic acid isomers	L(+)	L(+)	L(+)	D(—)	D(—)
Lactic acid produced in milk(%)	0.8—1.0	0.8-1.0	0.8—1.0	0.1-0.3	0.1—0.3
Acetic acid production (%)	-	-	0.2—0.4	0.2-0.4	
Gas (CO_2) production	-	+	±	±	
Proteolytic activity	+	+	+	±	±
Lipolytic activity	±	±	±	±	±
Citrate fermentation	-	-	+	+	+
Flavour/aroma	+	+	+++	+++	+++
Muco polysaccharide production	±	–	±	No dextran from sucrose	Dextran from sucrose
Hydrogen peroxide production	+	+	"+	–	±
Alcohol production	±	±	±	±	±
Salt tolerance (% max.)	4—6.5	4.0	4—6.5	6.5	6.5

Table 5.4 Attributes of thermophillic starters used in yogurt.

Characteristic	*Streptococcus thermophilus*	*Lactobacillus delbrueckii subsp. bulgahcus*	*Lactobacillus delbrueckii subsp. lactis*	*Lactobacillus acidophilus*	*Lactobacillus casei subsp. casei*
Cell shape and configuration	Spherical to ovoid, pairs to long chains	Rods with round ends, single, short chains, metachromatic granules	Rods with round ends, metachromatic granules	Rods with round ends, single, pairs short chains, no metachromatic granules	Rods with square ends, short/long chains
Catalase reaction	-	-	-	-	-
Growth temperature (°C)					
Optimum	40—45	40—45	40—45	37	37
Minimum	20	22	22	20—22	15—20
Maximum	50	52	52	45—48	40—45
Incubation temperature (°C)	40—45	42	40—45	37	37
Heat tolerance (60°C/30 minutes)	++	+	+	—	—
Lactic acid isomers	L (+)	D (-)	D (-)	DL	L (+)
Lactic acid produced in milk (%)	0.7—0.8	1.5—4.0	1.5—3.0	0.3-2.0	1.2—1.5
Acetic acid (%)	Trace	Trace	Trace	+	+
Gas (CO_2) production	—	—	—	—	—
Proteolytic activity	±	+	+	±	±
Lipolytic activity	±	±	±	±	±
Citrate fermentation	—	—	—	—	—
Flavour/aroma compounds	++	++	+	+	±
Mucopolysaccharide production	±	++	—	—	±
Hydrogen peroxide production	±	+	+	+	+
Alcohol production	—	Trace	Trace	Trace	Trace
Salt tolerance (% max.)	2.0	2.0	2.0	6.5	2.0

compatibility with a variety and levels of ingredients used; (e) Fermentation time and temperatures; (f) Survival of culture viability during shelf-life of dahi; (g) Possessing desirable health and probiotic properties and exhibiting survival in the human gastrointestinal tract for certain health attributes; and, (h) Minimum acid production during distribution and storage at 5°—10°C until dahi is consumed.

The activity of a starter culture is determined by direct microscopic counts of methylene blue stained culture slide. This exercise also indicates physiological state of the culture cells. The acid producing ability is measured by pH drop and titratable acidity rise in 12 per cent reconstituted skim milk powder (sterilized at 116°C/18 min) incubated at 37°C for 8 hours. A pH of 4.20 and titratable acidity of 1.05 per cent under the above conditions are expected.

Microbiological specifications of commercial cultures suggest that counts of mesophillic lactics, yeasts and moulds, coliforms, anaerobic spore formers and salt-tolerant micrococci should not exceed 10 cfu/g. *E. coli, S. faecium* and coagulase positive *staphylococci* should be <1cfu/g. The culture must be free of *salmonella, listeria* and other pathogenic contaminants. Some common factors that inhibit growth of starter cultures are:

Selection: Proper selection of culture strains is necessary to avoid possible antagonism between the component organisms. Also, certain abnormal milks (mastitic cows, hydrolytic rancidity in milk) are inhibitory to the growth of cultures. Seasonal variations in milk composition resulting in lower micronutrients (trace elements, non-protein nitrogenous compounds) may affect starter performance. Natural inhibitors secreted in milk (LP-system, agglutinins, lysozyme) are generally destroyed by proper heat-treatment.

Antibiotics: Antibiotic residues in milk and entry of sanitation chemicals (quaternary compounds, iodophors, hypochlorites, hydrogen peroxide) have profound inhibitory impact on the growth of the starter.

Sweeteners: Mishti doi mix contains appreciable quantities of cane sugar. Sugar exerts osmotic pressure on the system, leading to progressive inhibition and decline in the rate of acid production by the culture. Being a colligative property, the osmotic pressure-driven inhibitory effect would be directly proportional to concentration of the sweetener and inversely related to the molecular weight of the solute. Solutes inherently present in SNF part of the product mix accruing from starting milk and added milk solids would also contribute towards the total inhibitory effect on yogurt culture growth.

Acid producing ability of dahi culture is fairly normal in mixes containing 4—7 per cent cane sugar. Commercial strains, which are relatively osmotolerant, may allow higher usage levels without interruption in acid production during dahi manufacture.

Bacteriophages: Phage infection and accompanying loss in rate of acid production by lactic cultures results in flavour and texture defects as well as major product losses in fermented dairy products.

Dahi fermentation process is relatively fast (4 to 6 hours) at optimum incubation temperature. It is improbable that all the component strains of the starter would be simultaneously attacked by phages, which are specific for each strain of the organism. In the likelihood of a phage attack on one strain, acid production may be carried on by another strain, causing little or no interruption in production. However, phage problem in cultured milk plants cannot be ignored. Adherence to strict sanitation procedures would ensure prevention of phage attack.

Production of Starters: Dairy plants should purchase cultures on a regular basis from commercial suppliers or the National Dairy Research Institute. Dairy cultures are available in various freeze-dried, liquid and frozen forms. In India, freeze-dried cultures are generally used. Figure 5.1 illustrates steps involved in the production of starters which are used for fermentation of milk. Working knowledge and employee training in lactic cultures are advantageous in handling starters at the plant. It is essential to develop and maintain appropriate microbiological expertise in the propagation, maintenance, and control of lactic starter cultures.

The starter is the most crucial component in the production of high-quality fermented milks. Culture propagation should be conducted in a specified, secluded area of the plant where access of personnel is restricted. An effective sanitation programme coupled with filtered air and positive pressure in the culture area, preferably all the manufacturing areas including the packaging room, should significantly reduce airborne contamination. Consequently, culture failure due to phage and contamination with extraneous organisms may be controlled, and an extended shelf-life of the product may be attained.

The media for culture propagation generally consist of liquid skim milk or blends of skim milk powder dispersed in water so as to contain 9—10 per cent milk solids. Water, skim milk powder, and other media ingredients must be free from substances inhibitory to the growth of the starter.

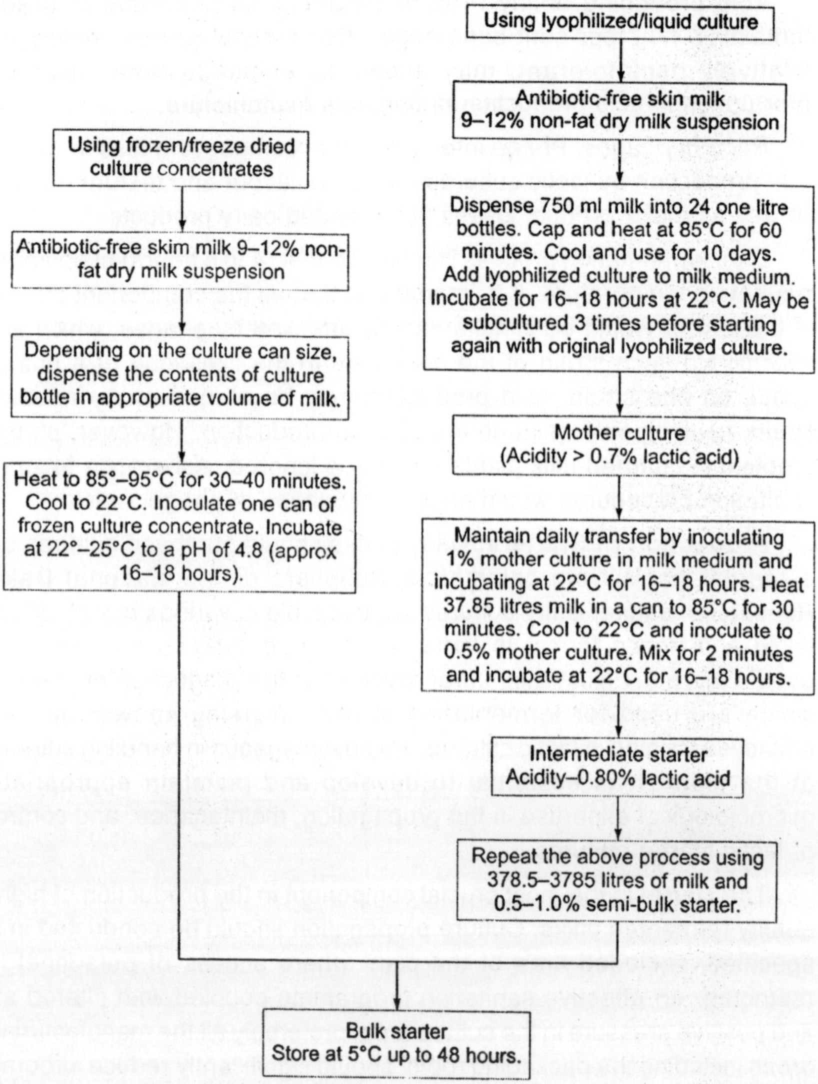

Figure 5.1 : Flow-chart for large-scale production of bulk starters using frozen/ liquid cultures.

Heat treatment is necessary to destroy the contaminants in the medium and alleviate unnecessary competition to the growth of a desirable lactic culture. Besides, heating of the medium produces desirable nutrients by heat-induced reactions in milk constituents.

Control of acid and flavour development in lactic starter cultures may be achieved by understanding their growth characteristics. By modifying the inoculation rate, incubation temperature and time, it is possible to direct the fermentation, in a limited way, to fit the plant schedules.

Mother cultures are propagated daily for a period of about two-three weeks after which a fresh lyophilized culture is activated. Microscopic examination of the culture is recommended to ensure integrity of the culture.

Technology: Dahi, lassi and cultured milk are made from fat-standardized milk. All ingredients should be of high bacteriological quality, conforming to specifications maintained by the quality control laboratory with a systematic sampling and testing programme. It is extremely important to standardize and control the day-to-day product to meet consumer expectations and regulatory obligations.

Because the total solids in milk of cows and buffaloes range from 11 to 17 per cent, the cultured products derived from them vary in consistency from a fluid to a custard-like gel. The range in casein content also contributes to the gel formation because on souring this class of proteins coagulates at its iso-electric point of pH 4.6. The whey proteins are considerably denatured and insolubilized by heat treatments prior to culturing. The denatured whey proteins are also precipitated along with caseins to exert an effect on the water binding capacity of the gel.

Equipment: A cultured milk plant requires a special design to minimize contamination of the products with phage and spoilage organisms. Filtered air is useful in this regard. The plant is generally equipped with a receiving room to receive, meter or weigh, store milk and other raw materials. In addition, a culture propagation room along with a control laboratory, a dry storage area, a refrigerated storage area, and a mix processing room, a fermentation room, and a packaging room form the backbone of the plant. The mix processing room contains equipment for standardizing and separating milk, pasteurizing and heating, and homogenizing along with necessary pipelines, fittings, pumps, valves and controls.

The fermentation room housing fermentation tanks is isolated from the rest of the plant. Filtered air under positive pressure is supplied to the room to generate clean room conditions. A control laboratory is generally set aside where culture preparation, process control, product composition, and shelf life tests may be carried out to ensure adherence to regulatory and company standards. Also, laboratory personnel establish a quality control programme. A utility room is required for maintenance and engineering services needed by the plant. The refrigerated storage area is used for holding fruit, finished products, and other heat-labile materials. A dry storage area at ambient temperature is primarily utilized for temperature-stable raw materials and packaging supplies. The sequence of processing in the manufacture of fermented milks is given in Table 5.5.

Storage Tank: Milk is stored in silos which are large vertical tanks with a capacity up to 100,000 litres. A silo consists of an inner tank made of food grade stainless steel (Grade AISI 304). To minimize corrosion, it is also used for the storage of acidic products. The stainless steel tank is usually covered with 125 mm of insulation material, which in turn is surrounded by an outer shell of stainless or painted mild steel or aluminium. The silo tanks generally have an agitation system (30 to 35 rpm), spray balls mounted in the centre for cleaning-in-place (CIP), an air vent, and a manhole. The air vent must be kept open during cleaning with hot solutions. This precaution is necessary to prevent a sudden development of vacuum in the tank and consequent collapse of the inner tank upon rinsing with cold water. For reconstitution of dry powders, such as skim milk powder, sweeteners, and stabilizers, the use of a powder funnel and recirculation loop, or a special blender, is convenient.

Heat Treatment: The common pasteurization equipment consists of vat, plate, triple-tube, and scraped, or swept surface heat exchanger. In case of milk, vat pasteurization is conducted at a minimum temperature of 63°C with a minimum holding time of 30 minutes. This temperature is raised to 66°C in the presence of sweeteners in the mix. For a high temperature-short time (HTST) system, the equivalent temperature-time combination is 73°C for 15 seconds or 75°C for 15 seconds in the presence of sweeteners. An ultra-high temperature (UHT) system employs temperatures > 90°C and as high as 148°C for 2 seconds. Alternatively, culinary steam may be used directly by injection or infusion to raise the temperature to 94°C. However, in this process allowance must be made for an increase in water content of the mix due to steam condensation. Certain undesirable odours such as of feed, onion or garlic associated with milk can be removed by vacuum treatment in deodouriser.

Table 5.5 : Stages in the manufacture of dahi and other fermented milks.

Step	Salient features
Milk procurement	Sanitary production of milk from healthy cows is necessary. For best micro-biological control, refrigerated bulk milk tanks should cool to 10°C in 1 hour and < 5°C in 2 hours. Avoid unnecessary agitation to prevent lipolytic deterioration of milk flavour.
Milk reception and storage in manufacturing plant	Temperature of raw milk at this stage should not exceed 10°C. Quality of milk is checked and controlled.
Centrifugal separation of fat	Milk is separated into cream and skim milk or standardized to desired fat level at 5 to 32°C.
Mix preparation	Various ingredients to secure desired formulation are blended together at 10°—50°C in a mix tank equipped with powder funnel and an agitation system.
Heat treatment	Using plate heat exchangers with regeneration systems, milk is heated to temperatures of 85°—95°C for 10—40 minutes, well above pasteurization treatment. Heating of milk kills contaminating and competitive micro-organisms, produces growth factors by breakdown of milk proteins, generates micro-aerophilic conditions for growth of lactic organisms, and creates desirable body and texture in the cultured dairy products.
Homogenization, if no cream layer is required	Mix is passed through extremely small orifice at pressure of 2,000—2,500 psi, causing extensive physico-chemical changes in the colloidal characteristics of milk.
Inoculation and incubation	The homogenized mix is cooled to an optimum growth temperature. Inoculation is generally at the rate of 0.5—5%. The inoculated milk is dispensed into cups and the lids are applied. The cups are placed in trays and transferred to incubation room. The optimum temperature is maintained throughout incubation period to achieve a desired titratable acidity. Quiescent incubation is necessary for product texture and body development.
Cooling, fruit incorporation and packaging	The coagulated product is cooled down to 5°C, depending upon the product.
Storage and distribution	Storage at 5°C ensures desirable shelf-life by slowing down physical, chemical, and micro-biological degradation.

In processing of dahi and other fermented products, the mix is subjected to much more severe heat treatment than conventional pasteurization temperature-time combinations. Heat treatment at 85°C for 30 minutes or 95°C for 10 minutes is an important step in the manufacture process. The four-fold effects of heat treatment are: (a) development of a relatively sterile medium for the exclusive growth of the starter; (b) removal of air from the medium to produce a more conducive medium for the growth of micro-aerophillic lactic cultures; (c) effecting thermal breakdown of milk constituents, especially proteins, releasing peptones and sulfhydryl groups which provide nutrition and anaerobic conditions for the starter; and (d) it denatures and coagulates milk albumins and globulins which enhance the viscosity and produce custard-like consistency in the product.

Homogenization: The homogenizer is a high-pressure pump forcing the mix through extremely small orifices. It includes a bypass for safety of operation. Homogenization is usually conducted by applying pressure in two stages. The first-stage pressure, of the order of 210 kg/cm^2 reduces the average milk fat globule diameter size from approx 4 microns (range 0.1 to 16 microns) to < 1 micron. The second stage, using 35 kg/cm^2 pressure, is designed to break the clusters of fat globules apart, with the objective of inhibiting creaming in milk. After homogenization, all the fat globules are below 3-4 microns. If surface creaming in dahi is not acceptable to the consumer, homogenization helps in preventing its formation.

Fermentation: The heat treated mix is cooled to 37°C and inoculated with starter by dosing pump and stored in a vessel for packaging. The inoculated milk is then packaged in cups of appropriate size and lids are applied. In some cases, foil lids are heat-welded to the cup opening, followed by insertion of removable lids. The cups are transferred to cases or crates and transported quickly to hot room for incubation. Here a constant optimum temperature is maintained for fermentation to proceed. The acidity of milk in the cups is checked at periodic intervals and when pH reaches 4.4-4.5, the cases of cups are transferred to a room maintained at 3-4°C. Dahi is cooled rapidly to 5°C by exposing cups to high velocity air in the cold room. The steps involved in the manufacturing of set-type type dahi/plain yogurt are shown in Figure 5.2.

Dahi/plain yogurt normally contains no added sugar or flavours. Consumers can relish it in its natural flavour or add flavourings with

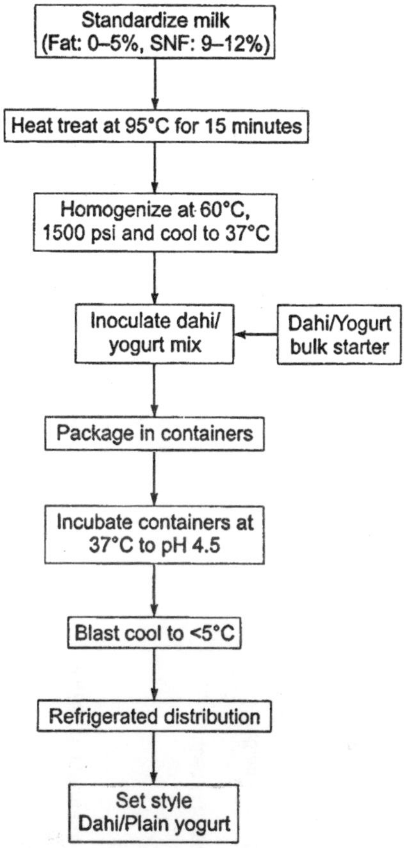

Figure 5.2 : Flow-chart for the manufacture of dahi/plain yogurt.

food materials of their choice. It may also be used for cooking or for salad preparation with fresh fruits or grated vegetables. Its fat content may be standardized to the levels as prescribed by the PFA or as per consumer preference for higher fat or SNF. Also, the size of the package may be geared to the market demand.

Packaging and Storage: Plastic cups and lids are the chief packaging materials used in the industry. Various packaging machines of suitable speeds (up to 400 cups/minute) are available to package various cultured dairy products in different sizes. For extended shelf-life of these products, storage at 1—4 °C is recommended.

Quality Control: A well-planned quality control programme must be executed in the dairy plant to maximize shelf-life quality of a cultured

Table 5.6 : Common quality problems in dahi.

Defect	Probable cause	Remedy
Insufficient flavour	• Low citrate level in milk • Diacetyl destroyed	• Add 0.02—0.05% (up to 0.1 %) sodium citrate prior to the mix • Cool rapidly after culturing • Agitate gently after breaking to incorporate oxygen in the product
Green/yogurt flavour	• Acetaldehyde accumulation	• Avoid use of *Lactococcus diacetylactis*
Oxidized (cardboard) flavour	• Copper contamination and/or exposure to fluorescent light or sunlight	• Avoid exposure to copper utensils • Protect product from direct sunlight/UV light exposure
Yeast-like/cheesy	• Contaminating yeast growth	• Sanitation check • Avoid return milk
Rancid flavour	• Lipolytic activity	• Do not mix pasteurized and raw dairy ingredients prior to homogenization
Weak body	• Insufficient heat treatment of the mix • Milk SNF too low • Agitation too severe after fermentation	• Heat treatment should not be less than 85°C/30 minutes for dahi/lassi and 95°C/30 minutes for yogurt and sour cream • Fortify with 0.5-1% skim milk powder for dahi and lassi and 3-4% for yogurt • Homogenize the dahi mix prior to fermentation
Grainy texture	• Acidity too high • Skim milk powder not dispersed properly	• Exercise rigid acidity control • Dispersion equipment check • Use in-line screen
Chalky/powdery texture	• Too much of skim milk powder	• Check on the quality and quantity of milk powder

milk product. Quality control programmes focus on product viscosity, flavour, body and texture, colour, fermentation process, and composition. Daily chemical, physical, micro-biological, and organoleptic tests constitute the core of quality assurance. The ingredients used may impart undesirable flavours such as stale, metallic, oxidized, rancid, or unclean. Lack of control in processing procedures may cause over-cooked, caramelized, or excessively sour flavour notes in the product. Proper control of processing parameters and ingredient quality ensures good flavour. Table 5.6 summarizes common quality problems of dahi and steps needed to rectify them.

To deliver the product with the most desirable attributes of flavour and texture, product standards of fats, solids, viscosity, pH (or titratable acidity), and organoleptic characteristics should be strictly adhered to. It is imperative to enforce a strict sanitation programme along with good manufacturing practices. Shelf-life of commercial dahi varies from two to three weeks from the date of manufacture, provided the temperature in distribution and retail marketing channels does not exceed 7°C. Lactic acid and some other metabolites produced by fermentation process protect fermented milk from most Gram-negative psychotropic organisms. In general, most quality issues in dahi and cultured dairy plant are not related to proliferation of spoilage bacteria. Mostly, the spoilage flora in fermented milks are yeasts and moulds, which are highly tolerant to low pH and can grow under refrigeration temperatures. Yeast growth is a more serious problem than mould growth during shelf-life of the product.

The control of yeast contamination is effected by following aggressive sanitation procedures related to equipment, ingredients, and plant environment. CIP chemical solutions should be used with special attention to their strength and proper temperature. Hypochlorites and iodophors are effective sanitizing compounds for fungal control on the contact surfaces and in combating the environmental contamination. Hypochlorites at high concentrations are corrosive. Iodophors are preferred for their non-corrosive property as they are effective at relatively low concentrations.

Yeast and mould contamination may also arise from contaminated starter, packaging materials, fruit preparations, and packaging equipment. Organoleptic examination of the starter may be helpful in eliminating the fungal contamination therefrom. If warranted, direct microscopic view of the starter may reveal the presence of budding yeast cells or mould mycelium filaments. Plating of the starter on acidified potato dextrose agar would confirm the results. Use of contaminated starter for production of cultured dairy product should be avoided.

Efficiency of equipment and environmental sanitation can be verified by enumeration techniques, involving exposure of poured plates to atmosphere in the plant or making a smear of the contact surfaces of the equipment, followed by plating. Filters on the air circulation system should be changed frequently. Walls and floors should be cleaned and sanitized frequently and regularly. The packaging materials should be stored under dust-free and humidity-free conditions. The filling room should be fogged with chlorine or iodine regularly.

6

Technology of Mishti Doi

For centuries, mishti doi, also known as payodhi and lal dahi, has been a well-established dessert in the eastern parts of India. It is a popular dessert in West Bengal where it is served with the meal accompanied by dried sweets. It is a delicacy of choice during religious festivities and is considered an auspicious item to serve while starting a journey, or any important work. In combination with rasogolla, mishti doi is regarded an extra special dessert on ceremonial occasions both in the rural and urban Bengal. The product is commonly available in earthen pots of different sizes.

According to ancient Bengali literature, milk meant for curdling was first thickened by boiling before adding caramelized palm jaggery, cane jaggery or sugar and then allowed to set as curd to yield mishti doi. This was often done in an earthen vessel, which contributes a characteristic earthy flavour and to some extent helps in absorbing free whey at the end of the fermentation process.

Mishti doi preparation is mainly confined to domestic or cottage scale operations. Due to lack of standardization in the composition and quality of raw materials, and manufacturing techniques, the market quality of the product varies considerably. However, standardized mishti doi is now being marketed in metro cities by dairy plants.

Product Description: Mishti doi is a fermented milk product, having creamish to light brown colour, firm consistency, smooth texture and pleasant aroma. In the absence of PFA/BIS standards, there could be different grades of mishti doi depending on the percentage of fat, SNF, and sugar in the product to meet the wide variety of consumer tastes. However, typical composition of mishti doi is given in Table 6.1.

Technology: Traditionally, mishti doi is prepared from cow or mixed milk. It is first boiled with a required amount of sugar and partially concentrated by simmering over a low fire during which milk develops a distinctive light cream to light brown caramel colour and flavour. This is

Table 6.1 : Composition of different grades of mishti doi

per cent

Constituent	Low fat	Medium fat	High fat
Milk fat	2-3	4.5	8-9
Milk SNF	13—14	11—13	10—11
Sugar	17—19	17—18	17—18
Total solids	32—35	32—36	35—38

then cooled to ambient temperature and cultured with dahi (lactic) culture. It is then poured into earthen vessels of consumer/bulk size and left undisturbed overnight for fermentation. When a firm body curd has set, it is shifted to a cooler place or preferably refrigerated. Use of earthen vessel absorbs any whey that may tend to separate during storage and distribution. Mishti doi is served chilled.

Industrial Production: A technological process has been developed for the manufacture of mishti doi in the organized sector. It facilitates use of a wide range of milk products (Table 6.2) for sourcing milk solids in the production of mishti doi.

Table 6.2 : Sources of milk solids for mishti doi.

per cent

Ingredients	Milk fat	Milk SNF	Sugar (Sucrose)
Fresh cow/buffalo milk	4—6	8.5—9.5	—
Cream	30—40	5.4—6.3	—
Skimmed milk powder	0.5	95.5	—
Whole milk powder	26	70	—
Evaporated whole milk	8	18	—
Sweetened condensed milk	9.1	22	40—42
White butter	80	1	—

By combining the ingredients in proper portion, a basic mix for mishti doi can be prepared, keeping in view the final compositional standard of the product in terms of fat, SNF, and sugar. Extreme care is needed in the selection and use of the raw material and sweeteners. The ingredients should be fresh, wholesome and of good microbial and sensory quality. Their quality has a direct bearing on the final product. When fresh raw milk is used for production of mishti doi, its acidity should not be more than 0.16 per cent. It should be clot-on-boiling negative and free from off-flavours.

The most common sweetener used is cane sugar. It should be of high bacteriological quality and free from extraneous matter. Corn sugar, corn syrup, maltose or beet sugar can be used to sweeten mishti doi or to partially substitute sugar if these are commercially available and priced cheaper than cane sugar. In some special varieties of mishti doi, fresh palm jaggery (gur) is used as a sweetener.

Mishti doi is coloured and flavoured commonly with caramel. Caramel is prepared by caramelizing sugar and is available commercially in the form of a viscous liquid. The pH of this caramel should be close to the pH of the product (around 5.0). The quality standards for commercial caramel are given in Table 6.3.

Table 6.3 : Quality standards for caramel.

Parameter	Criterion
Total solids (%)	76
Solubility in:	
Water	Miscible
Ether	Immiscible
Chloroform	Immiscible
50% alcohol	55% soluble
Neutral tannin test	No precipitate
Acid tannin test	A brown precipitate within 24 hours
Specific gravity	1.315—1.345

Synthetic flavours like caramel, vanilla, cardamom and rose may also be used with or without nuts and fruits for developing a wide range of mishti doi formulations.

Milk fat is the most expensive constituent of mishti doi. It enriches the characteristic top layer of mishti doi, giving it a creamy rich flavour. The main contribution of SNF in mishti doi is the body and textural characteristic of the product. Compared to milk fat, it is less expensive. Sugar is added to sweeten mishti doi and give it a smooth body and texture. It is the cheapest source of total solids in the product.

Starter Culture: The most critical step in the manufacture of the product is the selection of starter culture, since it affects the flavour and acidity development in the presence of sugar and caramel at relatively higher SNF levels. Mixed strain culture may be used since it yields a superior product and performs more reliably under variable conditions. Optimum performance of the mishti doi culture is expected in a narrow temperature range of 42 ± 1°C. A good culture develops 0.7 per cent acidity within 6—8 hours with 1 per cent inoculum.

Process: Milk and cream in required proportions are mixed in a multipurpose vat, connected to a conical hopper/venturi assembly for reconstitution of SMP to increase the total solids level. Sugar is also dry blended at this stage. Caramel is added @ 0.1 to 0.12 per cent before starting the heating of the mix. If caramel is added to the mix above 50°C, undesirable flakes would be formed. The mix is heated to 80°—90°C in a vat or a plate pasteurizer. It is necessary to have a filter in the process line to filter all suspended matter and lumps. Heat treatment at various temperatures has been tried out. It has been observed that heating the mix to 85 °C and holding for 15 minutes yields a product of desirable quality and texture. After holding, the product is cooled to 40—45°C either in the plate heat exchanger or by circulating water in the multi-purpose vat.

The bulk culture is stirred to a fine and smooth mass, and added to the mix @ 1 per cent and mixed well. The culture should be added to the mix at about 43°C so that after the mishti doi mix is filled in sanitized cups, the temperature should be around 41°C. Lids are heat sealed on cups to make them airtight and prevent leakage of the mix. The sealed cups are then placed in trays/crates, which can be stacked on trolleys with minimum shaking. Enough air space should be left in the cup after filling to avoid the top web/lid touching the top surface of the product. If this happens, the top fat layer of the product will get peeled off, cracked or broken, leaving an undesirable appearance. Too much of head space would give the impression of empty cups.

Incubation: Mishti doi mix is incubated at 42 + l°C for about 6 to 8 hours till the acidity develops to about 0.7 to 0.8 per cent, expressed as lactic acid. Trolleys with filled and sealed cups are moved in the incubation rooms with least disturbance. The time for incubation depends upon the activity of the starter culture used. During and after incubation, the product should be handled with minimum mechanical shock to retain a uniform texture in it.

Storage: Once the desired level of acidity (0.7%) is developed, the product should be shifted to a cold store (4°C) with minimum disturbance as the product at this stage has very weak body and unstable top layer.

Excessive shaking will result in cracks on the top layer or in the curd mass itself. The cold store temperature should be 0°C for the storage of the product for a longer period. If the temperature is below 0°C, freezing can take place. This will affect the body of the product due to ice crystals formation that disrupt the gel structure of the curd and result in a floppy body. Therefore, care should be taken to maintain the cold store at proper temperature to prevent any freezing of the product.

Transportation and Distribution: Mishti doi cups should be properly crated or cartoned. They should be transported in an insulated box, with cooling pad inside the box for marketing. The retailers should be instructed to keep the product under refrigeration until it is sold to the consumer. Mishti Doi stored below 10°C retains good quality for about 3 days without any significant deterioration in flavour and bacteriological quality. If stored below 4°C, its shelf life is increased to about five days. Keeping mishti doi at room temperature is not advisable, since its acidity starts increasing slowly.

Novelties: Mishti doi is in many ways similar to the western dairy product, yogurt. Initially, there used to be only plain yogurt which was liked for its typical mild acidic taste. Now, there are varieties of yogurt with many combinations of flavours, fruits and nuts. Similarly, several varieties of mishti doi can be prepared to compete with yogurt by adding flavour (cardamom, vanilla, butter scotch), fruits (mangoes, bananas), grains and nuts (almond, pistachio). Mishti doi can also be made without cream layer on the top by homogenizing the mix. The resultant product would have a smooth body and texture and reduced tendency for wheying off.

7

Shrikhand Manufacture

Shrikhand is a semi-solid, sweetish-sour fermented milk product, prepared from dahi (curd). Whey is drained off from dahi to yield chakka. Sugar, flavour, colour and spices are thoroughly mixed into chakka to form a soft homogeneous mass that resembles sweetened quarg of Germany. Shrikhand is a popular dessert and forms part of a meal on festive occasions, particularly in the States of Gujarat and Maharashtra. Like dahi, it is very refreshing, particularly during summer months.

Product Description: Shrikhand is obtained from chakka or skimmed milk chakka to which milk fat is added. It may contain fruits, nuts, sugar, cardamom, saffron and other spices. It should not contain any colouring and artificial flavouring substances. The standards prescribed for shrikhand by the Bureau of Indian Standards (BIS) and under the Prevention of Food Adulteration Act (PFA) are given in Table 7.1.

Table 7.1 PFA/BIS standards for shrikhand.

	BIS	PFA
Total solids (per cent, by mass), minimum	58.0	58.0
Milk fat (in dry matter, per cent by mass), minimum	8.5	8.5
Milk protein (in dry matter, per cent by mass), minimum	10.5	10.5
Titratable acidity (percent lactic acid),	1.4	1.4
maximum Sucrose (in dry matter per cent by mass), maximum	72.5	72.5
Total ash (in dry matter per cent by mass), maximum	0.9	0.9
Coliform count, cfu/g, maximum	—	10.0
Yeast and mould count, cfu/g, maximum	—	50.0

Technology: The shrikhand manufacturing process consists of the following steps:

- Coagulation of milk by fermentation with starter culture to obtain acidic curd or dahi;
- Preparation of chhaka by draining whey from the curd; and,

- Blending additives like sugar, colour, flavour, and spice to reach a desired level of composition and consistency.

Traditional Method: Milk of cow or buffalo, or mixed milk is heated to boiling and then cooled to 30°—35°C. It is inoculated with dahi (lactic culture) @ 0.5 to 1 per cent from the previous day's production. Milk is left at room tempenture (30°—35°C) until it sets firmly. It is then stirred and hung in a muslin cloth for 10 to 12 hours, to drain off whey (in some traditional practices, curd wrapped in a muslin cloth may be placed over an incline! bed of clean, washed and dried sand in a shallow container). The product so obtained is called chakka or maska. The chakka yield is about 65 kg per 100 kg of milk, depending upon the composition of milk.

The chakka is mixed with the required amount of sugar (usually 50—100 per cent of curd quantity), flavour, colour, herbs and spices. Commonly used additives include saffron, cream, charoli, almonds, nutmeg, cashew nut, mango pulp, raisins, and seasonal fruits. The shrikhand yield is about 1.5 to 2.0 kg per kg of chakka used. Shrikhand is served chilled. Consumers in Gujarat prefer its sweet variety while those in Maharashtra prefer the tangy/soury variety.

Innovations: A fully mechanized/continuous process has been developed for industrial production of shrikhand. Its manufacture has also been taken up at a lumber of centres in Maharashtra and Gujarat. The first nodern plant has been established at the Baroda District Cooperative Milk Producers' Union Ltd. (Sugam Unit), in Gujarat. It has been producing and marketing shrikhand since the 1980's under the brand names of 'Sugam' and Amul' in plastic cups of sizes ranging from 100 to 1000 grams. The industrial production involves the following steps:

Preparation of Curd: Skim milk (9% SNF, 0.05% fat) is heated to 90°C for 15 seconds in a HTST pasteurizer, cooled to 30°C and inoculated with 0.25—0.50 per cent dahi culture of mixed strains. After eight hours of incubation period, the required acidity (0.8 to 1.0% lactic acid) is achieved, and the curd is ready for further processing.

Preparation of Chakka: Chakka/maska is prepared by separating the whey from dahi. Earlier, a 28" diameter basket centrifuge at 1,100 rpm was used that produced 80 kg of curd per hour. Now, the process has been upgraded by using a quarg separator. Its capacity is 2,500 kg of curd per hour.

Preparation of Shrikhand from Chakka: Shrikhand is prepared by adding sugar at the rate of 80 per cent of the amount of chakka and mixed in a Scraped Surface Heat Exchanger (SSHE). Required amount of plastic cream (80% fat) is added along with sugar to chakka so as to give at least 8.5 per cent fat in the finished product on dry matter basis.

The processing conditions for the manufacture of shrikhand have been standardized. The final product contains 5 per cent fat, 42 per cent sugar and 60 per cent total solids. The acidity of the product is usually between 1.10 and 1.40 per cent (expressed as lactic acid). The protein content of the product is 10.5 per cent.

The process for shrikhand manufacture has been upgraded further and is shown in Figure 7.2.

Starter Cultures: The use of right type of culture is essential for the manufacture of shrikhand. A mixed culture containing *Lactococcus lactis subsp. lactis, Lactococcus lactis subsp. diacetylactis/Leuconostoc, Lactococcus lactis subsp. cremoris* in the ratio of 1:1:1 may be used. Other recommended cultures are yogurt containing *Streptococcus thermophilus* and *Lactobacillus delbrueckii subsp. bulgaricus* (1:1) or LF-40, a culture compromise of *Lactococcus lactis subsp. lactis* and *Lactococcus lactis subsp. diacetylactis.*

Separation of Whey from Curd: It is carried out in a quarg separator that can handle 2,500 kg of curd input per hour. This permits to scale up the production to 8 tonnes/day with installation of other equipment of matching capacity. This process has been further refined for enhancing shelf-life of shrikhand by pasteurization (heating and holding process).

Mixing of Chakka with Cream and Sugar: The mixing capacity in the earlier process was limited since the planetary mixer could only handle up to 40 kg/batch.

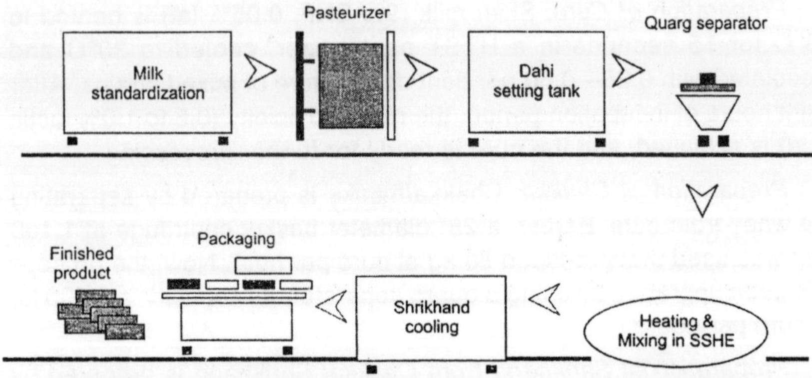

Figure 7.1 : Upgraded industrial process for manufacture of shrikhand.

Table 7.2 Physico-chemical parameters of shrikhand marketed in Gujarat and Maharashtra.

Parameters	Average values		
	Maharashtra[1]	Gujarat[1]	Industrial[2]
pH	4.09	4.10	4.33
Acidity (% as lactic acid)	1.30	1.08	1.13
Soluble nitrogen (%)	0.21	0.29	0.29
Free fatty acids (% as oleic acid)	0.58	0.40	0.26
Penetration Value (mm) at 10°C	28.54	27.35	32.71

1. Average values of product made in the non-organized sector.
2. Average values of product made by the mechanized process in the organized sector.

However, by using a scraped surface heat exchanger (SSHE), handling per batch may be increased up to 500 kg in 10 minutes. Two such SSHEs may be installed in the production line to facilitate continuity in production. When one mixer is in use, the other empties its mix to the shrikhand cooling tank.

Packaging of Shrikhand: In the earlier process, the use of preformed polystyrene cups for packing shrikhand limited the packaging capacity to 1,000 cups/hour. By employing a form-fill-seal (FFS) machine up to 6,000 cups may be filled/packed per hour.

Shelf-life: The keeping quality of shrikhand depends largely on its initial microflora like yeast, mould and other foreign organisms. Under ambient conditions (30°C), it tends to spoil within 2 to 3 days. Under refrigerated conditions (4°C), it may keep up to 40 days without spoilage.

Table 7.3 : Chemical composition of shrikhand sold in Gujarat.

Constituent	Traditional shrikhand	Industrial shrikhand
Moisture (%)	40.52	35.11
Fat (%) DM*	8.27	9.25
Proteins (%) DM	9.53	12.53
Lactose (%) DM	3.74	2.59
Sucrose (%) DM	76.25	70.00
Ash (%)	0.530	0.683
Titratable acidity (% LA)	1.075	1.310
pH	4.10	4.33
Soluble nitrogen (%)	0.290	0.286
FFA (% Oleic Acid)	0.395	0.265

* DM-Dry matter.

The industrial process used to get best shelf-life involves pasteurization (65°C/10 minutes) of shrikhand and its subsequent freezing. The frozen product can be kept in good condition from six months to twelve months at -18°C.

Physico-chemical Aspects: They vary from manufacturer to manufacturer. However, no consistent region-specific variations in shrikhand have been encountered in the market surveys as shown in Table 7.2. Further, the chemical composition *of* shrikhand sold in Gujarat is given in Table 7.3.

8

Chakka Powder

Manufacture of chakka powder involves preparation of dahi followed by partial removal of whey from it. The chakka is then ground in a colloid mill to obtain a smooth and uniform consistency in slurry. The slurry containing fat is heated to 38°C and then homogenized in a single-stage homogenizer at a pressure of 100 kg/cm^2. A spray drier is used to make the powder using 185°C inlet and 85°C outlet air temperature. Figure 8.1 shows the steps in the production of chakka powder from standardized milk. The proximate composition of chakka and shrikhand powder is given in Table 8.1.

Table 8.1 : Approximate composition of chakka and shrikhand powder on dry matter (DM) basis.

Characteristics	Standardized milk chakka powder	Standardized milk shrikhand powder
TS	96.18	96.08
Fat	36.48	19.82
Protein	44.96	24.12
Reducing Sugar	11.53	6.64
Sucrose	—	43.44
Ash	3.21	2.06
Acidity (% LA)	6.58	4.94

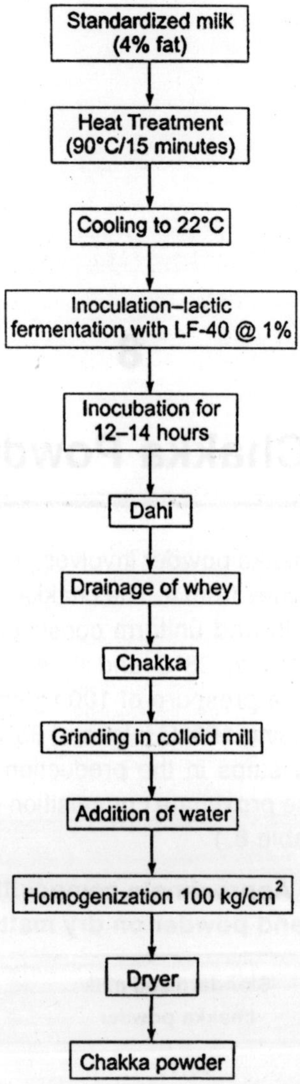

Figure 8.1 : Flow-chart for the manufacture of standardized milk chakka powder.

9

Shrikhand Wadi

Shrikhand wadi, a popular product, has its origin in the western region of India. It is an extension of shrikhand. It is obtained by desiccating shrikhand to a hard mass by heating in an open pan over direct low fire.

Approximate Composition: Moisture: 5-6 per cent, fat: 7-8 per cent, protein: 8—10 per cent, lactose: 15-17 per cent, ash: 0.75—0.8 per cent, sugar: 63—65 per cent, lactic acid: 1.0-1.2 per cent.

LASSI

Lassi (stirred dahi/yogurt) is a refreshing summer beverage, popular in North India. According to an old joke, the prosperous Punjabis use old washing machines to churn lassi in gigantic quantities, but judging from their generosity, you couldn't put it past them. Enormous glasses of fresh, frothy lassi are invariably pressed upon a visitor. If you offer money in return, your host will be deeply offended. Variations of lassi include butter-milk, chhach and mattha that are consumed with relish in other regions too.

Lassi is a white to creamy-white, viscous liquid, with a sweetish, rich aroma and mild to high acidic taste. It is flavoured either with salt or sugar and other condiments, depending on regional preferences. Lassi is obtained from pasteurized milk or part skim milk, cultured with lactic and aroma/flavour-producing organisms.

The term lassi is also used for a phospholipid-rich fluid fraction obtained as a by-product during the churning of dahi while making makkhan (desi fresh butter). Lassi making was earlier confined to the cottage sector or homes. It was mainly a rural product. Now, it is commercially prepared in several parts of North India. Commercial lassi is viscous, cultured fluid milk, containing a characteristic pleasing aroma and flavour. It is packaged in traditional milk cartons/sachets/

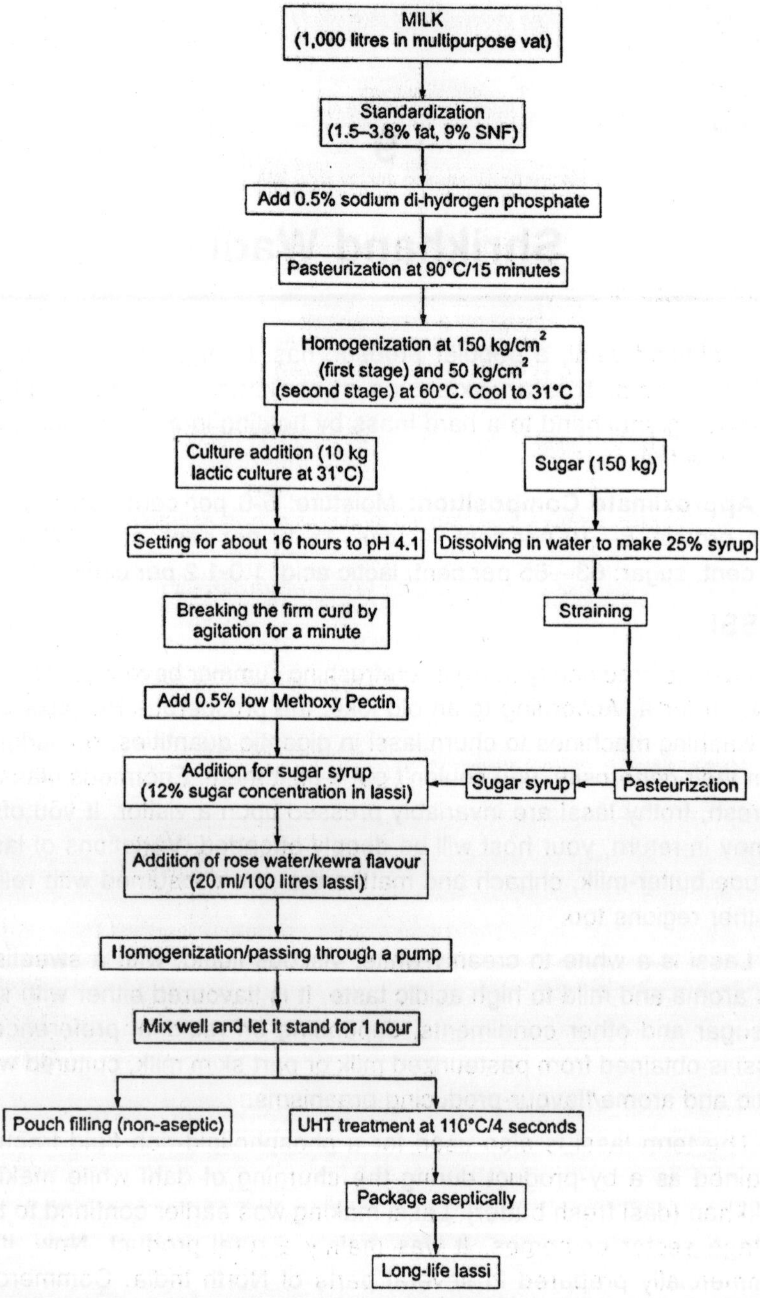

Figure 9.1 : Flow-chart for mechanised production of lassi.

UHT boxes. Salted lassi is marketed in a number of cities in the southern region of the country. Aseptically-packaged long-life lassi is also getting popular in the market.

Technology: The processes used in the manufacture of lassi include pasteurization, homogenization, and culturing systems. Traditionally, lassi is prepared by stirring dahi with a small quantity of cold water. Sugar is the preferred additive in the northern parts of the country. In the south, salt along with other seasonings such as crushed ginger, green chillies and curry leaves are commonly added. The South Indian version of the product is much less viscous but with a stronger/ pungent aroma than its northern counterpart. Lassi is also produced commercially by stirring dahi and adding to it a calculated quantity of sugar in the form of syrup. Water in the syrup also facilitates thinning of the product, thus eliminating the need to add cold water. The mixture is homogenized to improve body and texture. It is flavoured with rose water or kewra flavour and filled in bottles or pouches before refrigerated storage. Under refrigeration, the keeping quality of lassi is extended considerably. Further extension of shelf life is achieved by UHT processing after fermentation of the product and packaging it aseptically. Wheying off may occur but it can be avoided by using a suitable stabilizer and proper processing conditions. Aneja, et al, patented a processing method for manufacture of long-life lassi that does not settle down over extended storage in aseptic packs.

Innovations: Significant advancements have been made towards the industrial production of lassi through application of UHT. Standardized milk (9-10% SNF and 0.5-1.0% milk fat) is warmed to 85°C for 30 minutes or 91°C for 2.5 to 5 minutes and cultured with suitable lactic culture (dahi culture at 31°C). It is then fermented at 22°C to lower its pH to 4.5. Set curd is broken with the help of a stirrer while sugar solution (30% in water) is added to give 8—12 per cent sugar concentration in the blend. Lassi is then homogenized at 13.7 Kpa (2000 psi) and UHT processed at 135—145°C for 1-5 seconds and packaged aseptically employing standard equipment. Figure 9.1 presents the processing sequence for the mechanized production of lassi.

Physico-chemical Aspects: Lassi is a white to creamy-white viscous liquid, with a sweetish, rich aroma and mild to highly acidic taste. Its chemical composition depends on the initial composition of the milk, the degree of concentration of the milk solids and the quantity of sugar added. The quality defects commonly encountered in lassi are similar to those of dahi which have been discussed earlier in the section on dahi. The approximate composition of lassi is as follows:

Milk fat	1.5—3.8%
MilkTS	9.00%
Sugar	13—20%
Sodium dihydrogen phosphate	0.5 %
Low Methoxy Pectin	0.5 %
Acidity	0.7% LA minimum

10

Kheer Manufacture

India's favourite dessert par excellence, kheer is a sweet milk-rice confection. It has the status of a royal treat. No feast is considered complete without kheer. Hindu mythology refers to kheer as the celestial nectar, 'Amrit' or elixir, and gives it a place of prominence among foods as the secret of immortality—the life-giving food. The Hindi word kheer is derived from the Sanskrit 'ksheer' for milk and 'kshirika' for any dish prepared with milk. Kheer is popular all over the country. As a pre-eminent milk delicacy, it has been associated with festivities and celebrations from time immemorial.

A sweetened dish of rice cooked in milk first finds mention as 'payasa' in Buddhist-Jain literature in 400 BC. It seems unchanged to this day, being called payasam in South India and payesh in Bengal. Payasam and payesh both mean milk. Similar to payasa is the kheer of North India and the prathaman of Kerala. Its extension is the paramanna, a ritual kheer-like confection, given to a six-month old infant as his first solid food.

Kheer is prepared on all ritual and festive occasions as an auspicious item of food to placate the gods. Kheer khand bhojan is synonymous with a rich spread, while kheer-puri is the common man's idea of a great repast. Kheer is must at Diwali, India's national festival. Kheer and payasam are also made with sevian (Indian vermicelli), fruits (mangoes, apples, dates), vegetables (bottle gourd and sweet potatoes), makhaana (lotus puffs), sago and nuts (almonds, pistachio).

Product Description: Kheer is a heat-desiccated, cereal-based sweetened and concentrated milk confection. Kheer prepared from buffalo milk is whiter and thick bodied and is, therefore, preferred over that obtained from cow milk. In addition to milk, kheer also contains substantial amount of non-dairy ingredients such as rice, sugar, sabudana, semolina, etc., as well as nuts and spices such as saffron and cardamom, almonds, pistachio, etc. It is considered to be a nutritious food for people of all ages. It is characterized by a sweet, nutty and pleasant flavour that is highly acceptable to the Indian palate. It closely resembles 'rice pudding', a popular dessert in the United States and in north and central Europe.

Despite region-specific variations, kheer generally constitutes a homogeneous mass of milk and rice, in which the two major constituents—milk and rice—flow together. Concentrated milk engulfs cooked rice grains that adhere to each other. Usually, it is said that the weight of kheer after cooking should be almost equal to the weight of the raw milk taken. This is achieved as a result of swelling and cooking of rice grains, which upon gelatinization undergo three-four times weight gain. Colour of the product will generally depend on the extent of heat treatment given and may range from almost white to slightly brownish. However, a rich creamy shade is highly preferred.

Size of Industry: In the absence of organized manufacturing and marketing, no data are available on kheer's annual production. However, several brands of ready-to-reconstitute kheer mixes are gaining acceptance at the regional level, especially in the States of Maharashtra, Karnataka, Kerala and Tamil Nadu. Most of them are reconstituted in milk and offer convenience to consumers. The kheer mix is a blend of processed rice or semolina, ground sugar and dry fruits. Kheer has the enormous potential to make a sizable contribution to the growing market of traditional dairy products. An urgent need is to develop suitable processes for commercial manufacture of kheer both in liquid and dry forms.

Technology: Kheer is a partially desiccated product, similar to khoa, the ratio of concentration being three to four as compared to six for khoa. Preparation of kheer involves immersion of pre-soaked rice (5—6% by weight of milk) in simmering milk followed by sugar addition (6—8%) and heating the mixture further till the rice softens and shows signs of gelatinization, leading to substantial thickening. Chopped nuts and cardamom are then usually added. Kheer making has undergone a limited modification in that the open pan process employing direct fire has been successfully replaced by the steam-kettle. In the modified method, kheer is prepared by partial dehydration of whole milk, with sugar and rice added to it, in an open pan over direct fire. It is obtained by cooking of rice in sweetened milk and simultaneously concentrating the latter.

Process Upgradation: A steam-jacketed kettle for manufacture of kheer was employed, using the steam process. Kheer was made from cow milk with 4 per cent fat, using 2.4 per cent rice (pre-soaked) and 5 per cent sugar. Later, different compositional variables were studied. It was observed that a superior quality kheer could be prepared from buffalo milk containing 5 per cent fat and 9.7 per cent SNF, with an added 5 per cent rice and 12 per cent of sugar. Following further process modifications, an acceptable product was obtained by mixing sweetened condensed milk (diluted to 30% TS by adding buffalo milk) with pre-cooked rice (6%).

Processes have been developed in the United States and Europe to produce kheer-like products that go by the names of milk-rice ('Milch Reis' in Germany) and rice pudding. Rice grains (broken or whole) are exposed to saturated steam at a pressure higher than atmospheric pressure (> 0.03 bar) in an autoclave for sufficient time to gelatinize a major portion of starch. The rice grains are then mixed with milk for consumption in the form of a kheer-like product.

Production of in-can sterilized creamed-rice dessert has also been reported in which short-grained rice releasing starch on cooking was used. Homogenization of milk was found to improve the product quality. Gradual heating up periods and agitation were necessary during autoclaving to prevent localized over-heating. Even though browning and age thickening were reported, the product had a shelf-life of 12 months.

Rice pudding has also been manufactured employing a scraped surface heat exchanger (SSHE). Rice and milk are pumped into this system, heated up to 115°C, held for 26 minutes in a holding tube and then cooled down to 80°C in another cylinder. The rice pudding is transferred to a sterile buffer tank, and then filled into plastic pots. Flame sterilization has also been successfully used for canned milk-rice puddings. The pudding mix is packed in cans, which are immediately closed and run into the heating-section (137.8°C for 40—60 seconds).

Selection of Rice: Taste, appearance and nutritional criteria decide the type of rice required for preparing kheer and rice pudding. Types of rice generally used include brown rice, long grain rice, and medium grain rice. Rice-based dairy desserts, traditional or otherwise, may be prepared from rice in different forms, viz., whole or broken grains and grain fractions. A product containing whole rice grains is popular. Since different types and varieties of rice have widely varying cooking characteristics, they exert a considerable influence on the quality of kheer as well as its texture and other sensory attributes. In kheer-making, the processing/cooking is critical for the product quality. Evaluation of raw rice before and after cooking would provide important guidelines for selecting the suitable rice variety for kheer preparation.

In a recent study on manufacture of long-life kheer at the National Dairy Research Institute (NDRI), Karnal, several types of rice were analyzed for their suitability for kheer-making. These included whole grains and brokens of three varieties—basmati, parmal and parboiled. Basmati brokens were considered most suitable for kheer-making on the basis of various tests such as alkali spreading value (index of gelatinization temperature) and gel consistency test.

Usually, glutinous or waxy rice that has very little amylose content becomes very sticky on cooking. Hence, it is not preferred for kheer making. High amylose rice (indica type) varieties are normally used for kheer-making in India, Pakistan, Bangladesh and Sri Lanka.

Cooking Characteristics of Rice: Depending on the end use, rice processing may involve any of a wide range of unit operations such as cooking, flaking, roasting, puffing, etc. However, cooking or heating in the presence of water is the most common process, and the only one relevant to the traditional kheer-making process.

Amount of water needed to cook rice is an indication of the approximate increase in size of the grain (swell). However, rice grain increases more than twice in volume, even if it is cooked in only twice its volume of water. Long grain rice tends to swell more than short grain rice, and parboiled rice swells less than non-parboiled rice. Brown rice or unpolished rice swells somewhat less than polished rice. Rice swells more when cooked in milk than in water. Texture of the cooked rice is an important determinant of its acceptability. It is particularly significant in relation to a product like kheer.

Long-life Kheer: Though kheer is popular throughout India, its limited shelf-life, even under refrigeration, imposes severe restrictions on its commercial manu-facture and marketing. If a process could be developed to produce kheer in shelf-stable form, it would offer significant value addition and product diversification to the Indian dairy industry.

However, processing of particulate products poses certain challenges to food processors. The problems associated with thermal processing of heterogeneous products such as milk-rice (or kheer) may be sought to be circumvented by adopting newer technologies such as microwave heating, scraped surface heat exchangers, sterilization in retortable pouches, etc. In-package thermal processing offers certain unique advantages such as flexibility of scale of operation and obviate the need for aseptic packaging. Further, thermally processed and packaged desserts are expected to have adequate shelf-life to facilitate their transportation and shipping over long distances for widespread marketing.

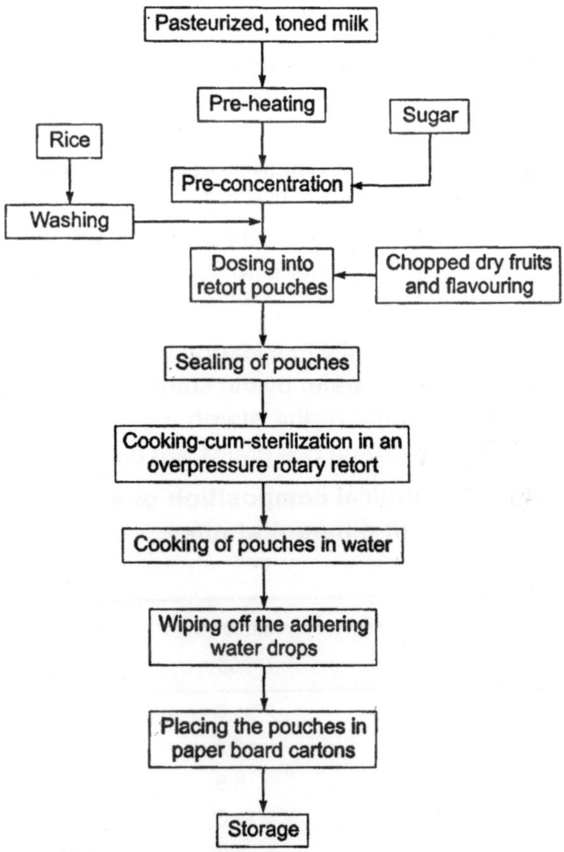

Figure 10.1 : Flow-chart for manufacture of long-life kheer employing a pilot-scale rotary retort.

A process has recently been developed at the NDRI, Karnal, for in-package cooking and sterilization of kheer in retort pouches with the objective to enhance its shelf-life at ambient temperature (Figure 10.1). Sterilization is done in steam-air environment, using a Rotary Pilot Scale Retorting System, employing a constant rotation of 2 rpm. Retort temperature and pressure are set at 121.1°C and 15 psi, respectively. An over-pressure of 30 psi is maintained to prevent bursting of pouches. Concentrated milk, raw rice (washed and soaked at 30°C/30 minutes) and sugar are filled in retort pouches (size 200 mm x 170 mm) having a configuration of polyester, aluminium-foil and 350-gauge cast polypropylene. Kheer obtained by this process exhibited proximate composition of 6.21 per cent fat, 10.75 per cent protein, 28.67 per cent total solids, 0.74 per cent ash and 10.97 per cent carbohydrates. The product had a shelf-life of more than four months at 37°C.

Physico-chemical Characteristics: During kheer manufacture, the changes in milk concentration are accompanied by physical changes in the rice grains being cooked. Both these changes contribute to rheological changes in the milk-rice mixture. Concentration of milk over a period of time also increases the fat and protein content in the final product. Results of several studies on the effect of varying fat content of milk on the average chemical composition of kheer are given in Table 10.1.

Gelatinization of starch is the most prominent change during cooking of rice. It results in uptake of water by the starch granules accompanied by expansion of the network of the starch molecule chains. Swelling and softening of the gelatinizing rice grains are concomitant processes.

Table 10.1 Chemical composition of kheer observed in different studies.

percentage by weight

Constituent	Manietal. (1955)*	Deetal. (1976)**	Chaudhary (1989)***
Total solids	31.0	32.98	38.23
Fat	12.2	7.83	6.38
Protein	5.9	6.34	5.44
Lactose	11.3	8.45	6.49
Ash	2.3	1.41	0.74
Sucrose	—	8.95	14.74
Other Carbohydrates	—	—	4.45

* Kheer made from milk of 4.1 per cent fat and 12.5 per cent total solids.

** Kheer made from cow milk of 4.0 per cent fat, 2.4 per cent rice and 5 per cent sugar.

*** Kheer made from milk of 5.0 per cent fat, 9.5 per cent SNF, 5 per cent rice and 12 per cent sugar.

Gelatinization of rice may take place even during soaking if the soak-water temperature is high enough. When the rice is milled, the cells of the grain are fractured and some of the embedded starch grains are exposed on the surfaces of the individual particles. If the rice grains are agitated during cooking, many of these starch granules are dislodged. These thicken the liquid around the individual particles of the rice, resulting in cooked rice with individual pieces embedded in a thick starch paste of a gooey consistency. Further, during the gelatinization or cooking process, water is believed to disrupt the protein matrix, part of the protein bodies and the starch granules. Amylose diffuses out of the granules that eventually collapse. This seems to enable a starch-protein interaction.

Even though changes in kheer during storage have not been analyzed because of its inherent poor shelf-life, changes during storage of long-life kheer have been fully characterized. The pH of long-life kheer is in the range of 6.04 to 6.10. This lowering of the pH may be attributed to the concentration effect of milk solids as well as the heat-treatment given to the product in the retort.

Rheological properties of kheer serve as important acceptability parameters. Studies on body and texture of kheer have found improvement in the sensory score from 6.9 to 8.5 (on a 9-point hedonic scale) when the fat content of milk is increased from 3 to 5 per cent. The pre-soaking of rice at 30 or 50°C for 30 minutes improved the body and texture. Higher visual consistency and lower grain hardness contributed to an appreciably higher texture acceptability score for basmati rice kheer. Viscosity of the milk-rice mixture increased logarithmically with increase in total solids. It was also observed that a creamy consistency of the shear-thinning liquid fraction was generally preferred. However, the overall textural acceptability of the product appeared to be determined by both the liquid phase viscosity and cooked grain tenderness.

Shelf-life: Short-shelf-life has been a major deterrent in large-scale commercial manufacture and marketing of kheer in traditional form. The shelf life of kheer when hot packed in tin cans was found to be only 2-3 days at 37°C that could be extended up to 3-4 days by adopting thermal treatment and up to 8—10 days by employing nisin as a preservative.

The shelf-life of steam kettle-processed kheer was only 7-8 hours at 30°C and 9 days at 5°C. Even the use of sodium metabisulphite could not appreciably improve the shelf-life of kheer at 30°C. Increase in shelf-life of thermally processed kheer to more than 6 months at room temperature has been achieved by using nisin at a concentration of 200 IU/g of the product. Nisin has been used to lower the process value for some canned Indian dishes including kheer. Products have been processed at different temperatures after the addition of nisin and following inoculation with *Bacillus stearothermophilus* NCA 1518. Results indicated that the level of nisin required for adequate processing and the processing time needed for kheer were 400 IU/g and 6 minutes respectively.

11

Dried Kheer Mix Manufacture

Manufacturing Method: The procedure for the production of the instant kheer mix involves separate preparation of the instant milk-rice powder, representing the liquid fraction of kheer as well as instant rice, representing the particulate phase. Fresh buffalo milk (6.9% fat and 9.5% SNF) is standardized to a fat: SNF level of 5.0 : 9.1 for the manufacture of kheer mix powder. Standardized milk is heated at 60°C for 15 minutes in the pre-heater of the triple-effect evaporator and then concentrated to 35 per cent total solids. Homogenization of the milk concentrate is done at a pressure of 183 bar during first stage and 36 bar during second stage. Homogenized milk concentrate is mixed with ground rice and sugar and the resultant milk-rice-sugar slurry is heated to a temperature of 80°C for gelatinization of rice in a steam-jacketed heating-cum-mixing vessel. The milk-rice-sugar slurry representing the simulated liquid phase of kheer is dried in a two-stage spray dryer. This kheer mix powder is blended with ground sugar. Using a fluidized bed dryer instantizes rice. Instant rice grains are separately packed in polythene pouches. Kheer mix powder can be packaged in metallized polyester LDPE bags, and a separate polythene pouch containing instant rice can be placed in them. This process is shown in Figure 11.1.

Reconstitution of kheer mix involves rehydration of instant rice in boiling water for 10 min. followed by dispersal of the powdered component into the rice-water mixture. The reconstituted product could be suitably flavoured and enriched with dry fruits, etc. This product has been found to have a high acceptance rating in a consumer study. Such a dry mix has great commercial potential in the Indian Dairy Products Market.

Physico-chemical Characteristics: In a systematic study, instant kheer mix powder was stored at 30°, 37° and 45°C to predict its shelf-life at ambient conditions. Several important parameters that might influence product quality and in turn its acceptability were monitored.

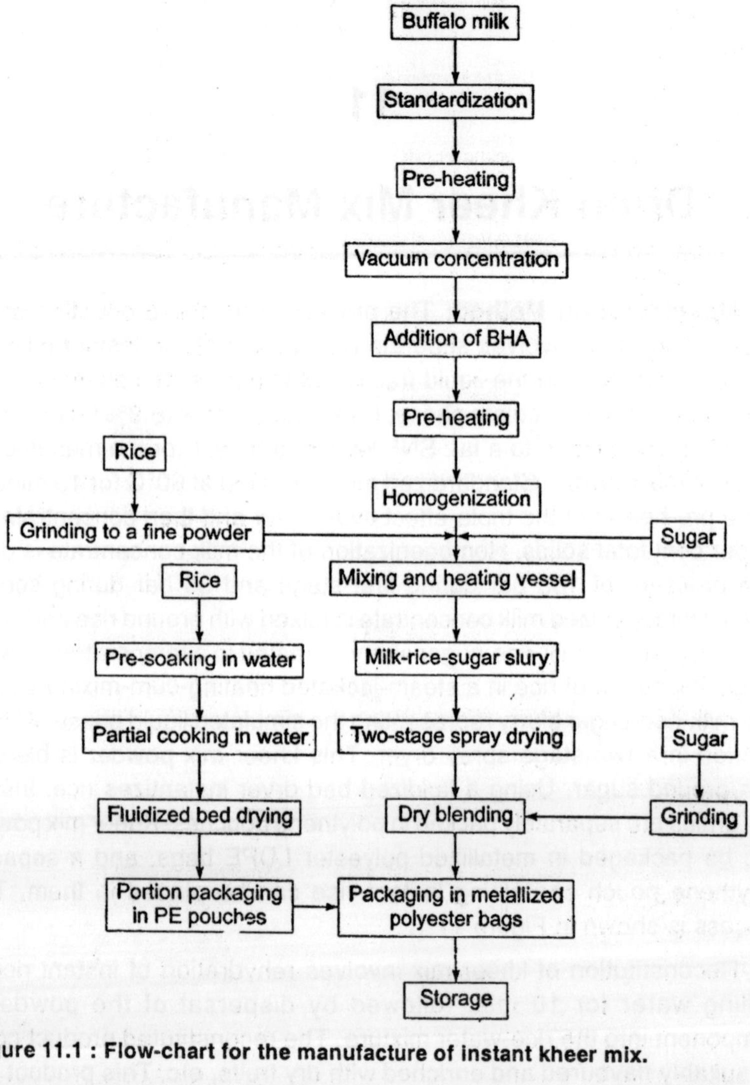

Figure 11.1 : Flow-chart for the manufacture of instant kheer mix.

These included colour (absorbance), thiobarbiturric acid test (oxidative stability), total and free hydroxy methyl furfural contents (browning indices), wettability, flowability, bulk density, dispensability, insolubility index, particle density, occluded air content, interstitial air content, porosity and pH of reconstituted liquid.

Proximate chemical composition of kheer mix has also been analyzed. Moisture, fat, protein, ash and carbohydrate contents of this powder are 1.98,18.2,16.0, 2.64 and 65.8 per cent respectively. Average composition of this product compares favourably with dairy whitener. Flowability, which is the ease with which powder particles move with each other, has been measured in terms of angle of repose, and found to be 40.09°. Wettability, primarily a measure of hydrophilic properties, was two minutes. Loose bulk density of kheer mix powder is 0.69 g/cc whereas packed bulk density is 0.81 g/cc. A relatively high bulk density can be attributed to the rice particles in the powder. Dispersability of kheer mix powder is 75.38 per cent, whereas its insolubility index is 4.0 ml. Particle density, occluded air content, interstitial air content and porosity are 1.21 g/cc, 6.63 cc/100 g, 45.00 cc/100 g and 44.8 per cent, respectively.

Shelf-Life: Kinetic approach to predict the shelf-life of any food product requires generation of information relating to the physico-chemical parameters and loss of sensory quality as a function of storage time and temperature. If an overall acceptability score of 4 on the hedonic scale for reconstituted kheer is considered as the minimum acceptable score then a period of 92 weeks at 37°C can be considered to be the potential shelf-life of the instant kheer mix powder.

12

Payasam Manufacture

Payasam is a milk-based delicacy popular in the southern parts of India. It resembles kheer of North India and has similar ritualistic connotations. Payasam forms an integral part of the cultural ethos of South India, closely associated with ritualistic ceremonies such as weddings, religious functions, and birth and death anniversaries. The manner and time of consuming payasam during a meal is also strictly laid out. A wedding feast in South India is served on a large banana leaf, with cold items laid out at specified positions. Among them is a small serving of thick vermicelli payasam, which is consumed to start off the meal. The meal also ends invariably with another variety of payasam, served in larger portions and treated as a dessert. In Bengal, a similar delicacy called payesh (made of rice and thickened milk) accompanied by fruits like mango is served at the end of a festive meal.

Product Description: There are several varieties of payasam with distinct characteristics that may be attributed to the area of their origin and traditional methods of preparation. The popularity of different varieties also differs from state to state. While vermicelli payasam is relished in all the four southern states, a variety with khus-khus (poppy seeds) is a speciality in Karnataka, palada payasam in Kerala and Thirattupal in Tamil Nadu. Shirkurma and Gil-e-Firdaus are special varieties of Hyderabad city, where there is a predominantly Muslim population. In Karnataka, paramanna is a prized kind of rice payasam in milk, which is repeatedly extolled in ancient texts as the finest type of payasam. This ritual confection of rice and milk with honey and sugar is given to an infant as his/her first solid food at the annaprasanna ceremony.

Wedding feasts in Kerala include payasams based on milk, coconut milk, rice, dal and bananas. Payasams of Kerala containing a combination of coconut milk and milk are termed as prathamans. Besides milk and/or coconut milk, the prathaman contains fruits or dal or paper-thin shreds of a rice-roll, cooked separately and added to the sweetened milk to give palada prathaman. Table 12.1 lists the regional varieties of payasam of South India.

Classification: Based on the use of ingredients other than milk and sugar, payasam is classified as pulse, cereal, tuber crop product, fruit and seed-based (Table 12.1).

Pulse-based Payasams: The common pulses used for the preparation of payasam are green/Bengalgram dal. A sweet payasam of horse gram is a common "shraddha" food item. The quantity of dal used

Table 12.1 : Regional varieties of payasam in South India.

State	Popular varieties	Others
Andhra Pradesh	Vermicelli, Sago	Shirkurma, Gil-e-Firdaus, Phirni
Karnataka	Vermicelli (Shyavige), Bengal gram dal (Kadale bele)	Poppy seeds (Khus khus), Green gram dal (Hesaru bele)
Kerala	Pal, Palada	Vermicelli (Semiya), Bengal/green gram (Parippu)
Tamil Nadu	Pal, Vermicelli	Thirattupal

Table 12.2 : Types of payasam based on ingredients used.

Type	Ingredient(s)	Specific name(s)
Pulse-based	Bengal gram dal, Green gram dal	Kadale bele, Hesaru bele, Parippu
Cereal-based	Rice, wheat	Halu kheeru, Pal, Gil-e-Firdaus, Godhi
Cereal product-based	Beaten rice, suji, vermicelli, ada	Avalakkai, Happal kuthida, Rava, Akki nutchu, Phirni, Shyavige, Semiya, Palada, Shirkurma
Tuber product-based	Sago	Sabbakki, Kaddu ki kheer
Fruit-based	Mango, jackfruit	Mavina, Halasina, Manga prathaman, Chakka prathaman
Seed-based	Poppy	Khus khus

* Contributed by Dr. S. Kulkarni, Principal Scientist, National Dairy Research Institute, Bangalore.

is about one-fifth of the weight of the product. The pulses are either cooked in water directly or after roasting in ghee, they are added to milk and boiled. Sugar or jaggery may be used as the sweetening ingredient. When jaggery is used, it is added after removing the preparation from the fire, or after reducing the heat, to avoid coagulation of milk. Even other additives such as coconut gratings, raisins and cashew nuts are added after the temperature of the product is reduced. Whenever coconut milk is used, as in the prathamans of Kerala, the product is never reheated to avoid coagulation.

Domestic preparation involves roasting/frying of Bengal gram/green gram dal (lentil) with a little ghee, followed by steaming to soften the dal. It is then cooked with milk (1:1). In the last stages of cooking, jaggery, grated coconuts, cardamom and dry fruits are added to taste.

For the preparation of prathaman payasam, green gram dal (200 grams) is first roasted with a little ghee, followed by cooking in water. Water is drained off, and dal is mashed. The mashed mass is mixed with 500 ml of milk, and cooking continued. Towards the middle stage of cooking, molten/strained jaggery (600 grams) is added and cooking continued after adding coconut milk (prepared by three successive extractions of one full grated coconut). The mixture is brought to a gentle boil. Final garnishing is done with roasted cashew nuts and raisins.

Cereal-based Payasams: The main ingredient of the cereal-based payasam is rice or wheat. Significant differences exist in the traditional methods of preparation. To prepare halu kheeru payasam, soaked rice is ground to a fine paste along with coconut and cardamom and then cooked in milk. The product is garnished with a fair amount of dry fruits. The godhi payasam is similar to this, but ground wheat is used instead of rice. To prepare pal payasam medium-sized rice grains are cooked in milk. It is a concentrated product, which generally contains no additives other than sugar.

While the quantity of rice used is one-fifteenth of the amount of milk in pal payasam, it is as high as half the quantity of milk in halu kheeru payasam. Superior quality rice (basmati) is used for preparing Gil-e-Firdaus. The rice (one-tenth of the quantity of milk) is fried in ghee and a fair amount of additives of dairy origin (khoa, malai and condensed milk) and non-dairy origin (almonds, pistachio and cashew nuts) are used in the preparation of Gil-e-Firdaus.

Domestic preparation of halu kheeru payasam involves pre-soaking of 250 grams rice for 1 hour. To the washed rice, 100 grams of coconut and 1 gram of cardamom is added and the mixture is ground to a fine paste. Milk is added to the paste (1 :1), and the mixture is boiled. Boiling is continued till fully cooked. In the last stages of cooking, 500 grams of sugar is added and finally, garnishing is done with saffron and raisins. Halu kheeru payasam may be served hot or cold.

Besides the above described payasams, some other varieties are prepared from vermicelli, rice suji, wheat suji, beaten rice and a rice dough-product (ada).

Vermicelli Payasams: Shyavige and shirkurma are the common vermicelli-based payasams. In the preparation of shirkurma, a specialty of Hyderabad city, condensed milk is used in addition to milk. Sweetened condensed milk (800 grams), cooked dry dates and fried raisins are added in the final stages of cooking. For making shyavige, 100 grams vermicelli is first roasted in ghee. Then one litre milk is added and cooking continued for 30 minutes. Finally sugar, raisins and powdered cardamom are added. Shyavige may be served either hot or cold.

Rice Suji-based Payasam: It is called Akki nutchu payasam. Suji from basmati rice is used for preparing it. Usually, rice suji is cooked in water. However, the finer version of the product is cooked in condensed milk. To prepare akki nutchu payasam, rice suji (500 grams) is first roasted light brown in ghee and then cooked with one litre of milk and 600 grams of sugar. To this cardamom, saffron and dry fruits are finally added before serving hot or cold.

Wheat Suji-based Payasam: Its two main varieties use the wheat suji along with coconut paste and papads made of wheat suji dough. The papads are deep-fried in ghee and constitute the major suspended ingredient of payasam. To prepare wheat suji payasam, 400 grams of suji is first roasted in ghee, and then cooked in water till soft. To this 200 grams of coconut paste and 1 litre of milk are added and cooking continued. Finally, sugar (600 grams), cardamom and raisins are added and served.

Avalakki (beaten rice-based) Payasam: Beaten rice consists of flat flakes of rice, brownish gray in colour. To prepare avalakki payasam, 300 grams of avalakki is deep-fried in ghee. It is then cooked with one litre of milk. Towards the end of cooking, sugar (400 grams), cardamom, saffron and raisins are added and payasam served.

Ada-based Payasam: This variety is called palada payasam. Ada is a cooked product made from rice dough. Its preparation is a long process since the rice dough is cooked for a long time to obtain a consistency at which it can be cut into flakes. The texture of ada flakes should be tough so as to withstand vigorous stirring during the preparation of palada payasam. Ready-to-use ada is now commercially marketed in Kerala. Flow diagram for preparation of palada payasam is shown in Figure 12.2.

Table 12.3 : Product profile of different varieties of payasam.

Name	Characteristics
Pulse-based payasams	
Bengal gram dal (Kadale bele) payasam	Light cream colour, highly viscous (often semi-solid) consistency with coconut gratings, dried grapes and nuts. Colour darker if jaggery is the sweetening agent.
Green gram dal (Hesaru bele) payasam	Light yellowish brown colour, semi-solid with a sticky, pasty texture. Sweetening agent either sugar br jaggery. Raisins and cardamom are added.
Cereal-based payasams	
Rice (Halu kheeru) payasam	A viscous, free-flowing, non-homogeneous product with rice settling at the bottom. Liberal addition of raisins and cashew nuts.
Pal payasam	Highly viscous, slightly pasty, homogeneous product. Light brown in colour, pleasant caramelized flavour.
Gil-e-Firdaus	Creamy rich, highly viscous homogeneous product. Light brown in colour, pleasant nutty flavour. Garnished with high levels of fruits and nuts.
Wheat (Godhi) payasam	Highly viscous, semi-solid, pasty product with visible coconut gratings. Brown in colour. Nutty/ cardamom flavour.
Cereal product-based payasams	
Vermicelli payasam (Shyavige)	Low to medium viscous, non-homogeneous free flowing product with large amounts of raisins. Appealing cream colour, nutty flavour.
Shirkurma	Highly viscous, creamy rich, homogeneous product having liberal amount of nuts and raisins. Light brown in colour, pleasant caramelized/nutty flavour.
Rice suji (Akki nutchu) payasam	Homogeneous, thick viscous product with suspended dry fruits. Light cream in colour. Cooked/pleasant flavour of added spices.
Phirni	Highly viscous homogeneous product. Light yellowish brown in colour. Nutty/fruity flavour.
Wheat suji payasam	Thick, viscous, homogeneous product with suspended raisins and cashew nuts.
Happala kuthida payasam	Free flowing product with suspended papad crumbs. Cardamom flavour.
Beaten rice (Avalakkai) payasam	Low viscous, free flowing white product with visible coconut gratings. Pleasant cooked flavour.
Palada payasam	Medium viscous product with ada flakes uniformly distributed. Brown colour. Pleasant nutty flavour.

Name	Characteristics
Tuber crop product-based payasams	
Sago (Sabakki) payasam	Free flowing product with suspended sago granules. White colour.
Kaddu ki kheer	Medium viscous product with smooth body and suspended granular particles. Light cream in colour. Cardamom flavour.
Fruit- and seed-based payasams	
Mango (Mavina) payasam	Medium viscous homogeneous product with suspended fruit pieces. Light yellow colour with strong mango flavour.
Jackf ruit (Halasina) payasam	Low to medium viscous, non-homogeneous product. Yellowish in colour. Mild, pleasant fruity flavour.
Poppy seed (Khus khus) payasam	Free flowing, rich, homogeneous product. Light cream in colour. Medium/strong poppy/ cardamom flavour.

Table 12.4 : Proximate chemical composition of selected varieties of payasam.

weight per cent

Type	Total solids	Suspended solids	Fat	Protein	Lactose	Sucrose
Kadale bele	48.10	25.80	3.20	6.40	2.20	24.20
Hesarubele	42.40	16.10	1.70	5.50	2.40	22.70
Halu kheeru	38.40	14.40	2.30	1.90	2.60	19.90
Pal	43.10	7.80	3.70	3.40	4.10	24.60
Godhi	42.40	12.80	3.40	2.60	1.80	21.90
Avalakkai	35.20	8.80	3.70	2.80	1.80	17.70
Akki nutchu	39.80	4.00	1.40	2.20	1.90	21.60
Rava	40.10	5.10	3.50	2.30	1.90	20.80
Shyavige	30.90	4.80	1.80	1.80	1,90'	20.80
Shirkurma	36.50	5.80	3.40	3.30	6.20	17.80
Palada	51.90	6.20	3.70	4.20	4.90	32.00
Kaddu ki kheer	40.10	11.90	1.10	1.20	2.60	22.70
Halasina	32.40	3.10	2.00	1.70	2.50	22.90
Mavina	31.20	—	1.40	1.60	2.80	20.60
Khus khus	40.00	—	7.20	6.20	2.40	20.30

Tuber Crop-based Payasams: Sago is a granular product processed from tuber crops such as tapioca. Sago-based payasams, either alone or in combination with pulses, are popular in Karnataka and Andhra Pradesh. One variety in this category is Sabakki payasam. To prepare it, 300 grams of sago is first washed and cooked in water till soft. Water is drained off and further cooking is done with one litre of milk and 500

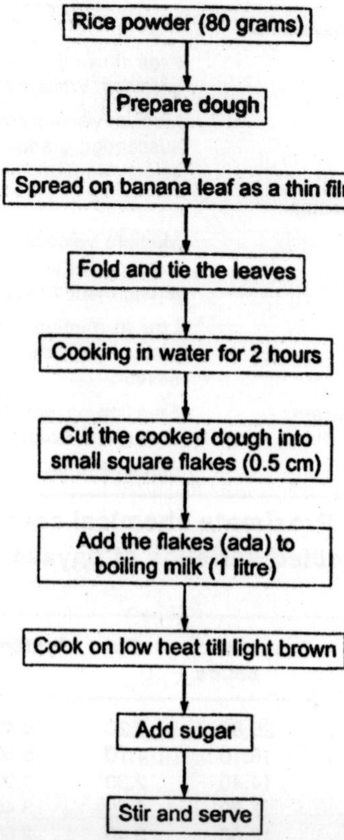

Figure 12.1 : Flow-chart for preparation of palada payasam.

grams of sugar. When cooking is over, payasam is garnished with powdered cardamom and dry fruits.

Fruit-based Payasams: Mango and jackfruit are commonly used in fruit-based payasams. In the mango variety, mango extract is used while fried pieces of jackfruit are used to prepare jackfruit payasam. In Kerala, the mango prathaman and chakka prathaman make use of coconut milk, milk and the respective fruits. In Karnataka, mavino payasam is made by boiling one litre of milk with 500 grams each of mango juice and sugar. When cooked, it is garnished with powdered cardamom and served hot or cold. Alternatively, for making halasina payasam, in place of mango juice, cut pieces of jackfruit may be used.

Seed-based Payasams: Khus khus (poppy seeds) form the main suspended ingredient in this payasam. About 300 grams of khus khus is ground to a fine paste with grated coconut (200 grams) and a small quantity of rice (40 grams) before addition of one litre of milk. The sweetening agent may be either jaggery or sugar (500 grams). The mixture is boiled till fully cooked. This form of payasam is preferably served cold.

Physico-chemical Characteristics: They vary widely in different types of payasam depending on the ingredients used. In general, payasam is thinner in consistency than kheer, although its varieties range from free flowing to solid. The payasam colour varies from white, light cream, cream and light brown to brown. It is distinctly brown in payasams which contain jaggery as a sweetening ingredient. They have a pleasant cooked flavour, while some have added nutty or fruity flavour. Caramel flavour is associated with those products that are concentrated by heating during preparation. Caramel flavour may also be present if condensed milk is used as a raw material. Cardamom is the most popular flavouring ingredient used in payasam. Product profiles of payasam varieties are listed in Table 12.3.

The chemical composition (total solids, total suspended solids, fat, protein, reducing sugar and sucrose) of selected varieties of payasam estimated at the Southern Regional Station of the NDRI at Bangalore is given in Table 12.4.

Excellent scope exists for mechanizing the payasam manufacture process to tap its wide popularity. A number of options exist for integrating new technologies, such as UHT equipment for particulate foods, retort sterilization in flexible pouches, etc., with the commercial processes. Long shelf-life forms of payasam packaged in flexible pouches or polystyrene cups would need to be adopted for marketing on a national network.

13

Phirni Manufacture

A delicious variant of kheer, phirni is prepared by cooking milk with rice paste and sugar. Generally served in shikora (earthen cup), phirni is covered with a thin silver foil (vark). In Hyderabad, phirni is made with pineapple bits and is named Gil-e-Firdaus or "clay from paradise", an obvious reference to the shikora. Not much work has been done on its industrial production.

INGREDIENTS :

(a) *Milk:* Buffalo milk or mixed milk (pH 6.5 to 6.7, titratable acidity 0.14 to 0.16%), fat (6.0 to 6.2%) and SNF (9.0 to 9.2%) is usually used for phirni preparation.

(b) *Rice:* Generally Basmati rice is used. It is washed with cold water and macerated wet in a mixer to get the paste. Rice is used in the proportion of 100 grams per kg of milk.

(c) *Sugar:* Cane sugar at the rate of 15 per cent (w/w) may be used. The concentration will depend on the individual taste and market preference.

Technology: The standardized milk is heated in a stainless steel container and boiled vigorously for 2—5 minutes. The milk is constantly stirred to avoid burning at the bottom and sides. The required amount of rice paste is incorporated into the boiling milk with constant stirring until the milk starts to thicken. When the desired consistency is achieved, appropriate amount of sugar is added slowly with stirring into the hot milk. It is then cooled to room temperature, dispensed into individual serving containers, and further cooled to 4°C under refrigeration.

Phirni can be made from skim milk or from standardized milk with 3.5 to 5 per cent fat or even with high fat milk. Although skim milk phirni has low calories, the use of standardized milk, with 3.5 per cent fat, is most preferred for taste. Good quality phirni can be made from milk of 6 per cent fat.

14

Sevian Manufacture

Sevian is a sweet dish relished all over India. It is a variant of kheer. At various religious festivals like Id, it is customary for housewives to prepare this dish and distribute portions of it to friends and relatives. Mainly homemade, a wide variation in product profile of sevian is noted from region to region and even from household to household. Standardization of its traditional production process in terms of techniques, sensory profiles, and compositional and physico-chemical attributes is necessary for getting a uniform product of assured quality.

Product Description: Sevian is sweet dish prepared by cooking milk and roasted vermicelli. In northern parts of the country, the thicker and shorter variety of vermicelli made from hard wheat is used to make this delicacy. The sevian relished by Muslims is thicker in consistency than its South Indian counterpart, semiya payasam.

Technology: A traditional recipe for sevian uses approximately 225 grams vermicelli, 600 ml of milk and 225 grams of sugar. After frying crushed cardamoms and cloves in ghee, vermicelli is added into the vessel and roasted. Ample care is taken to ensure that vermicelli does not get broken during roasting. Milk is added, and the mixture stirred gently, but thoroughly. Thereafter, the vessel is covered and cooking resumed on medium heat for about ten minutes, with occasional stirring. When the milk is almost evaporated, sugar, almonds, pistachios and rose water are added. Sevian is consumed either hot or cold. The product is served garnished with finely beaten silver foil (vark).

15

Sohan Halwa

The origin of the word halwa can be traced to the Arabic word 'hal', which means 'to dissolve'. Traditionally, halwa was a fudge-like sweet made by mixing any ground grain with sugar syrup. The manufacture of sohan halwa is confined to North India. Its product profile differs from region to region, even from halwai to halwai. Standardization of the traditional process in terms of manufacturing techniques, sensory profiles, and compositional and physico-chemical attributes is necessary for attaining a uniform product of assured quality.

Product Description: Sohan halwa is a wheat-based product with an extremely chewy texture, which is attributed to wheat gluten. Wheat used is first allowed to germinate and then ground. The atta so obtained is termed angoori atta, the name probably derived from the word ankurit, which in Hindi means sprouted or germinated. Its softer fudge-like variation is 'dodha', resembling burfi.

Technology: Whole buffalo milk is boiled and left outside to allow development of a certain degree of acidity (about 0.18% LA). Angoori atta and normal atta in the ratio 1 : 2 are mixed in milk (about 150 grams of the mixture in one litre of milk), ensuring that there are no lumps. The mixture is boiled with constant stirring. Sugar (10—15% of milk) is added when almost all the moisture has evaporated. Stirring is continued and when the mixture is dry, ghee (5% of milk) is added to facilitate stir-frying. When the halwa attains a brown colour, it is turned on to a flat surface and levelled. Garnishing with nuts is optional. When the product is set, it is cut with a sharp knife into any desired shape.

16

Gajar-ka-Halwa

Gajar-ka-halwa (fudge-like halwa of carrot), a popular dessert of North India, is specially favoured during the winter season. Carrot (gajar) is valued for its growth promoting nutrients such as carotenoids (source of vitamin A) and fibre. It is called "Gajrella" in certain parts of Punjab and Kashmir, where saffron is used as colouring material. It is mostly prepared at the household level and by local sweet-makers on cottage scale. Carrot-milk based sweets, like carrot halwa, carrot burfi, gajrella and gajar deeth have gained popularity by virtue of their pleasing aroma, chewy texture and attractive colour. The health attributes of carrots have been well documented in ancient Indian literature.

Product Description: Gajar-ka-halwa is bright reddish brown with certain darkened but glossy fragments of grated carrot. It has a lumpy body with a few pieces of shredded carrot and bits of khoa that may be sometimes used for garnishing. Its texture is crunchy but with a typical mellowness. The characteristic aroma of gajar-ka-halwa is a blend of cooked carrots, heat-concentrated milk and caramelized sugar. Invariably, the product is garnished with khoa, crushed cardamom, cashew nuts, almonds and raisins. In some regions, ground rice is used to provide it thickness, and saffron is used both as flavouring as well as colouring agent.

Technology: In traditional preparation method, carrots are first cleaned, pealed thinly to remove the inedible surface skin, grated finely and pre-cooked with steam to impart the requisite tenderness. Milk and sugar are then added and cooking continued on a low flame with intermittent stirring during which milk boils and froths. As the cooking progresses, shredded carrots and concentrated milk form a lumpy mass. With further cooking, free fat oozes out from the lumpy mass, imparting a moderate frying effect. Halwa then acquires golden/reddish-brown colour partly due to the controlled caramelization of sugar and milk. Rate of scraping and stirring is increased towards the finishing stages, when saffron, cardamom, raisins, slivered almonds and shredded cashew nuts are added and the surface is topped with silver foil. The final product is mostly served hot.

Since the traditional process is labour intensive, certain sweet-makers use ground rice for the sake of convenience to provide the thickness to the product and even use khoa rather than heat-concentrated milk while cooking carrots. Such a process variation yields a product with reduced flavour. This process variation is commonly used for preparing the product on a cottage scale.

Typical process of manufacturing gajar-ka-halwa, commonly employed at home and for small-scale production, consists of grating the carrots, boiling the grated mass with milk in a big heavy bottom pan on a slow flame. Cooking is continued until liquid is almost gone, with continuous stirring so as to prevent sticking and burning. Butter or vegetable fat is added and the mixture is cooked for another half-hour. Sugar and raisins are added with continuous stirring and the mixture is further cooked to a thick consistency till oil starts to separate out. Now the halwa is ready, and it is usually served hot. The product is milky in appearance.

Innovations: A process has been developed for making instant carrot-halwa mix. The method consists of washing, peeling and grating carrots, cooking under pressure, drying in a fluidized bed dryer, blending with other ingredients (like sugar, milk powder, cardamom) and conditioning and packaging. The product stores well for a year in PFP (paper-aluminium foilpoly-ethylene) packs. For reconstitution, equal quantities of the mix and water are blended thoroughly and heated for 5 minutes.

Quality Factors: Quality of raw material greatly affects the acceptability of finished halwa. Carrots should possess a high peel to core ratio, high total soluble content, high carotenoid content and low fibre content. Processing variables like cooking temperature, cooking period, and blanching of grated carrots also have a pronounced effect over the product quality. A longer cooking period at lower temperature leads to development of the product with superior flavour.

Packaging: Mould growth and development of off-flavour is generally encountered during retail storage of carrot halwa. In sweet shops, halwa is heated too often before serving. Such heating may lead to oxidation of fats and carotenoids, manifested by an unfavourable odour.

Instant carrot halwa mixes developed at the Defence Food Research Laboratory (DFRL), Mysore, had a low moisture range (2.0—2.6%). Moisture control during processing as well as during storage is very critical for adequate shelf-life. Discolouration due to Maillard reaction and oxidation of carotenoids decrease the overall acceptability of the product. Soaking of grated carrots in sodium metabisulphite solution considerably reduced the susceptibility of instant carrot halwa mix to undesirable reaction during storage. Two packaging materials, namely polypropylene (PP) and paper- aluminium foil-polyethylene (PFP) laminate, were evaluated for storage at various temperatures. Instant carrot halwa remained stable for 12, 6, 2 months in PP and 12, 12 and 4 months in PFP packs at 0°C, room temperature and 37°C, respectively.

17

Kaju Burfi Manufacture

Among Indian sweets, kaju burfi or cashew nut *(Anacardium occidentle L.)* burfi is one of the most popular because of its delicate texture, good flavour and excellent mouthfeel. Other cashew nut-based sweets are halwa, cashew nut katli (wafer-thin slice), and cashew nut chikki and cashew sweet milk. Despite their high costs, cashew nut products are always in demand. Recently, their export to the Middle East and European Countries has assumed importance. In these countries, people of Indian origin constitute a sizeable proportion of the population.

Product Description: Kaju burfi is a delicacy, containing cashew nut, sugar, milk solids, and at times certain minor ingredients like jaggery and coconut. Typically, it is prepared in the form of thin slices (3—5 mm) cut into diamond shape with silver foil coating. Hundred grams of burfi provide 480 kcal, containing 24 per cent fat, 8.7 per cent protein and 56.8 per cent carbohydrates.

Technology: Grated khoa and sugar are mixed thoroughly, and the mixture is heated in a heavy bottom shallow pan with continuous stirring to completely dissolve the sugar. When the right temperature and consistency are reached, ground cashew and powdered cardamom are added. Cooking is continued with constant stirring till a soft lump is formed that does not stick to sides. It is then spread over greased trays by rolling on the flat surface to the desired thickness. Silver foil is then applied, and the product allowed to cool and set. The product is stable for six months. Table 17.1 gives the composition of kaju burfi.

A modified method developed at the Defence Food Research Laboratory (DFRL), Mysore, for making kaju burfi is outlined in Figure 17.1. The composition of the standardized recipe was: cashew nut 22 per cent, whole milk powder 11.05 per cent, sugar 44.2 per cent, vanaspati oil 11.05 per cent, cardamom powder 0.55 per cent and water 11.05 per cent.

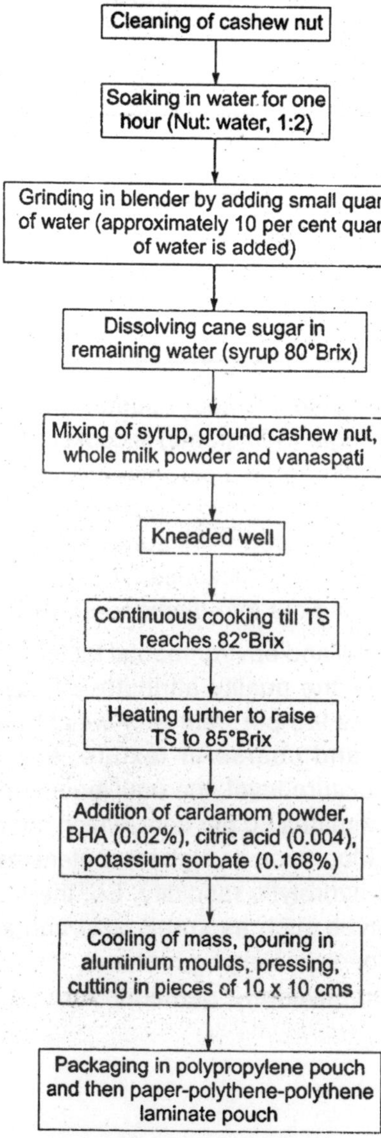

Figure 17.1 : Flow-chart for preparation of kaju burfi.

Kaju katli, another cashew nut sweet, is quite similar to kaju burfi in taste but differs in thickness. It is less thick than kaju burfi. To make kaju katli, cashews (500 grams) are soaked in water for two hours and ground to a fine paste. Precaution should be taken to use just as little

Table 17.1 : Composition of kaju burfi.

Constituent	Quantity (%)
Moisture	8.5—10
Fat	24-25
Crude protein	7-8.5
Ash	1-2
Fibre	0.5-1
Carbohydrates	55-57
Energy	400 Kcal/100 g

water as is required to make a smooth paste. In a heavy sauce pan, this paste together with sugar (300 grams) is cooked on a slow to medium flame, with continuous stirring till a soft lump is formed. Then, a small quantity of ghee and cardamom powder are added and mixed well. The mix is spread on a clean greased work surface and rolled lightly using a rolling pin to about 2-3 mm thickness. A single layer of silver foil (vark) is applied over it and cut into diamond-shaped katlis.

Several compositional and environmental factors are known to have important influence over the quality attributes of cashew nut sweets. Moisture reduction below 9.5 per cent (dry weight basis) renders the product hard in body and coarse in texture, thereby affecting its acceptability. At this moisture level, the equilibrium relative humidity of cashew nut burfi approximates 80 per cent, which permits the growth of most common moulds. Moreover, its high fat content makes it vulnerable to oxidative as well as hydrolytic rancidity. So, there is need for using anti-mycotic preservatives such as sorbic acid and antioxidants such as BHA, along with proper packaging material, for ensuring adequate shelf-life. These preservatives are permitted for use in food products (PFA, 1954).

18

Ghevar Preparation

A milk sweet preparation with admixture of wheat flour that was known as ghrataputra (also called havispura) is today's ghevar, a rare delicacy of Rajasthan. As a sweet, it complements the colourful costumes, festivals and customs. Popular sweets—ladoos of Jaisalmer, malpuas of Pushkar, ghevar of Jaipur and rasogolla of Bikaner to name a few—distinguish each region of Rajasthan. Every festive occasion in Rajasthan is associated with some traditional sweet. In case of the Teej festival, ghevar is the sweet. It now also finds market in Western Uttar Pradesh, Haryana and parts of Gujarat, especially during the Teej and Raksha Bandhan festivals.

Product Description: Ghevar is a favourite festive disc-shaped sweet, having cream-yellow to orange-brown shades of colour (attributable to the surface layer of caramelized sugar). Its body has a characteristic miniaturized honeycomb structure that is spongy and chewy. Sugar layer formed all over the body provides a glossy appearance, and a characteristic texture and flavour to the product. An elite variation of ghevar has its surface topped with a fine layer of rabri that imparts a comparatively more mellow body. Ghevar has a shelf-life of 10—12 days under ambient conditions. LMB (Lakshmi Mishthaan Bhandar) of Jaipur claims pride of place in ghevar production.

Technology: Solidified ghee (120 grams) is taken in a large bowl and is rubbed vigorously with ice-cubes till it becomes white. Plain wheat flour (maida 350 grams), milk (60 ml), and water are added to the ghee and mixed thoroughly to prepare a smooth but fairly thin batter. In an aluminium or steel cylindrical container (height about 30 cm and diameter 15 cm), melted ghee is filled up to the half of the container and heated. When it becomes smoky hot, approximate 50 ml of batter is poured in one continuous stream, at the centre of container and the foam is allowed to settle down. One glassful of batter is poured so as to form a circular cavity in the centre. When the foams again settle, ghevar is loosened with an iron skewer. It is lifted carefully and placed on a wire mesh to drain excess fat. Hot syrup of one thread consistency is kept in a wide flat-bottomed container.

Ghevar is dipped in syrup and removed, kept aside on a mesh to drain excess syrup. Alternatively, hot syrup may be poured evenly all over it. After cooling, few drops of saffron milk are splashed and chopped dry fruits and a few pinches of cardamom powder are sprinkled over the product.

LAUKI HALWA

A vegetable-based milk sweet, lauki halwa is popular in North India. For preparing lauki halwa, ghee is melted in a pan and grated bottle gourd (2.5 kg) is fried in it for about 20 minutes until light brown. Sugar (250 grams) and edible grade yellow colour (2 gram dissolved in little water) are added and mixed thoroughly with the fried grated gourd. Remaining ingredients such as khoa (500 grams) and cardamom powder are added and heated with constant stirring till free fat starts separating and a uniform lump is formed. Before serving, the halwa is evenly spread on a plate and garnished with sliced almonds and pistachio, thus further enriching the product.

PADUSHA (MAKKHAN BADA)

This South Indian sweet is made of flour mixed with curds. Maize or wheat flour is mixed with dahi and ghee (in the ratio of 8 :1 :1) with some baking soda (@ 0.01%), and kneaded into dough, using milk. The dough is then made into small balls and flattened into a patty-like shape. Simultaneously, sugar syrup is prepared in a separate vessel by boiling sugar with water. The sugar syrup is clarified during boiling by adding a few teaspoonfuls of milk. Impurities in sugar,

if any, separate out as scum. The syrup is flavoured by saffron, powdered cardamom and borneol and main-tained at about 60°-70°C.

The flattened balls are fried in ghee at about 130°-150°C, taking care that they retain their shape and fry to a slight brown surface. Frying is preferably carried out in a shallow pan where seven to eight pieces can be conveniently fried at a time with the aid of special ladles. These ladles should be of stainless steel and should be perforated for satisfactory final drainage of ghee from the fried pieces. The fried discs, while still hot, are dropped in the sugar syrup and kept immersed till they draw in sufficient syrup. They are then removed individually and allowed to drain. Each piece is finally top dressed with coconut shreds and sliced pistachio.

The product is traditionally packed in cardboard cartons with a parchment lining and individual pieces are covered on the top and sides with silver foil.

JILLI

This popular South Indian sweet is made of coconut milk. Its ingredients are: whole milk 375-400 grams, coconut milk (prepared by grinding the kernel from a ripe coconut into a paste and straining the milk through double-folded muslin) 175-250 grams, milk of rava or semolina (suji: coarse ground wheat passing through a 20-mesh sieve; prepared by grinding suji with a little water and straining the milk through double-folded muslin) 175-200 grams, cane sugar 200-300 grams, ghee 75-100 grams, saffron 1 gram and borneol 50 mg.

Technology: Buffalo whole milk, coconut milk and milk of rava are mixed together in proportion of about 2 :1:1 and concentrated in a wide-mouthed vessel over gentle fire with constant stirring, taking care to avoid charring at the bottom. As the concentrate gets thickened, sugar (1 part) is added and the stirring continued. When sugar gets completely dissolved, ghee is added followed by saffron and borneol (added in the form of a concentrated solution in a little quantity of water). With continued stirring the content of the pan assumes the consistency of a paste, which does not stick to the sides of the vessel. At this stage, the dough is emptied into a shallow pan coated with a little ghee on its sides. The dough is spread as a uniform 1.25-2.5 cm layer. This layer is sub-sequently cut into cakes of required size and shape.

The product should be very smooth and non-sticky in texture. It is packed in cardboard cartons with a parchment lining and individual pieces are covered on the top and sides with silver foil (vark).

MOHANDAS

This South Indian sweet has cashew nuts as its base. They are cut into small pieces, mixed with gram flour (7 parts), and the mixture fried with a little ghee in a bronze or cast-iron pan over a gentle fire until a pleasant cooked smell develops. Then, the content is mixed thoroughly with an orange colour and emptied into a shallow pan. Simultaneously, syrup of sugar with concentration sufficient to produce perceptible stickiness is prepared by boiling sugar with water about one-third its weight. The gram flour fried earlier and khoa (1.5 parts) are mixed with the syrup. The mixture is continuously stirred and heated. After this, a part of the.ghee (a total of about 1.5 parts) is poured into the mixture, which is stirred again to obtain a dough, which does not stick to the sides of the vessel.

Rest of the ghee is now poured and heating and stirring continued a little longer. Towards the end, the dough is removed from the fire and mixed thoroughly with saffron and cardamom and emptied into a shallow pan coated with a little ghee inside and a thin layer of sliced pistachio. The dough is spread over this layer of pistachio and smoothened out to form a uniform layer of 2-3 cm thickness, top dressed with slices of pistachio and cut into the desired shape and size.

19

Rasogolla, Kheer and Pal Payasam

The three rising stars in the mithai basket of the organized sector are rasogolla, kheer and pal payasam. At present, they are not being produced on an industrial scale. They are waiting for some enterprising entrepreneurs to take up their production. Already, the UHT long-life kheer is a long-established and popular dessert in Europe. In this and the following page, the mass balancing diagrams for these three products are given.

Rasogolla is India's national sweet. Its creation by Nobin Chandra Das in 1868 is a fitting tribute to the inventive genius of traditional mithai-makers. They blended distinct taste and flavour with hard-headed economic sense in terms of value addition to the products developed. Similarly, kheer is India's favourite dessert par excellence. It contains all the milk solids in a highly concentrated form with considerable food and nutritive value on account of addition of nuts and spices such as almonds, raisins, cardamom and saffron. Its shelf-life can be extended significantly by addition of nicin to the hot product at the end of the manufacturing process and before packaging. Pal payasam is another variety of kheer and is popular in South India.

Also shown in the schematic drawing on the facing page is the assembly-line production of shrikhand.

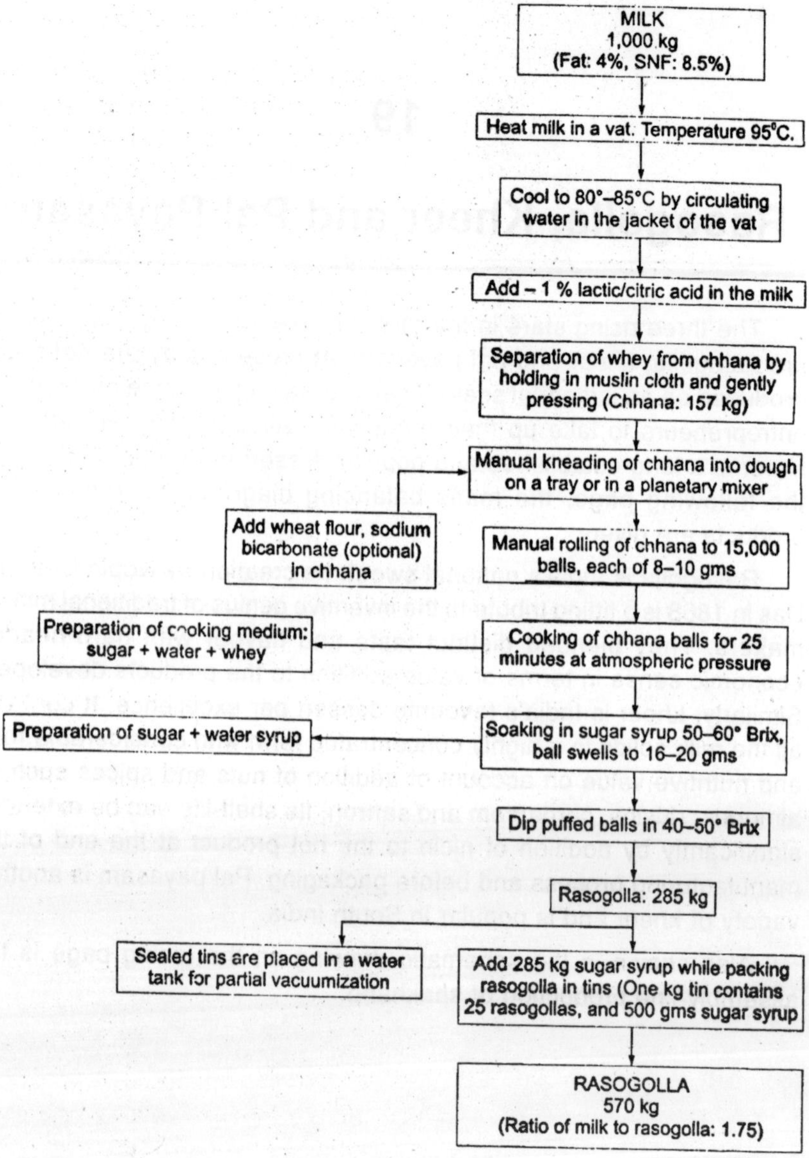

Note : One kg chhana yields 95—100 rasogolla balls, weighing around 10 gms each, prior to cooking and soaking in sugar syrup.

Figure 19.1 : Mass balance for production of resogolla.

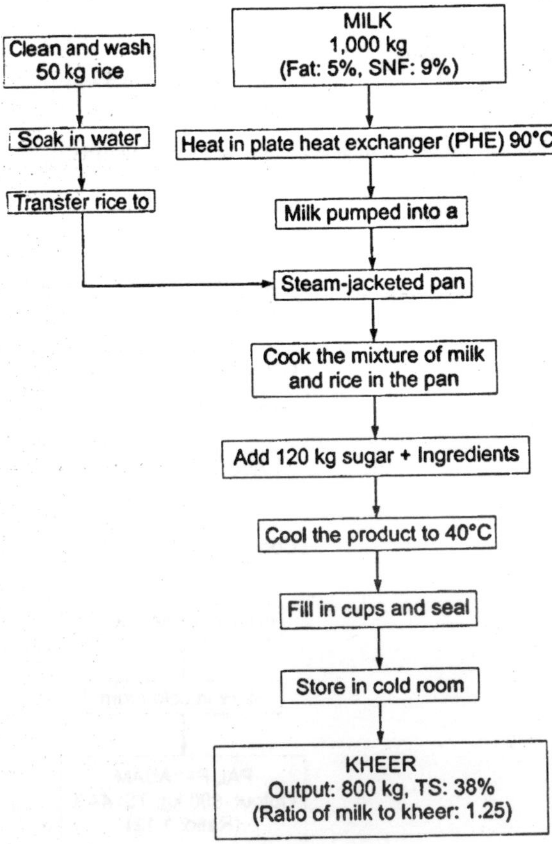

Figure 19.2 : Mass balance for production of kheer.

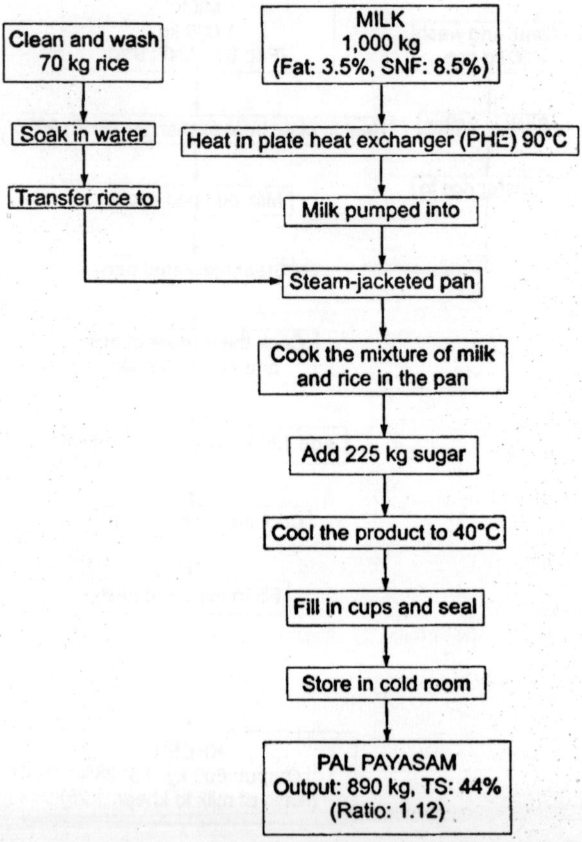

Figure 19.3 : Mass balance for production of pal payasam.

20

Preparation of Lassi

INTRODUCTION

Lassi is a sweetened, flavoured, fermented milk product consumed by large sections of the population throughout the country, lassi is a by-product obtained during the preparation of country butter from dahi by indigenous methods. This product is used with or without sugar or salt depending upon the consumer's preference. Lassi, also called chhas or matha.

Lassi is an excellent refreshing beverage for quenching thirst. There is a large variation in the quality. Characteristics of lassi sold in the different parts of the country - in rural India, lassi is also known as butter milk. Lassi is a creamy viscous fluid with rich aroma and mildly acidic in taste. It is prepared by mixing a calculated quantity of sugar, flavour and cold water with dahi by agitation. It is desirable to homogenise the product for improved body and texture. Lassi contains 79 per cent water, 3 per cent fat, 2.8 per cent protein, 4.5 per cent lactose and 12 per cent sugar. Lassi is filled in sterilized containers and stored at 4—6 °C until consumed.

COMPOSITION

The composition of lassi varies considerably since there is no standard method available for the preparation of this product. The factors affecting the composition of lassi are the type of milk used, extent of dilution during churning and efficiency of fat removal. The average composition of lassi is presented below in table 20.1.

Table 20.1 : Composition of lassi (Percentage).

Water	Total solid	Fat	Solids not fat	Protein	Lactose	Ash	Lactic Acid	Ca.	p.
96.2	3.8	0.8	3.0	1.3	1.2	0.4	0.44	0.6	0.04

Adopted From : Table 9.5 of Indian Dairy Products by Rangappa and Achaya (1974).

METHOD OF PREPARATION

Materials Required

Stainless steel (s.s.) Kettle/Vat/degchi

Stirrer/plunger

Thermometer (0—110°C)

Cow/buffalo milk

Incubator

Lactic starter culture

Sugar and flavours

Agitator/Centrifugal pump

Preparation of Sugar Syrup

Take water and sugar equally i.e. in 1:1 ratio and mix thoroughly. Heat the mixture up to 70°C/15 min and cool to 5—10°C.

Preparation of Lassi

Dahi is prepared as per the procedure described in preparation of Dahi.

The curd so obtained is passed through the centrifugal pump in order to break the curd and get uniform product.

Sugar is added 15% in the form of syrup. The desired flavour may be added 1ml/kg. Dahi.

Lassi is packed in bottles or pouches.

The product is stored at 5—10°C.

Lassi could be preserved for more than six days at 37°C by the addition of 0.03 to 0.35% sodium metabisulphite. The characteristic sulphur flavour imparted to the product during storage could be masked by the addition of 0.07 to 0.09% crushed green ginger and 0.5—0.7% salt.

MICROFLORA OF LASSI

The microflora of lassi and its microbiological quality are almost comparable to those of dahi from which it is derived.

21

Shrikhand Preparation

INTRODUCTION

Shrikhand is a fermented indigenous sweet made by mixing chakka, an intermediate product, with sugar and other ingredients (flavours, spices etc.). Chakka may be defined as a semi-solid product obtained by draining off the whey from the curd obtained by acid fermentation of cow's/buffalo's/mixed/ skimmed/standardized milk or reconstituted milk. Shrikhand has very good therapeutic and nutritive value.

The composition of the Shrikhand depends on the initial composition of the milk, the degree of fermentation, the extent of whey removal and the quality of sugar added. The standards outlined by BIS (Bureau of Indian Standards) are in Table 21.1.

Table 21.1 : BIS Standards for Chakka and Shrikhand (IS: 9532-1980.)

S.No.	Characteristic (by weight)	Skim milk Chakka	Whole milk Chakka	Shrikhand
1.	Total solids % Min.	20	30	58.0
2.	Milk fat (%) DM	5.0 (Max.)	33.0 (min.)	8.5
3.	Milk protien(%) Min. on DM	60.0	37.0	10.5
4.	Titratable acidity (%) L.A.	2.5	2.5	1.4
5.	Total ash(%) max. on DM	5.0	3.5	0.9
6.	Sugar(%) Max. on DM	-	-	72.5
7.	Conform (Perg) Max.	10	10	10
8.	Yeast and mould (perg.) max.	20	20	50

MATERIAL REQUIRED

1. Preparation of Shrikhand by traditional method—
   (i) Stainless Steel (S.S.) kettle/vat./degchi
   (ii) Stirrer/Plunger.

(iii) Thermometer (0—110°C).

(iv) Fat and acidity testing unit.

(v) Incubator.

(vi) Muslin cloth.

(vii) Mixer/Kneader.

(viii) Sugar.

(ix) Milk.

(x) Lactic Starter culture.

(xi) Flavouring substances.

(xii) Packaging material.

2. Preparation of Shrikhand by Industrial Method—

(i) Cream separator,

(ii) Plate pasteurizer,

(iii) Storage/incubation tanks,

(iv) Basket centrifuge,

(v) Planetary mixer with variable speeds,

(vi) Filling machine,

METHOD OF PREPARATION

Traditional Method

The traditional method of making Shrikhand is as follows:-

— Take fresh or skimmed milk of good quality.

— Heat the fresh/skimmed milk to a temperature of about 90°C for 5 minutes, followed by cooling to 22°C.

— Inoculate the milk with 0.5 - 1.09 per cent lactic starter culture or dahi of the previous batch and incubate till desired acidity is attained (normally 0.9 per cent lactic acid).

— Allow most of the whey to drain by tying up the dahi in a cloth bag and hanging it up and applying gentle pressure for sufficient time, to drain the whey leaving a semi-solid product called chakka or maska.

— Add about equal weights of sugar to the chakka. The amount of sugar can be reduced or increased depending upon the acidity.

— Knead and blend the chakka and sugar to obtain a product of homogenous consistency.

— Incorporate additives, like flavour, fruits, nuts, colour etc., depending on the preference of the consumers.

— Keep the final product under refrigeration until consumed.

2 *Industrial Method*

The Industrial method of making Shrikhand is as follows:-

— Select good quality milk and separate it into cream and skim milk using a centrifugal cream separator. The skim milk should be completely devoid of fat. Cream should preferably be of high fat (70 per cent or above).

— Heat the skim milk to 90°C for ten minutes followed by cooling to 30°C. Alternatively, a batch pasteurizer can also be used. Simultaneously, pasteurized the required quantity of cream at 85°C for 16 seconds for later use.

— Take the heated skim milk in a pre-sterilized incubation/ storage vat and add 0.5 per cent lactic starter and mix well with the help of a mechanical agitator. Maintain the temperature of the vat at about 30°C with the help of circulation of the warm water.

— Incubate it for about eight hours.

— After the curd has properly set and acidity developed in the range of 0.8 - 1.0 per cent, stop incubation.

— Separate whey by centrifuging the curd for 60 minutes using a basket centrifuge (at about 1100 rpm). Thus, chakka is obtained.

— Transfer the known quantity of chakka into a planetary mixer.

— Add the required amount of pasteurized cream (the fat in the final product should be about six percent) and sugar (about forty two per cent in the final product) to the chakka.

— Mix the contents by running the mixer at variable speeds. Normally, it takes 40 minutes at 110 rpm for getting a homogeneous mass.

— Flavour and other additives may also be added during the mixing of the chakka, sugar and cream.

— Cool the final product and fill in the wax coated paper cups/ polystyrene cups (100 or 500 gm. capacity).

— Store under refrigerated condition.

22

Technology of Khoa Manufacture and Storage

INTRODUCTION

A large quantity of surplus milk becomes available in distantly located villages, for marketing. Although, the dairy professionals and planners strive to collect as much surplus milk as possible from the milk shed areas for centralized processing and distribution, about 5 per cent of the milk produced in the country is still used for the manufacture of Indian milk products. In the absence of adequate resources and proper infrastructure, it is not possible to collect all the surplus milk twice a day from 5.76 lakh tiny villages, scattered in 3.29 million km^2. Quite often, milk collection through any organized system becomes a financial liability involving high costs of transportation and other overheads. The milk producers are unable to establish direct contact with the consumer and there are no regulated markets for milk in the nearest town or city. The extreme climatic conditions such as high temperature and humidity prevailing in the sub-tropics, together with nearly unhygienic systems of milk handling cause rapid spoilage of milk. In such a situation, the milk producers cannot derive the fullest financial benefits from the surplus milk. The Indian dairy products which have a comparatively longer shelf-life are, therefore, manufactured from the surplus milk. Besides economic utilization of milk, Indian milk products form a base for the preparation of a variety of confectionary and related products. Next to ghee, Khoa occupies a prominent place among all the traditional milk products.

DEFINITION

Khoa (mawa, kava, palghoa, etc.) is a concentrated whole milk product obtained by open pan condensing of the milk of cow or buffalo or a mixture thereof. The rapid evaporation of moisture is achieved on a brisk fire with constant stirring and scraping until the desired levels of total solids, flavour and consistency are obtained. According to the Prevention of Food Adultration Act (1955), as amended in 1976, Khoa shall contain not less than 20 per cent fat on an 'as it is' basis and shail be free from the ingredients not commonly found in milk. The manufacture, sale of trading of Khoa containing less than 20 percent fat will attract severe punitive action under the PFA rules.

VARIETIES AND GRADES OF KHOA

The different varieties and grades of khoa sold in the market e.g. pindi, dhap and danedar are needed for various uses. Pindi is used for preparing burfi, peda, gujhia, pista-burfi, coconut burfi and chocolate burfi. Dhap is used in the preparation of gulabjamun, panthoa, carrot and other types of halwa, toffees and coconut balls. Danedar is used in the manufacture of kalakand, malai-ke-laddoo, polangtod, milk-cake, etc.

CHEMICAL COMPOSITION OF KHOA

The chemical composition of khoa varies according to the quality of milk used, the method of preparation, degree of heat-treatment, manner of handling of the product and duration of storage. The average chemical composition of market samples of khoa and that of laboratory samples is given in Table 22.1.

Table 22.1 : Chemical Composition of Khoa.

Sl.No.	Type of sample	Total Solids %	Fat%	Protein %	Lactos e%	Ash %
1.	Pindi	65.0	22.5	19.5	19.4	3.5
2.	Danedar	61.5	20.9	18.4	18.9	3.4
3.	Dhap	56.0	19.4	17.1	16.7	2.9
4.	Laboratory	66.1	22.4	19.6	20.3	3.0

MICROBIOLOGICAL QUALITY OF KHOA

The microbiological load in khoa is used to assess the standard of cleanliness during production, packaging, transportation and storage and to ascertain its keeping quality. The microbiological quality of fresh khoa is presented in Table 22.2. Since micro-organisms multiply at a very fast rate at ordinary temperature and very slowly in the cold it is, therefore, recommended that khoa be stored in cold rooms or refrigerators after manufacture and be transported in refrigerated vessels.

Table 22.2 : Microbiological Quality of Fresh Khoa.

Sl.No.	Type of Organism	Average count per g. of khoa
1.	Total Bacterial count	2700
2.	Acid Producers	600
3.	Proteolytic Bacteria	200
4.	Chromogenic Type	100
5.	Spore Count	200
6.	Yeast and Mould Counts	20
7.	Coliform Count	Nil

METHODS OF MANUFACTURE

The three approaches are suggested for the manufacture of khoa depending upon the needs and facilities available:

— Preparation of khoa at the village level, employing small scale technology, followed by systematic collection, transportation and marketing.

— Collection of surplus milk at the rural milk processing centres located within a radius of 20 km., especially established for the purpose, and conversion of milk into khoa, employing the middle or intermediate technology.

— Large scale manufacture of khoa in modern dairy plants using the mechanized or continuous system.

SMALL SCALE PREPARATION OF KHOA

The small scale technology is the least expensive in terms of capital investment, locally available tools and equipment, and use of local fuel resources. The equipment is manually operated, and a high level of sophistication is not needed. The posts are low and dependence for spare parts outside is totally avoided.

Equipment

In the manufacture of khoa by the traditional method, the equipment required includes:

(i) Heavy bottomed, round steel pan, fitted with two loop handles (Karahi).

(ii) Scraper with a long wooden handle.

(iii) Fire place (hearth) of bricks and a non-smoky fire.

(iv) Milk cans for transport of milk from the producers.

(v) Aluminium containers of one kg capacity for moulding and shaping of khoa.

(vi) A refrigerator for product storage.

(vii) Fat testing facilities.

Quality of Milk

Buffalo's milk is preferred in the trade, because, besides giving higher yield than cow's milk it results in a product of short body and smooth texture, which are the most desirable attributes of khoa for the preparation of sweets. Buffalo's milk is concentrated to four-fold and cow's milk to five-fold giving 25 and 20 per cent yield respectively. It is important to provide guarantees of legal requirements for khoa, minimum fat content of 4.4 per cent in cow's milk and 5.5 in buffalo's milk will ensure quality. These are also the right amounts of fat essential for the production of a smooth textured product suitable for sweet making. Although, a higher fat level improves the quality of khoa, it increases the cost of the product, while any developed lactic acidity tends to produce a grainy, coarse texture and sour taste.

Traditional Process

The standardized milk (4 litres buffalo's milk with 5.5 per cent fat or 5 litres cow's milk with 4.4 per cent fat) is poured into an iron pan and brought to boil by placing over a brick, non-smoky fire. The milk is stirred vigorously by means of a stirrer. This is simultaneously used to scrap off any dried milk film which may otherwise tend to stick and get burnt on the metal surface of the pan. As a consequence of vigorous boiling and constant stirring and scraping, a fairly rapid evaporation of moisture takes place and the milk viscosity increases progressively. The heating is continued till the product's viscosity nearly reaches the rabri stage. At this stage the product starts leaving the sides of the pan and tends to accumulate at the bottom. On a coal fired furnace this stage is usually reached in about 8 to 10 minutes. Soon after, the pan with the contents is removed from the fire and the second pan, with another lot of milk, is placed on the hearth. The contents of the first pan are constantly worked up and down to use the residual heat for final evaporation. Big sized grains, formed as a result of heat coagulation, are broken to achieve a smooth texture with the help of a hand operated wooden bar/stick. The product is then filled in an aluminium container printed with identification mark and kept for cooling. The containers are emptied out from the mould after one hour and transferred to a cool place.

Improved batch method for khoa preparation

A modern assembly for the batch method of khoa manufacture may consist of a stainless steel, jacketed, steam-heated open pan with a steam regulating valve and a pressure guage. However, the cost of such a set up, requiring a stainless steel pan and baby boiler for supplying steam, will increase considerably. About 4 to 5 litre of fresh milk are poured into the kettle. The milk is brought to boil and stirred vigorously by means of a stainless steel stirrer. The stirrer is simultaneously used to scrap the bottom and surface of the kettle to avoid burning of milk solids. As a result of these actions, viz. boiling, stirring and scraping, fairly rapid evaporation of moisture takes place. This process is continued till the consistency of milk reaches a dough stage. At the end of the manufacturing process, the flow of steam is reduced to 0.5 kg/cm^2 from an initial pressure of 2 kg/cm^2 maintained in the beginning. This is necessary to prevent the burning of milk solids. As soon as the product shows signs of leaving the sides of the kettle and forms a bolus at the bottom, the steam supply is totally cut off. The contents of the pan are emptied in a pre-sterilized aluminium container. It takes usually 15 minutes to convert 5 litres of milk into khoa at a time. For best results, the milk should boil vigorously (95°C and above) till the contents reach a pasty consistency and thereafter, the temperature should be lowered to 75 and 80°C. Continuation of high working temperature towards the later stage may result in browning, and a hard body, coarse texture and burnt flavour in the finished product. The higher the speed of stirring (80—90 strokes/minutes), the more desirable is the body and texture of khoa. Dairy plants having the facilities of steam and stainless steel kettles can divert a part of their surplus milk for khoa making and complete with the traditional system in terms of cost, quality and convenience.

PACKAGING AND STORAGE OF KHOA

In most cases, khoa made in the villages is transported to marketing centres in open containers during which it loses weight and gets unduly exposed to atmospheric contamination. Such khoa has a storage life of 3 to 5 days at room temperature, wrapping the khoa in parchment paper or polyethylene will increase the life to about one week. For freshly made khoa, with moisture content ranging from 30 to 35 per cent, packed hot (around 80—85°C) in pre-sterilized tin, cans and sealed immediately with similarly treated lids, a minimum storage life of 15 days at room temperature is assured. Under refrigerated conditions, khoa should normally keep well for 75 to 80 days. Tin containers are, however, very expensive. The flexible packages and their laminates offer the alternate choice for packaging of dairy products. The flexible packages should be sterilized with the help of 100 ppm chlorine solution allowing 5 minutes contact time or pre-sterilized by other methods such as dipping in 2 per cent hydrogen peroxide or potassium sorbat (2 per cent solution). Three-ply laminates of 40 g/m^2 poster paper/0.02 mm aluminium foil/100g low density polyethylene and fore-ply laminates of 50 g/m^2 poster paper/ 0.02 mm aluminium foil/150 g. low density polyethylene are effective for single service containers (500 g. to 1 kg) in which the shelf life of khoa at 30°C and 70 per cent relative humidity could be increased to about two weeks and more than 75 days at 7°C. Addition 0.2 per cent of sorbic acid by weight of khoa at the last stage of its manufacture, enhances the shelf-life up to 20 days at 30°C and for 125 days in cold storage. The addition of preservative to khoa will, however require clearance from PFA authorities.

23

Peda

INTRODUCTION

There are numerous varieties of peda and the methods of their manufacture vary from region to region, depending on the consumer's requirement. Consequently, the sensory and chemical attributes of peda vary considerably. Some prefer white colour, while others may ask for peda with a yellowish colour. Highly cooked to burnt flavour remains the attribute of choice in certain parts of the country. The preference for texture also varies from soft to grittiness. The choice of size and shape is of minor consideration.

COMPOSITION

The quality of khoa, quantity of sugar added and the extent of heating influences the composition of peda. The average chemical composition of peda is given in Table 23.1.

Table 23.1 : Constituents Percentage of Peda.

Constituents	Percentage
Fat	18.00
Proteins	19.50
Lactose	16.31
Ash	2.28
Sucrose	31.80
Moisture	13.50

METHOD OF MANUFACTURE OF PEDA

About 5 liters of buffalo's milk is taken in a pan and heated on a brisk smokeless fire. As soon as the pat formation stage is reached, 400—450g of sugar is added and stirring and scraping is continued until a pasty consistency is obtained. The vessel is removed from the fire and the paste is spread on the walls of the pan for cooling. The product is then removed to a tray where flavour additives may be added, for a less brown colour or cooked flavour, sugar is added at the last stage of khoa-making. Finally, the product is rolled and shaped into circular balls of about 25 g each, measuring 4 cm in diameter and 1.5 cm in height. Paper board cartons or boxes of 250 g to 1 kg capacity are used for packaging. The use of new packaging materials in polystyrene containers may significantly improve the keeping quality of peda besides being a good barrier to moisture evaporation.

24

Khoa Based Sweet - Kalakand

INTRODUCTION

Like burfi and peda, khoa is used as a base material for the manufacture of Kalakand. Though, the chemical composition of kalakand is somewhat similar to burfi, there is a difference between the two on the basis of physical traits. Kalakand has a more distinct cooked flavour and brown colour than burfi. The body of kalakand is also more greasy with a grainy texture, and it has large sized hard grains.

CHEMICAL COMPOSITION

All those factors which are responsible for variations in the chemical composition of burfi and peda, also affect the composition of kalakand. The gross composition of kalakand does not differ significantly from that of burfi.

METHOD OF MANUFACTURE OF KALAKAND

Buffalo's milk, because of its higher fat percentage and lactose, is preferred for kalakand. However, the quality of milk need not be as good for making kalakand as for burfi. Slightly acidic milk (up to 0.20 percent lactic acid) or returned milk can also be used for its preparation.

Standardized milk (6 per cent fat and 9.0 per cent SNF) is taken in a kettle and the heating started. At the first boil 0.01 per cent citric acid, dissolved in small quantity of water, is added to the milk. If milk is slightly acidic there is no need for adding citric acid. Boiling, with simultaneous stirring and scraping, is continued till the pat formation stage. Then sugar at the rate of 30 per cent of khoa or 7 per cent of milk is added to the khoa and heated for another 5 minutes in the kettle the kalakand is removed to be packaged in suitable materials. Large scale production of kalakand is possible from concentrated milk.

25

Khoa Based Sweet - Gulab Jamun

INTRODUCTION

Gulab Jamun is a popular milk sweet all over India. Khoa is conventionally used for its preparation. However, ready to use gulab jamun mix powder is also available in the market. At Amul Dairy, Anand, gulab jamun is made on a commercial scale and marketed in many parts of the country. The desired attributes of gulab jamun are light brown colour, smooth and spherical shape, soft and spongy body, free from both lumps and a hard central core, uniform granular texture, mild cooked and oily flavour, free from doughy feel and fully saturated with syrup. It should have optimum sweetness.

COMPOSITION OF GULAB JAMUN

The gross chemical composition of gulab jamun. Varies widely depending on numerous factors. Some of these are the composition and quality of Khoa, proportion of ingredients (maida), concentration of dough and sugar syrup. Gulab Jamun, prepared under standard conditions, has 25—35 per cent moisture, 65—75 per cent total solids, 7.5—10.5 per cent fat, 6—7 per cent protein, 0.9 to 1.0 per cent ash and 43—48 per cent starch + sucrose. The shelf-life of gulab jamun at ambient temperature, when kept in syrup, is 5—7 days.

METHOD OF PREPARATION

Preparation of gulab jamun in the market is on a small scale batch process. About 1.5 kg dhop khoa (having around 40 per cent moisture) is taken. To this 500 g maida and 7.5 g baking powder are mixed. Balls of uniform size, shape are made after kneading the mixture thoroughly. If the dough appears to be hard and difficult to roll, a little more water is added. The balls should not show any signs of cracks on the surface. In case of delay in frying, cover the balls with a wet clean cloth to prevent drying of the surface.

The balls are fried in a kettle, in hydrogenated oil or ghee at about 130°C for 15—20 minutes. They are removed from the ghee with the help of a perforated ladle and transferred to sugar syrup maintained at 60—65°C. The balls are allowed to soak in the syrup for at least 2 hours.

Sugar syrup is previously prepared by boiling together equal amounts of sugar and water for 15 minutes. Any dirt or impurity that gathers on the surface of the surface of the syrup during boiling is removed with a ladle.

For making gulab jamun from gulab jamun mix powder, the prescribed quantities of powder and water are mixed and kneaded into a uniform dough. The procedure for making balls, their frying and soaking in sugar syrup is the same as discussed above, for gulab jamun. Packaging of gulab jamun, when hot, in heat sealable polystyrene containers enhances its shelf-life.

26

Milk Based Sweet - Burfi

INTRODUCTION

Burfi is a popular milk based confection in which the base matereial, sugar, is added in different proportions and other ingredients are incorporated according to the demand of the consumers. Several varieties of burfi are sold in the market depending on the additives present, viz. plain mawa, nut, chocolate, and rawa burfi. A lot of variations can be observed in the physical attributes of market samples. However, good quality burfi is characterized by moderately sweet taste, soft and slightly greasy body and uniform texture with fine grains. The colour of burfi unless it is chocolate burfi, should be white or slightly yellowish.

COMPOSITION OF BURFI

The chemical composition of burfi depends on the quality and composition of the raw material i.e. milk, amount of sugar and other ingredients. The average quantities of different constituents of burfi are given in Table 26.1.

Table 26.1 : Average Constituents of Burfi.

Constituents	(%)
Fat	20.48
Proteins	14.92
Lactose	15.82
Ash	2.75
Sucrose	30.36
Moisture	15.67

METHOD OF PREPARATION OF BURFI

Buffalo's milk is preferred for making burfi. Milk used for this purpose should not have any objectionable odour/smell and taste, and not more than 0.16 per cent lactic acidity. The COB test should be negative. It should be filtered through a muslin/nylon cloth before use.

Standardized milk (about 6 per cent fat and 9 per cent SNF), 4-5 litres per batch is taken in a kettle and heated on a non-smoky/brick fire. Alternatively, a stainless steel double jacketed kettle can be used where steam heating is possible. Milk is boiled continuously with constant stirring and scraping, to avoid burning at the bottom and sides of the kettle. When a semi-solid consistency is attained and solids start leaving the sides of the kettle, heating is discontinued. Spread the solids on the surface of the kettle for about 5 minutes and then add sugar at the rate of 30 per cent of khoa. Ground sugar will yield a better textured product. Blend the mixture thoroughly with the help of a wooden kneader which has a long handle with one flattened end. When a homogenous mass is achieved, the blend is transferred to trays/moulds. Finally, pieces of rectangular shape of the desired size are cut and packaged in appropriate packaging material. The shelf-life of burfi is considerably enhanced when it is packaged while still hot in ore-treated containers.

Burfi can also be prepared from premade khoa. In this case, hot sugar syrup (300 g of sugar with the minimum possible water) is added to 1 kg khoa and kneaded properly to a homogenous mass. The mixture is heated slightly.

Burfi of acceptable quality can also be made from alternate sources of milk solids, for example, from concentrated milk and mixture of cream and skimmed milk powder.

MICROBIOLOGICAL STANDARDS

The microbiological standards for burfi prescribed by ISI is given in table 26.2.

Table 26.2 : Microbiological standard for Burfi Prescribed by ISI.

Product	Standard Plate Count (cfu/g)	Coliform Count (cfu/g)	Yest and Mold Count (cfu/g)
Burfi	30,000 Max.	-	10 Max.

The '-' Sign stands for 'not recommended'.

27

Chhana Based Sweet - Rasogolla

INTRODUCTION

Rasogolla is the most popular chhana based sweet in Bengal and the adjoining states. In recent years, rasogolla has been exported to some of the western and gulf countries. Its actual preparation is largely in the hands of experienced halwais and no dairy industry has taken up the production on a commercial scale. Rasogolla has a white or slightly yellowish colour. It is round in shape. The most important desirable attribute of this sweet is its sponginess and elasticity.

COMPOSITION OF RASOGOLLA

The average composition of rasogolla is given in Table 27.1.

Table 27.1 : Composition of Rasogolla.

Sl.No.	Constituents	Laboratory samples %	Market samples. (Kernal) %
1.	Moisture	37.0	30.9
2.	Total Solids	63.0	69.1
3.	Sucrose	51.9	55.1
4.	Proteins	6.8	8.0
5.	Fat	4.2	5.7

A wide variation in gross composition may, however, be observed in samples due to variations in the quality of the raw material, method of preparation, concentration of sugar etc.

METHOD OF RASOGOLLA PREPARATION

Cow's milk having 4.0 per cent fat is considered most desirable for making chhana for rasogolla making. The quality of milk should be organoleptically and chemically good. The method of preparation is as follows:

Chhana is the base material for the preparation of rasogolla. Therefore, the quality of the final product will depend on the quality of the base/raw material. For making good quality chhana, cow's milk is standardized to about 4 per cent fat. The milk is heated until it boils, on a non-smoky fire, followed by cooling to 82°C. At this temperature it is coagulated by adding 1 per cent solution of citric/ lactic acid. During coagulation the milk should be stirred gently. The appearance of yellow whey indicates completion of coagulation. The coagulated mass is collected in a muslin cloth and immersed in running tap water to cool for about 10 minutes. Finally, the chhana is hung on a stand for drainage of free moisture/whey.

Chhana is ground in a meat - grinder and, then kneaded by hand to make a soft and smooth dough. If the balls show sign of cracks, a small amount of maida (8—10 g. for 100g. chhana) may be added. The dough is then rolled into small balls by revolving between the palms. The required amount of freshly clarified (50—60 per cent) sugar syrup is brought to the boil in a kettle. The chhana balls are dropped into the boiling syrup. After some time, sufficient foam is produced which covers the balls and facilitates cooking. After about 20 minutes, heating is stopped for a few seconds to determine whether the rasogolla balls have soaked completely in the sugar syrup. This is a sign of complete cooking. During cooking, the balls should be stirred gently with a perforated ladle. At the end of cooking, the rasogolla absorb the sugar syrup and swell to about three times the original size. At this stage, rasogollas are transferred to hot clarified sugar syrup of about 40 per cent consistency. After cooling to room temperature, the product is stored in a refrigerator.

4. MICROBIOLOGICAL STANDARDS

The microbiological limits for satisfactory quality of canned rasogolla prescribed by Indian Standards Institution (ISI) is given in table-2.

Table 27.2 : Microbiological Standard limits (ISI) of Canned Rasogolla.

Product	Standard Plate Count (cfu/g)	Coliform Count (cfu/g)	Yest and Mold Count (cfu/g)
Canned rasogolla	500	Nil	—

The Sign '-' stands for 'not recommended'.

28

Preparation of Kulfi

INTRODUCTION

Kulfi is an indigenous frozen milk product. The method of manufacture of kulfi varies very widely. The conventional method of kulfi-making consists of boiling of milk, addition of sugar, concentration of milk (2:1) and addition of khoa, malai, flavour etc., to the concentrated cooled milk. The mix is then filled in metallic cones and the top of the cone is closed with a lid. The mixture in the moulds is frozen in large earthen vessels containing ice-salt mixture in the ratio of 1:1.

MATERIALS REQUIRED

Milk

Sugar

Khoa

Malai

Flavour

Ice

Coarse Salt

Kulfi Cones

Earthen Pitcher

Wheat flour

Steam jacketed kettle

Stirrer

PROCEDURE

Collect the milk and filter it.

Place the milk in the steam jacketed kettle and heat it with constant stirring.

Add sugar almost at the end of concentration so as to obtain 13 per cent in the final product.

Continue heating and stirring till the milk is concentrated to half of its original volume.

Cool the concentrated milk.

Add khoa, malai, and a flavouring ingredient.

Fill the mix in the cones made-up of aluminium or galvanized sheet.

Place of lids on the mouth of the cones and seal them by placing dough made with wheat flour.

Prepare a brine mixture by mixing salt and ice (1:1). The greater the percentage of salt, the lower the temperature of freezing that can be obtained. Kulfi will be frozen faster in the higher salt-ice ratio.

Place the cones in the brine mixture and cover the vessel.

Shake the earthen pot intermittently.

29

Yoghurt

DEFINITION

Yoghurt is a fermented milk product obtained through the controlled lactic acid fermentation of milk by S. thermophilus and L bulgaricus.

The FAO/WHO standards No. 11 (a) and 11 (b) define yoghurt and flavoured yoghurt respectively as the cogulated milk product obtained by lactic acid fermentation through the action of L-bulgaricus and S. thermophiius from milk. This definition which was used in the first draft of the standard prepared by the secretariat of the milk committee in 1969-70 remained unchanged.

HISTORY

The origin of yoghurt is not very clear. According to some peoples it originated in Asia, where ancient Turks lived as nomads.

TYPES OF YOGHURT

The types of yoghurt produced world-wide can be divided into various categories based on the chemical composition, method of production, flavours and post-incubation processing.

(a) **Types Based on Chemical Composition:**—According to FAO/ WHO (1973), yoghurt may be designated on the basis of fat content as full [above 3.0%] medium (3.02-0.5%) or low (0.5% or below) fat yoghurts.

(b) **Types based on method of production:**—Based on method of manufacture and physical structure of the coagulum, yoghurt can be classified as : (i) set yoghurt, (ii) stirred yoghurt, and (iii) fluid yoghurt.

(i) **Set Yoghurt:-** It is the product where incubation/ fermentation of the milk takes place in the retail container and hence the characteristic coagulum is a continuous semi-solid mass.

(ii) **Stirred Yoghurt:**—It is the type of yoghurt produced after the fermentation has been carried out in bulk and then the coagulum is broken prior to cooling and packaging.

(iii) **Fluid Yoghurt:**—It can be considered as stirred yoghurt with low viscosity e.g. 11% total solids or less.

(C) **Types based on flavour:**—Three different types of yoghurt are in vogue on the basis of flavour :

(i) **Natural or Plain Yoghurt:**—This is the traditional type with sharp acidic taste.

(ii) **Fruit Yoghurt:**—This can be made by the addition of fruits and sweetening agents to the natural yoghurt.

(iii) **Flavoured Yoghurt:**—This is the yoghurt type in which fruit ingredient is replaced with synthetic flavouring and colouring compounds.

(d) **Types Based on Post Incubation Processing:**—Various types of modified yoghurts can now be prepared based on post-incubation processes :

(i) **Pasteurized Yoghurt:**—This type of yoghurt can be processed by conventional methods but after fermentation, yoghurt is heat treated to extend its shelf-life.

(ii) **Frozen Yoghurt:**—This again is prepared in a conventional manner but is subsequently deep-frozen to at least —20°C. It requires higher level of sugar and stabilizers for maintaining the consistency of the coagulum during freezing.

(iii) **Dietetic Yoghurts:**—These are low-caloric yoghurts, low lactose or vitamin/protein fortified yoghurts.

(iv) **Concentrated Yoghurt:**—It has total solids of around 24%.

(v) **Dried Yoghurt:**—It has total solids between 90—94%.

Method of Manufacture:—The common flow diagram for manufacture of different types of yoghurt is presented belowin Fig. 29.1.

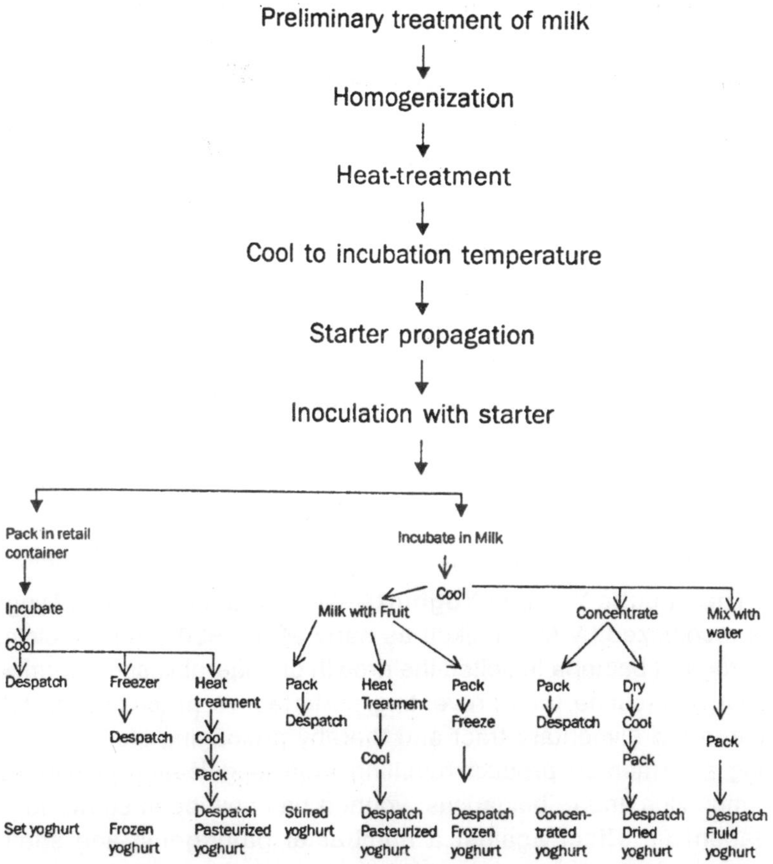

Fig. 29.1 : Flow Diagram for the Manufacture of Yoghurts.

Traditional Method of Yoghurt Making

(i) Concentrate the milk to evaporate ¼ to ⅓ water. Alternatively, add four to five per cent (Non-fat Dried Milk (NFDM) to the whole milk. Heat in the range of 82 to 93°C for 30 to 90 minutes.

(ii) Cool to 42-43°C and inoculate with two to three percent starter (Lactobacillus bulgaricus and Streptococcus thermophilus).

(iii) 'Incubate at 42-43°C for 2.5 to 3.5 hours (acidity of 0.65 to 0.70 per cent as lactic acid) chill the product to 5°C. Further acidity up to 0.9 per cent may develop while the product is being chilled.

(iv) Yoghurt can be kept satisfactorily up to one to two weeks at 5°C.

Industrial Method of Yoghurt Making

(i) Weigh a desired quantity of milk and heat it to 80—90°C for 10 to 20 minutes.

(ii) Cool the milk to 45° to 48°C.

(iii) Add two to three per cent of yoghurt culture and mix well with the milk.

(iv) Keep the milk in clean and sterilized containers for setting.

(v) Incubate the milk in the containers at 45°C till firm coagulum is obtained (approximately) in three to four hours.

(vi) Remove the product from the incubator and keep it at 5°C until distributed to the consumers.

(vii) Clean the equipment and keep it ready for next operation.

Therapeutic Value of Yoghurt:—The therapeutic value of yoghurt was recognized by Metchnikoff as early as in 1900 when he claimed, that yoghurt bacteria inhibited the growth of anaerobic spore formers in the large intestine thus preventing purtrefactive process from taking place in the alimentary tract and thereby prolonging life. By virtue of being a fermented product resulting from acidification of milk by S. thermophilus and L. bulgaricus, yoghurt has now been shown to have antagonistic effect against a number of pathogenic and spoilage organisms both in vivo and in vitro.

Examination of Yoghurt:—The standard methods used for the examination of yoghurt are the standard plate count, yeast and mold count and coliform count. The routine application of these methods in the quality control labs can tremendously improve the quality of the product. In addition to these, the activity of the starter cultures used in the manufacture of yoghurt also needs to be critically monitored periodically to get a product of uniform quality.

Defects of yoghurt:—Flavour defects are common to yoghurt just as they are to any milk product. Perhaps the most common fault is the absence of typical yoghurt flavour and aroma. Assuming that the mother culture contains the desired balance of cocci and rods, insufficient flavour development in the final product usually results from inadequate acid formation. Optimum flavour development occurs only after the acidity reaches about 0.85 per cent but ripening much beyond 0.95 per cent yields a product that is too sour. Aroma compounds are formed over a considerably wider range of acidity. Absence of typical yoghurt flavour and aroma also can result from use of strains of Lactobacillus bulgaricus that produce little of the flavour and aroma substances.

Unclean and bitter flavours in yoghurt sometimes result from using poor quality milk or contaminated starter. Certain strains of Lactobacillus bulgaricus can caruse a bitter taste.

Slow acid production by yoghurt cultures has been traced to bacteriophage attacking the cells of Streptococcus thermophilus. Phage resistant cultures have been obtained, but the body of yoghurt made with these cultures is not as firm as is desired.

Weak curd formation is a serious problem with yoghurt made from milk of normal solids content. According to the results of Pette and Lolkema, a weak curd is most likely to result if the solids content of the milk is low or if a significant amount of the milk is from cows early in the lactation cycle. Also, some cows give milk that inherently forms a weak curd. Firmness of the curd from "Weak Curd" milks can be increased by adding 1 to 2 per cent of dry milk solids or by homogenizing the milk at about 54°C (129.2°F) and a pressure of 3000 pounds per square inch just before inoculation. Addition of a small amount of rennet also increases firmness, but it harms the flavour and texture of the yoghurt. The temperature at which the milk is heated before inoculation also can influence the strength of the curd. Pette and Lolkema advise a heat-treatment of 80°C to 90°C (176°F to 194°F) for 10 minutes to obtain maximum firmness of body.

Some times, but not always, associated with weak curd formation is whey separation, which, according to pette and Lolkema, is caused by an incorrect salt balance in the milk. These workers were able to minimize the defect by reducing the heat-treatment as much as possible and by adding small amounts of calcium chloride to the milk.

30

Production of Sandesh

INTRODUCTION

With an annual milk production of 81 million tones, India now stands as the largest milk producing country in the World. Pattern of milk utilisation in the country indicates that 37.7% of the total milk produced is being converted into various types of indigenous products. Modernisation of the traditional dairy products is long over due in India. The country represents one of the World's largest and fastest growing markets for milk and milk products. Market for indigenous products far exceeds the market for western dairy products. With the increase in availability of liquid milk, refinement in marketing network and improvement in per capita income, there is an increased pressure for restructuring of the indigenous milk product industry.

Indigenous dairy products of the country can be grouped into—

* heat desiccated (*khoa* based),
* heat and acid coagulated (*chhana* based),
* fat rich (*ghee* based), and
* fermented (*dahi, lassi*) products.

Of these, khoa based products are popular in the Northern and Western region, chhana based products in the Eastern region while fermented and fat rich products are popular in all parts of the country. India produces about 900000 tones of *khoa* valued at 45 billion, 900000 of *ghee* valued at 85 billion and 120000 lakh tones of *chhana* valued at 6 billion annually. *Khoa* and chhana form the basis for the preparation of a variety of milk sweets in the country. It is estimated that the value of *khoa* and *chhana* based sweets put together could exceed 100 billion, which is double the value of milk handled by the organised dairy sector. This underlines the significance of indigenous dairy products to the national economy.

Sandesh is a chhana based milk sweet popular not only within the country but in our neighbouring countries as well. Current estimates show that about 80% of chhana produced in the country is used for the manufacture of *sandesh.* This shows the wide popularity of this milk sweet. *Sandesh* is preferentially made using chhana obtained from cow milk. However, technology has been developed to modify buffalo milk in the preparation of *chhana* to make it suitable for the manufacture of *sandesh.* Inspite of the wide popularity and increasing market for *sandesh,* no attempt has so far been made to mechanise the production of this traditional milk product.

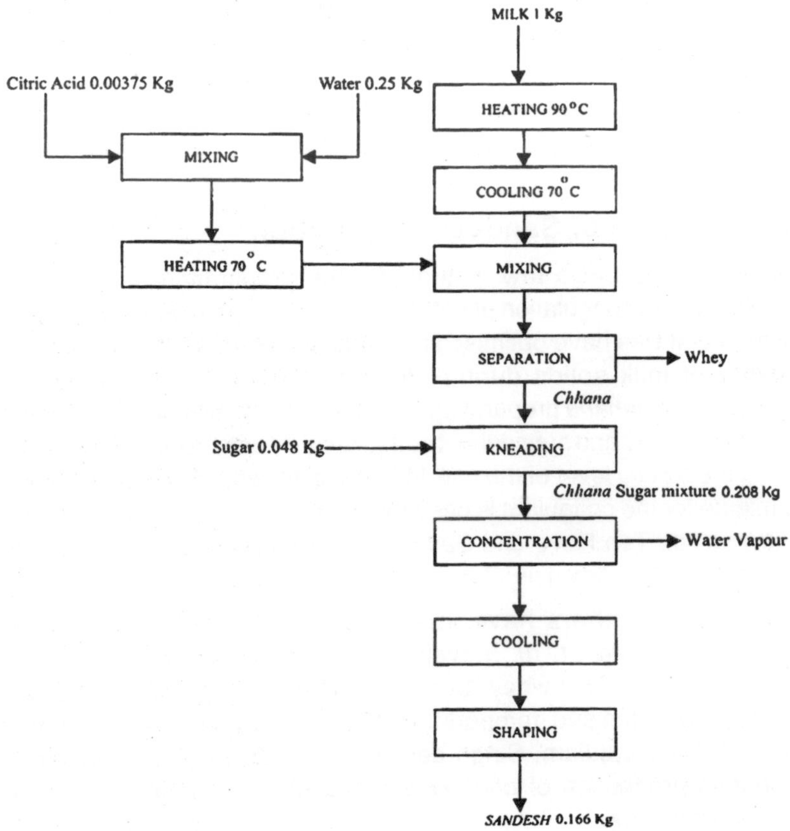

[1] Head, KAU Dairy Plant, Kerala Agricultural University, Trichur. [2] Professor, Agricultural and Food Engineering Department, Indian Institute of Technology, Kharagpur.

Fig. 30.1 : Process and Material Flow Chart for Production of Sandesh.

Traditional Method of Sandesh Preparation

Traditionally, sandesh is prepared by the local *halwais* on a small scale to meet local demands. In the traditional method of manufacture, *halwais* produce *sandesh* by heating a mixture of kneaded *chhana* with cane sugar in a shallow iron pan kept directly over fire with continuous stirring until the mixture develops the required consistency and characteristic flavour. The pan and the scraper form the essential part of the equipment for its production. Scrapping of the *chhana-sugar* mixture during heating is very important that in many cases the operator's skill is the single most important factor governing the quality of the finished product.

As a part of the effort made to standardise the production of various indigenous milk sweets to make it suitable for industrial scale production, the technology of manufacture of *sandesh* has been standardised. The various unit operations required for the manufacture of *sandesh* have been identified and shown in the process and material flow chart (Fig.30.1).

Mechanisation of Sandesh Preparation

Chhana, the basic raw material for the preparation of *sandesh* is obtained by acid coagulation of hot milk and subsequent drainage of whey. Jonkman and Das have optimised the various factors, which influence the recovery of milk solids during *chhana* preparation. The optimised parameters for *chhana* preparation includes heating milk to 95°C, followed by cooling to 70°C and subsequent coagulation by adding citric acid solution to bring the acidity level of the milk to 0.4% lactic acid. A residence time of one minute for the coagulam is desirable before draining the whey through a muslin cloth. Ten Hove and Das have given a prediction model for the recovery of milk solids using fat content of milk as a variable.

Many researchers have attempted mechanisation for chhana preparation. Aneja *et. al.,* developed a mechanical strainer for the continuous drainage of whey. Considering the heating and cooling rates for milk and optimised temperature for acid coagulation and time of residence for coagulam, Singh designed and developed a system for continuous production of *chhana,* which gives the maximum recovery of solids from milk.

Mechanisation of *sandesh* manufacture requires a method for the proper mixing and kneading of *chhana* sugar mixture, cooking of *chhana* sugar mixture in a suitable heat exchanger to get the proper consistency and texture, followed by shaping the product to the required shape.

Mixing of cane sugar and its proper kneading is an important unit operation in *sandesh*-making. In the traditional method, mixing of *chhana* and sugar is done with hand. This operation can be done in a batch process. For mechanisation of this process, a planetary mixer, which is used for dough-making in bread and cake industry can be used for mixing of *chhana* sugar mixture.

For the mechanised method of *sandesh* manufacture, it is desirable to have a high temperature short time process for maintaining the desirable qualities and nutrition of the product. Extrusion is a versatile high temperature short time cooking process, which has become established for the continuous manufacture of new and traditional products. Extrusion cooking applications in food industry today cover a wide range of food products based on starches, cereals, proteins, and sugars. Extrusion cooking technique helps in utilisation of raw material that so far never had a serious economic importance. The range of food processing requirements and introduction of new products has resulted in the development of a variety of food extruders.

Vented extruders are significantly different from non-vented extruders in design and in functional capabilities. This type of extruder is equipped with one or more openings called vent ports in the extruder barrel, through which volatiles can escape. Thus vented extruder can extract volatiles from the material being processed in a continuous fashion. These types of extruders are mainly used in polymer industry.

Development of suitable heat exchangers for the concentration of viscous food material has always been a challenge to food engineers. Extruder can be considered as a heat exchanger. Apart from having a good heat exchange surface, the barrel wall is wiped clean at each passage of a screw flight, thus making the extruder a scraped surface heat exchanger. The conventional heat transfer equipments are not suitable for certain evaporation application, particularly those involving heat sensitive and viscous material. Considering the capability of vented screw extruder in the removal of volatile compounds including moisture in polymeric extrusion, an attempt was made to develop a vented extruder for application in the cooking of *chhana* sugar mixture for the mechanisation of *sandesh* production.

Optimisation of Processing Parameters for Mechanised Production

As a part of the effort made to mechanise the production process of sandesh, Rajendra Kumar and Das (2002), had optimised the parameters for mixing, kneading and cooking of *chhana* sugar mixture. The effect of initial moisture content of *chhana,* temperature and time of cooking the *chhana* sugar mixture was determined on final moisture content, hardness and texture of the prepared *sandesh.* In their studies, the initial mixing of *chhana* and sugar was done in the planetary mixer. They observed that after 5 minutes of mixing in the planetary mixer, kneading of the *chhana* sugar mixture was necessary. Kneading reduces the size of the *chhana* and sugar particles, extending further the degree of mixing of the cane sugar with *chhana.* Kneading also helped to produce smaller grain size in *sandesh.* A stainless steel screw kneader was fabricated for this purpose. The chhana sugar mixture after mixing was fed into the hopper of the kneader. The gap between the screw tip and the end cover was adjustable by rotating the end cover. Passage of *chhana* sugar mixture through this gap carried out the kneading. The kneader screw was rotated at 75 rpm (revolutions per minute).

To optimise the cooking parameters, Rajendra Kumar and Das (2002), used an experimental set-up for conducting batch experiments where cooking temperature could be varied. Experiments conducted to optimise the various cooking parameters showed that the heating should be done under controlled conditions since the product texture is greatly dependent on the temperature of heating. To get the product with good sensory qualities, it has been found that temperature of heating should be kept below 75°C.

As it is evident that the method of *sandesh* making involves low temperature cooking of chhana sugar mixture, maintenance of hygienic conditions during its preparation is very much essential to produce the product within allowable microbial load. To achieve this, mechanisation of its production process is the only solution.

The optimised time of cooking as obtained from batch experiments conducted in their study for production of *sandesh* was 4.6 minutes and the temperature of cooking 75°C. The initial moisture content of *chhana* for the mechanised cooking process was found as 48%.

Vented Extruder for the Continuous Cooking of Chhana Sugar Mixture

During cooking, water evaporation and concentration of solids in *chhana* sugar mixture take place. In the study, a vented extruder was developed for the cooking, removal of water vapour, cooling and shaping operations used for the production of *sandesh.* For shaping the product, a round die was used at the exit of the extruder. In this and in all other extruders, the barrel is wiped clean at each passage of screw flight, thus making the extruder a scraped surface heat exchanger.

The single screw vented extruder developed in this study had : (i) feed section, (ii) evaporation section, and (iii) cooling section. In the evaporation section, the volume of the material in the screw channel after each rotation of the screw gets reduced due to evaporation of moisture. As this would have resulted in a partially filled screw, the screw helix angle after each turn of the screw was reduced such that the volume of screw channels after each rotation was reduced. In the cooling section, as no water evaporation takes place, the helix angle was kept constant.

In the present extruder, the initial helix angle in the feed section was fixed at 17.4°. Rajendra Kumar and Das developed a theoretical model for calculating the various dimensions of a single screw vented extruder. Using this theoretical model, the dimensions of the vented extruder were obtained and the helix angle of each flight in the evaporation section was calculated by iterative procedure using a computer programme. The designed feed rate of the extruder was 4.5 kg h^{-1} at 7 rpm screw speed.

Heating of the feed during its conveyance through the evaporation section of the extruder was done by steam. A steam jacket around the screw barrel was provided for this purpose. The thickness of the jacket was 0.025 m and in order to prevent heat loss, 0.025 m glass wool insulation was provided with stainless steel cladding outside the jacket.

The barrel of the extruder was cut open with a rectangular slit 6 mm wide through which water vapour could escape. To prevent spillage of product escaping outside through the vent port, a rectangular hopper was fixed on the barrel fitting to the size of the vent port.

In the cooling section, facility for cooling the concentrated product leaving the evaporation section was done by providing a cooling water jacket. In this section, the helix angle of the screw was kept constant.

Temperature of barrel was controlled by regulating the flow of steam through a steam control valve. A fuzzy logic microprocessor-based process controller was used for this. The arrangement of the temperature controller u§ed for the vented extruder is shown in Fig. 30.2.

Testing of Vented Extruder

The optimised parameters obtained from the experiments conducted by Rajenda Kumar and Das were used for the testing of a vented extruder developed for *the* continuous cooking of *chhana* sugar mixture for the mechanised production of *sandesh.*

The extruder was put into operation after the temperature settings in the PID controller. Saturated steam from the boiler was allowed to pass into the motorised steam control valve, which automatically regulated the flow of steam into the steam jacket of the vented extruder depending upon the output signal it received from the PID controller. Extruder was run initially for twenty minutes to stabilise the temperature of the barrel so that temperature fluctuation during running with the product could be minimised.

For the preparation of the feed material *(chhanna*-sugar mixture), cow milk was used. The *chhana* after gravity drainage was centrifuged in a basket centrifuge rotated at 1500 rpm for 8 minutes for further

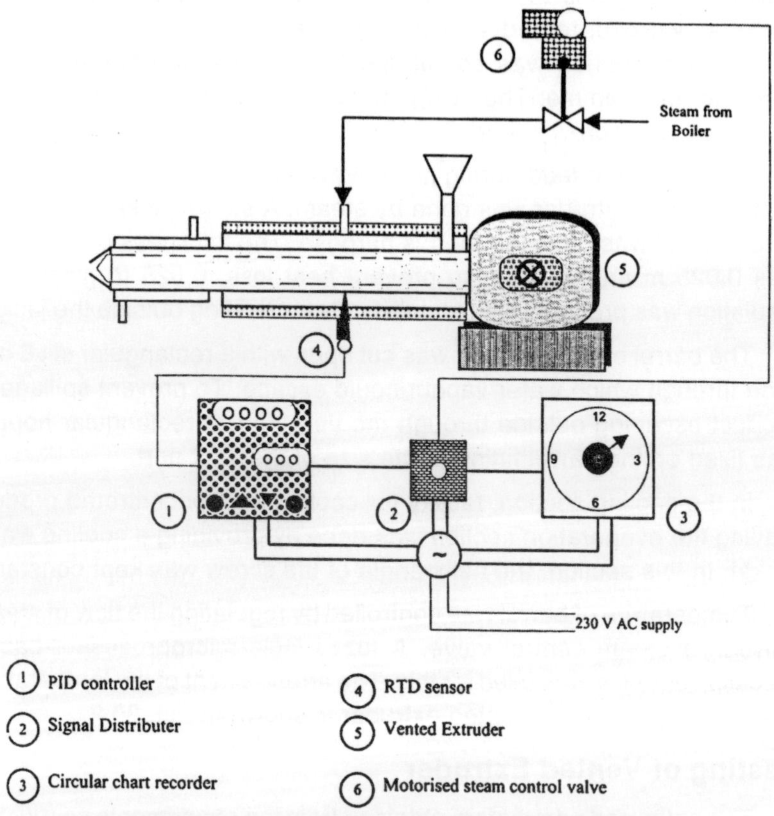

Fig. 30.2 : Schematic Arrangement of the Vented Extruder.

expulsion of whey. Centrifugal drainage of whey was necessary to further reduce the moisture content of *chhana* quickly. After the initial mixing of sugar with *chhana* in the planetary mixer, kneading of the mixture was done in a screw kneader.

After stabilization of barrel temperature, feed was introduced into the extruder through the feed hopper. Cooling water was admitted into the cooling section of the extruder. Feed, which consisted of kneaded *chhana* sugar mixture was taken by the screw flight while rotating and conveyed forward through the evaporation section, cooling section and finally extruded through the round die provided at the exit. During movement of feed through the evaporation section, no vent flow of product was noticed through the vent port. This infers that no pressure build-up took place in the evaporation section. The comparatively lower rpm of the screw might have also helped in preventing vent flow of the product. Product coming out of the extruder was found to be continuous and uniform in the shape of a rod. Product was collected in a clean container and then packed in pre-sterilized polyethylene bags and kept under refrigerated storage.

Evaluation of *Sandesh*

The moisture content of extruded *sandesh* varied from 0.281 to 0.290 (28.1—29%) with an average value of 0.286 (28.6%). Hardness is one of the important textural properties, which decides the sensory property of soft grade *sandesh.* Hardness of *sandesh* depends on the temperature and time of cooking. Hence its objective measurement is an important parameter that decides the optimum temperature and time of cooking. Hardness of *sandesh* was measured using Stevens Texture Analyzer

Hardness of extruded *sandesh* was observed to be between 90 and 95 with an average value of 93 grams. This is within the desirable limits for soft grade *sandesh.* The extruded *sandesh* obtained showed great resemblance to the *sandesh* available in the market. The water activity of extruded *sandesh* was measured using Aqua Lab. The value was found to vary between 0.921 and 0.925 with an average value of 0.923. Sen and Rajoriah have reported the value of water activity as 0.92 for *sandesh* samples analysed from market.

31

Manufacture of Shrikhand by Ultrafiltration Process

INTRODUCTION

The production of shrikhand is so far limited to individual houses and small dairies. The traditional method involves the preparation of curd or dahi, preparation of chakka by draining off whey from the curd by suspending for about 12—18 hours in muslin cloth bags and blending additives like sugar, flavor and colour. Thus, the conventional shrikhand-making technology is a tedious and time-consuming process. Traditional method of shrikhand making also allows the whey proteins to drain along with whey during the process of chakka making. Whey contains about 20 per cent of milk proteins of high biological value. Thus, there is a need for popularizing the production and consumption of this highly nutritious product by, introducing improved methods of manufacture, storage and marketing of the product so as to meet the required standards of quality, nutritive value and organoleptic preferences of the people in different regions of the country.

Ultraftltration is a pressure-driven process, which has found its way to several industrial applications during the last two decades. By the application of this technology, to make, so-called ultrafiltered chakka, the whey proteins having high biological value could be recovered. This technology also helps to get higher yield of chakka due to the recovery of whey proteins and easy automation, and better process control.

This investigation was therefore undertaken with the following objectives:

- To study the effect of processing temperature and pressure during ultrafiltration (UF) of whole milk, on the permeate flux pattern and the rejection factor of major components.

- To study the effect of degree of concentration of UF whole milk on the permeate flux pattern, rejection factor of major components, physico-chemical and organoleptic properties of shrikhand.

MATERIALS AND METHODS

Ultrafiltration (UF) Unit

The membrane processing system, installed at the Student's Experimental Dairy Plant of the Dairy Science College, KVAFSU, was used for the study. The unit was procured from PMI Process Systems, Jayanagar, Bangalore. The membrane module was of spiral wound type and the material was polyethersulphone with a molecular weight cut-off (MWCO) of 10,000 Daltons. The surface area of the membrane was 5.57m^2. Samples of feed, permeate and retentate were taken for analysis and the flux values given are average of three runs.

$$\text{Rejection factor} = \frac{C_1 - C_p}{C_1}$$

C_1 = concentration of the component in the feed.

C_p = concentration of the component in the permeate.

Rejection factor lies between 0 and 1.

$$\textbf{Concentration factor}\ \text{(CF)} = \frac{\text{Volume/weight of the feed}}{\text{Volume/weight of the retentate}}$$

BASKET CENTRIFUGE

Basket centrifuge (REMI, Bombay) was used for whey drainage from the curd to prepare chakka.

SHRIKHAND MAKING

Samples of retentate and permeate were taken for analysis of total solids, protein, minerals and lactose content. Total solids was done by gravimetric method, protein was analyzed by kjeldahl, minerals by ashing and lactose was determined by difference method. Results were analyzed using Completely Randomized Design (CRD) to test the statistical significance.

Whole milk

↓

Standardisation (4 % fat & 8.5 % SNF)

↓

Heat treatment (95°C / 5 min)

↓

Cooling to 30°C

↓

Addition of 2 % culture *(Lactococcus lactis* and *Lactococcus lactis spp. diacetilactis,* 1:1)

↓

Incubation (30°C, 14—16 hours, till acidity reaches 1 % lactic acid)

↓

Curd

↓

Whey drainage (8 hours)

↓

Chakka

↓

Sugar (40 % by weight of chakka)

↓

Kneading

↓

Shrikhand

Fig. 31.1 : Shrikhand by Traditional Method (Control).

Sensory Evaluation

A panel of judges judged the samples of shrikhand. The scores were awarded on 9-point hedonic scale, ranging from 9 (liked extremely) to 1 (disliked extremely).

Whole miik

↓

Standardization (4% fat & 8.5% SNF)

↓

Heating (to the optimum temperature of 50°C)

↓

Ultrafiltration (at 50—C/0.4 MPa)

↓

→Permeate

Retentate (CF 3 / 4 / or 5)

↓

Heating (95°C / 5 min.)

↓

Cooling to 30°C

↓

Inoculation (30°C) using lactic culture @ 3/ 4/or 5 % of the retentate

↓

Incubation (30°C) till acidity reaches 0.8% lactic acid

↓

Curd

↓

Basket centrifuge (1100 rpm / 90 min.)

↓

Pressing (0.1 MPa / 10 min.)

↓

Chakka

↓

Sugar (40 % of the weight of chakka)

↓

Kneading

↓

Shrikhand

Fig. 31. 2 : Shrikhand by Ultrafiltration process.

RESULTS AND DISCUSSION

Standardised whole milk was ultrafiltered to concentration factor 3 (CF3) at different temperature and pressure combinations in batch mode. The permeate flux values at three different pressures of 0.3/ 0.4 / or 0.5 MPa were recorded at constant temperature (50°C) and also at three different temperatures of 45/50 or 55°C were recorded at a constant pressure of 0.4 MPa. From the time of start, there was a gradual decrease in flux. This phenomenon was also reported by Kuo and Cheryan and Rao. The gradual decline in flux may be due to concentration polarization (CP) or fouling of the membrane. In the study, the initial permeate flux was highest for the treatment 0.5 MPa, but no significant difference was observed between the treatments in final permeate flux values.

The rejection of major components like total solids, minerals, fat, protein and lactose at different temperature - pressure combinations were studied and the results are given in Table 31.1. At constant temperature (50°C) the rejection of total solids, minerals, protein and lactose decreased with increase in TMP, also at constant pressure (50°C), the rejection of the major components decreased with increase in TMP. The membrane was found to retain almost all the fat in the feed stream. The treatment 50°C / 0.4 MPa resulted in considerably high retention of total solids and protein and lower retention of minerals and lactose when compared to other treatments. Hence, 50°C / 0.4 MPa was selected for further studies. According to Rao, 50°C is ideal for processing dairy fluids by UF. Moreover, Sharma and Reuter, used the similar temperature-pressure combination for the preparation of UF-shrikhand from skim milk.

Table 31.1 : Effects of Various Degree of Concentration of Whole Milk on Permeate Flux values during Ultrafiltration at 50°C and 0.4 MPI in batch mode.

Time (Minutes)	Flux ($lh^{-1}m^{-2}$)		
	CF3	CF4	CF5
5	10.42	10.42	10.42
10	9.61	9.61	9.61
15	8.97	8.97	8.97
20	8.52	8.52	8.52
25	7.18	7.18	7.18
30	—	6.21	6.21
35	—	5.39	5.39
40	—	—	4.75
45	—	—	4.62
50	—	—	4.49

Standardised whole milk was also ultrafiltered at 50°C/ 0.4 MPa to CF 3/4 or 5. The permeate flux pattern, the rejection factor of major components, composition of whey, chakka and shrikhand, penetration values of chakka and shrikhand and sensory attributes of the final product were studied. CF3 took lesser time for processing when compared to CF4 and CF5.

The rejection of major components (Table 31.2) viz., total solids, minerals, protein and lactose increased with increase in concentration levels. The increased content of minerals and lactose may be attributed to the increased clogging of the membrane pores leading to concentration polarization and fouling which results in higher retention of these components in the final product. With increase in concentration factor of whole milk, though there is higher rejection of protein, there is also higher retention of minerals and lactose that are undesirable.

Table 31.2: Effect of different Temperature and Pressure Combinations on rejection factor of Major Components during Ultrafiltration of Whole Milk in batch mode.

Temperature/ Pressure Combinations	Rejection Factor				
	Total Solids	Minerals	Fat	Protein	Lactose
50°C/0.3 MPa	0.57^{a}	0.80^{a}	0.98^{a}	0.84^{a}	0.04^{a}
50°C/0.4 MPa	0.55^{a}	0.70^{b}	0.98^{a}	0.83^{a}	0.02^{ab}
50°C/0.5 MPa	0.49^{b}	0.50^{d}	0.97^{a}	0.70^{c}	0.01^{b}
45°C/0.4 MPa	0.56^{a}	0.78^{a}	0.98^{a}	0.84^{a}	0.04^{a}
55°C/0.4 MPa	0.54^{b}	0.64^{c}	0.97^{a}	0.81^{b}	0.01^{b}
CD	0.051	0.041	0.018	0.018	0.020
F-value	3.847	87.545	0.605	113.00	3.737

All values are averages of 3 replications. $^{a, b, c, d,}$ within a column, means bearing at least one common superscript are statistically similar ($p < 0.05$).

With increase in CF levels, sensory scores for colour and appearance, body and texture, flavour and overall acceptability of UF shrikhand reduced. This may be due to high total solids and high mineral content in treated samples. Judges also felt that at higher levels of CF shrikhand was heavy and slightly salty in taste. This is probably due to higher retention of some minerals in UF concentrated milk. Control had significantly higher score than the treatments, but no significant difference was observed between the control and the treatment CF 3 with respect to the above sensory attributes. The result is in accordance with the

Table 31.3: Effect of Concentration Factor of whole Milk on rejection factor of Major Components during Ultrafiltration in batch mode.

Concentration Factor	Rejection Factor				
	Total Solids	Minerals	Fat	Protein	Lactose
3.	0.54[b]	0.55[c]	0.98[a]	0.78[b]	0.02[b]
4.	0.56[a]	0.58[b]	0.98[a]	0.79[b]	0.04[a]
5.	0.57[a]	0.62[a]	0.97[a]	0.81[a]	0.05[a]
CD	0.016	0.016	0.016	0.014	0.014
F-value	3.00	37.00	1.00	7.429	29.714

All values are averages of 3 replications. [a, b, c, d] within a column, means bearing at least one common superscript are statistically similar ($p < 0.05$).

findings of Sharma and Reuter. Among the treatments, the judges accepted CF 3 shrikhand. The sensory attributes are shown in Tables 31.4 and 31.5. In colour and appearance attribute, there is no significant deference between control and CF3. But scores of CF4 and CF5 were significantly lower than that of control. Moreover judges felt that in CF4 and CF5, the

Table 31.4: Effect of Concentration Factor on Sensory Characteristics of Shrikhand.

Sensory Characteristics	Control	CF 3	CF 4	CF 5
Appearance	Semi-solid, bright and glossy in appearance	Semi-solid, slightly hard in appearance	Solid and hard body	Solid, very hard body
Body & texture	Semi-solid, soft, smooth uniform consistency showing a characteristic firmness & pliability and shall show smooth texture without any sign of graininess.	Semi-solid, slightly hard showing firmness and pliability, smooth texture with a few grains	Semi-Solid, moderately hard, firm and not pliable with some big grains	Solid, hard, very firm non-pliable, very grainy
Flavour	Clean, pleasant, sweetish-sour flavour, representing blend of added flavour	Clean, pleasant, with sweetish sour slightly chalky flavour sugar and of fermented milk solids	Clean, sweetish sour, chalky	Sweetish sour, salty and lacks in clean

product appeared to have hard body. Similarly in body and texture, CF3 was comparable to control, whereas CF4 and CF5 possessed moderately hard to hard body, moderately grainy to very grainy texture, which was found to be unacceptable. In flavour, CF 3 has clean, pleasing flavour which was similar to that of control. Whereas in other two treated samples, these characteristics were lacking. These were also reflected in the scores awarded by the judges (Table 31.5). Hence CF 3 was judged as the best among the three treatments tried out.

Table 31.5: Effect of Concentration Factor of whole Milk during Ultrafiltration on Sensory Attributes of Shrikhand.

Treatments	Sensory Attributes			
	Colour and Appearance	Body and texture	Flavour	Overall Acceptability
Control	8.00^{a}	8.20^{a}	7.50^{a}	7.80^{a}
CF3	7.00^{a-b}	7.30^{ab}	7.40^{ab}	7.40^{a}
CF4	6.60^{b}	6.50^{b}	6.70^{b}	6.50^{b}
CF5	6.00^{a}	5.40^{c}	6.10^{b}	5.90^{c}
CD	1.218	0.905	0.764	0.589
F-value	4.283	15.525	6.603	6.805

All values are averages of 3 replications. $^{a, b, c,}$ *within a column, means bearing at least one common superscript are statistically similar ($p < 0.05$).*

32

Preparation of Traditional Sweets

KARAH (HALWA)

The halwa prepared from either flour or semolina forms a part of parsad and ritual servings. It is prepared and served in sacred shrines, gurudwaras, temples and during several religious ceremonies. The consumption of halwa is thus enormous. It is prepared by toasting semolina/flour in ghee to a peculiar browning and aroma to which a thin syrup of sugar and water is added and then it is cooked to the required consistency. It may be enriched and garnished with dry fruits. A quick cooking mixture for this can be prepared after dry toasting of semolina to which fat and water may be added at the time of consumption.

Toasting semonlina/flour in ghee to peculiar browning and aroma to which a thin syrup of sugar and water is added and then it is cooked to the required consistancy. It may be enriched and garmished with dray fruits. A quick cooking mixture for this can be prepared after dry toasting of semolina to which fat and water may be added at the time of consumption.

INSTANT MIX FOR HALWA

It is prepared by roasting/cooking and drying of individual ingredients and blending in suitable proportions. The mixes are generally packed in polyethylene, polypropylene of metallised polyerter packs. Because all the ingredients undergo heat treatment during cooking/drying operation, infestation during storage is not a serious problem but care should be taken to avoid chances of contamination during packaging. Uniform distribiution of ingredients in the manufacture of instant imxes is amajor technoogical constraint. Loss of volatiles during storage and resulting chager in flavour vis., off-flavours resulting from oxidation of lipids is one fo the limiting factor in shelf-life determination. Use of oleoresin and microencapsulatee flavours is likely to prove useful in proper blending of flavour and in minimising losses of vloatiles during storage. Recentrly some of rnicroencapsulated cardamom oil has been tried in halwa mix by DFRL. About 80% of the added flavour was reatained in microencapsulated flavour incorporated halwa mix as compared to 50% retention in powdered cardamon added product.

Degree of sturation and ftty acid composition of oils used during roasting or seasoning mainly determines the stability of the mix. Generally, vanaspati has been found most suitable in imprating longest shelf-life to halwa, as compared to refined groun nut oil, palmolein and cottonseed oil. Dsepite very good quality of instant mixes, their market share among processed foods is negligilbel. However, these are items of common Indian dietary and their demand is expected to increase in the coming years.

SHELF STABLE HALWA

Besides instant halwa mixes, processes have also been developed for preservation of halwa in ready toeat state by using either Hurdle Technology or thermal processing in retort pouches by DFRL. Thermally processed halwa is regularly supplied to Department of Ocean Development for members of Antarctica Expeditions. Except slight fading of colour and brown discolouration, no spoilage has been observed in retort pouch processed halwa. The know-how for retort pouch processing of halwa is avilabie from DFRL, Mysore through NRDC. However, due to high cost of cans and retort pouches, thermally processed halwa is relatively costly in comparison to instant mixes. *Ready to eat halwa* has also been preserved by Hurdle Technology using antimycotic agents and original taste. Becasue of lower cost on packaging and machineries, cost of finished products processed by hurdle technology is much less as compared to retort pouch processed halwa.

CHOORMA/PANJIRI

Are prepared and consumed in winters. Panjiri is consumed by women in abundance after child birth.

PINNIS

Pinnies are prepared by raosting wheat flour/powdered dals (moong sabut and mashdhuli) in lots of pure ghee. The taste of pinnies prepared by grand mother still lingers on tongues. These are invariably prepared in winters with lots of desi ghee and dry fruits. Grand mother notion says that these sharpen brain and provide takat (mental strenght) to school/college going generation. Product is very popular in the north.

33

Gulab Jamun/Rasgullas

GULAB JAMUN/RASGULLAS:—Gulab Jamun/Rasgullas arecommon sweets that contain what flour and are consumed enormously in the north. *Instant gulab jamun mix, Jelabi mix and Rasgulla mix :* Such mixes based on chemical leavening are prepared by blending wheat flour, milk flour, milk powder, vegetable oil and leavening agents in suitable proportions and are marketed mostly by packing them in plastic film pouches followed by duplex board cartons. Among these instant gulabjamun mix is most popular and has highest sales. Since only one unit operation of dry blending of ingredients is involved, these are no major constraints faced during the manufacture of instant mixes except occasional problem of uneven mixing of chemical leavening. During storage, however, all the mixed lend to develop infestation. Heating of wheat flour and /or low dose (50—100 krads) irrdatiation of packaged mixes have been found to be effective. Control of granularity, moisture land adequate missing are other essential requirements for adequate product acceptability.

CHAAMP, KALEJI, KEEMA: Prepared from wheat gluten are being sold in Paharganj since decades. Sales are enormous.

RICE PRODUCTS

India is the second largest producer of rice in the world. The predominant varieties of rice recommended for cultivation in Punjab are PR 106, PR 111 (superfine), IR 8 and Jaya (coarase) and Basmati 370, 386 and Pusa Basmatti (Basmati). Rice is being consumed in the form of traditional products which are listed as follows :

MARUNDA: Marunda is prepared from rice and sugar. A product resembling marunda in mechanised units (Grain slices), prepared a from broken or whole rice is becoming popular in Europe.

PHIRNI : Rice paste is cooked with milk. Chilled and served as sweet dish.

KHEER : Kheer is a variation sweet dish. The rice is cooked in milk and served hot or cold after addition of wager (dry fruit).

GUR WAALE CHAWAL : are prepared by mixing cooked rice, jaggery and ghee and are served steaming hot as a sweet dish.

BHELPURI: Contains expanded rice mixed with spices. It is a variation snack in homes or off day outing treat.

CHIRVA : Chirva with makhane form part of prasad in many shrines. It is also used to prepare sweet, salty and sour evening snacks.

MURMURA/KHEEL : Puffed and expanded products. Forms part of Rajasthani bhujia or fried salty snacks.

PULAV : Rice pulav with pre-cooked vegetables or meat is called biriani. It is consumed to quite an extent in the north.

KHICHRI : Rice and split channe ki daal is a common easily digestible meal for people with weak stomach. It is also used with curd forms as a part of ritual for people going to attend important job.

PHULWARIAN : Phulwarian are like extruded rice pallets which expand on frying and are consumed as snacks. In India many extruded products are prepared by housewives themselves or by skilled artisans from rice and legumes and served after frying as snacks. With the advent of cooker extruders, a few companies have started marketing extruded pellets (fryums) which need frying before use and ready to eat expanded and spiced snacks in attractive packs. Both these type products are prepared from wheat flour with or without potato or corn flour.

Extruded pellets are prepared from wheat, rice or maize flours or from their blends. After proper conditioning and equilibration, the ingredients are cooked in a primary extruder. The cooked material is then cooled and densified in a secondary extruder. In the secondary stage the temperature of the extrudate is kept below 100 °C to eliminate product expansion. Immediately after expansion the moisture content is around 20—25.5 which is brought down to 7-8 % by hot air drying in tunnel dryer. The dried pellets are packed in attractive plastic film packs. These pellets equilibrate to 0.45—0.60 a and remain stable for more than six months at room temperature. Before consumption these have to be fried in oil which imparts crispness, softness and about 4—6 times volume expansion. The products have excellent storage stability and impart resistance and can be transported easily. These are also relatively less costly to expanded ready to eat snacks.

34

Winter Products

MARUNDA : Is a sweet product prepared from puffed rice. Sugar with water is heated to desire consistency and puffed rice rolled into it to a sheet of uniform thickness and cut to pieces of desired sizes and shapes.

GACCHAK : Is a product prepared from jaggery and groundnut. Peanuts are dry roasted and jaggery heated and modified to desired consistency. Both are mixed and moulded into desired sizes and shapes.

REORIAN : Is a product prepared by heating sugars till they could be drawn into single thread. Now on they are pulled on or off a wooden speck for quite some time (process is quite labour intensive). Now it is cut to pieces and at higher temperatures coated with sesameseeds (oilseeds) which get fixed on sugar balls resulting into an attractive candy.

All they above products are consumed to a considerable extent during winters in India. These products have markets worth trillions of rupees. Unfortunately, there exists no quality control and no standards have been laid down for such products. These products are prepared and sold very unhygenically. They have a number of problems of getting soggy, sugar sticking to hand when they absorb moisture. With variation in market batches of rice, sesame and peanuts, quality of these products varies considerably. There are also wide batch to batch variations due to uncontrolled conditions.

Hence work on such products, standardization of recipes, development of machinery and technology would go a long way in encouraging trade between countries. Food processing industry though in infancy in India is expanding at a rapid pace and would welcome international collaboration with foreign companies in production and export of such traditional products.

SUMMER DRINKS

SATTU (BARLEY WATER) : Is a very popular summer drink and is supposed to have a medicinal value and safeguards against sunstroke as per popular belief amongst people. It is prepared by soaking, toasting, grinding barley and preparing a drink with sugar or jaggery,. With increase in working couples in India and families going nuclear such products are waning off and are difficult to prepare at home. A ready beverage thus will have a great scope. It would help integrated use of rice milling machinery that operates seasonally.

GANNE KA RAS (CANE JUICE): People prefer to consume it fresh. On heat sterilization sugars and flavours change character. A cheap product in pouches of 200 ml with freshness and reasonable pricing would capture mass markets and would compete with carbonated beverages.

KANKI : Is a saltish fermented drink prepared from black carrots and a mix of condiments. It is tasty and highly preferred traditional drink in summers.

Unfortunately, no work by any institution in India on the standardization of these products has been done despite the fact that they are the major consumables of the masses in different weather. It is also evident that there are a large number of grain based convenience foods which are traditionally prepared and marketed either by small scale artisans or by cottage and small scale industry. Many of the products are also prepared in homes or served in food service establishment. The technology of their production has remained more of an art and little emphasis has been laid in infusing new technological developments in their production and marketing. Though some information has been generated in laboratories and research institutions in scientific evaluation of processing parameters and physico-chemical aspects of products, R & D efforts in design of equipments and machineries for up scaling of technologies of their production has not made much headway. Also whatever information has been generated in research institution has not percolated to industries mainly because of poor technological absorption capacity of industries and lack of adequate interaction between research institutions and industries. It is, therefore, suggested that technological needs of this sector be identified and more stress be laid on design/fabrication of indigenous machineries to upgrade the technological base of convenience food industry.

APPENDIX -I

SOME SELECTED RECIPES OF TRADITIONAL FOODS

Mathi

Ingredients :

Maida	:	100 gms
Salt	:	pinch
Ghee (melted)	:	20 gms
Ajwain	:	2-3 gms (½ tsp)
Oil	:	for frying

Method

Mix maida , salt and ajwain thoroughly. Rub in ghee till a grainy even texture is obtained. Use water to make a very stiff dough. Keep covered with wet cloth and leave for 15—20 minutes. Divide into 10 portions. Heat oil in a frying pan and when hot lower the time. Roll each ball thin, then prick with a fork and fry till golden brown.

Matri

Ingredients:

Flour	:	100 gms
Chillies	:	1/2 tip
Salt	:	to taste
Oil	:	for frying

Method

1. Knead flour with salt and chilles to make the dough.
2. Make small balls and rolls them into 2 long strips.
3. Deep fry on slow fire till golden brown.

SEVIAN

Ingredients :

Vermicelli	:	1 cup
Sugar	:	1, 1/2 cup
Ghee	:	1 cup
Cashewnut broken	:	25 mgs
Milk	:	3 cups

Method

Heat ghee in a pan and fry vermicelli in ghee till golden brown. Then add boiled milk in it and cook it for 15—10 minutes till the vermicelli are done.

SUJI HALWA

Ingredients :

Suji semolina (suji)	:	100 gms
Sugar	:	100 gms
Ghee	:	100 gms
Water	:	300 gms
Almonds	:	optional
Raisins	:	optional
Cardamum (green elaichi)	:	optional

Method

Heat the ghee, add semolina and stir on a slow fire till the mixture becomes light creamy in colour and the ghee leaves the sides of the pan. Mix sugar in water and make a sugar syrup. And add to the syrup and stir briskly till it is absorbed in the semolina. Mix the crushed cardamon, almonds. Serve hot.

PINNIS

Ingredients :

Wheat flour/urad flour	:	1 kg
Ghee	:	750 gms
Powdered sugar	:	850 gms
Dry fruits		

Method

1. Heat ghee in a large pan,
2. Add flour and roast it till golden brown,
3. Add dry fruits and roast for 2-3 minutes,
4. Add sugar, remove from five and mix well.

MALL PURA

Ingredient :

Wheat flour	:	50 gms
Maida	:	50 gms
Suji	:	50 gms
Powdered Milk	:	25 gms

Powdered sugar	:	10 gms
Sugar	:	100 gms
Baking Powder	:	9 Pinch
Ghee	:	for frying
Water	:	for making syrup

Method

1. Mix wheat flour, suji, maida together and add powdered milk, powdered sugar and pinch of baking powder in it and make into a thick paste with water.
2. Heat ghee in a deep vessel and add spoon full of mixture and fry till golden brown.
3. Then make a syrup of 2 thread consistency with sugar and water and put the fried malpoora in the syrup for 5—10 minutes and then serve hot.

GULAB JAMUN

Ingredients :

Khoya	:	200 gms
Paneer	:	50 gms
Maida	:	60 gms
Soda bicarbonate	:	¼ tsp
Sugar	:	750 gms
Ghee	:	for frying

Method

Mix khoya, chenna, maida, soda bicarbonate and knead to a very smooth dough. Make small sails and fry them till golden brown. Ad water to the sugar and make sugar syrup. Add the fried balls to the sugar syrup and keep them for sometime so that sugar syrup penetrates in the balls. Serve hot or cold. It can be garnished with coconut powder.

POORIES

Ingredients :

Wheat flour	:	375 gm
Ghee or Oil	:	20 gm
Salt	:	to taste

Method

1. Prepare a stiff dough with above mentioned ingredients using water and keep it for some time.
2. Divide into small balls and roll out to 3-4 inch diameter puris.
3. Deep fry on both sided in oil or ghee till puffed and brownish in colour.
4. Serve hot.

JALEBI

Ingredients :

Wheat flour	:	½ kg
Gram dal flour	:	124 gms
Ghee	:	1½ kg
Sugar	:	2 kgs
Water	:	10 cups

Method

1. Prepare a batter by mixing and nicely beating wheat flour and gram dal flour.
2. Make a thick syrup by boiling sugar in about 7-8 cups of water.
3. Remove the pan from fire and keep it on boiling water so that it may not get cooled.
4. Boil ghee in deep karahi.
5. Fill in jalebi mould with batter and let down the better through the hole of the mould in to the ghee so as to form circular jalebi with 3 or 5 continuous inner circles.
6. Fry till done on both sides.
7. Remove each jalebi, dip it in the hot syrup for about a minute and drain.
8. Serve hot.

Note : Jalebi mould can be made out of any vessel with a hole in the centre.

SAMOSA

Ingredients :

For covering—

Flour	:	2 cups
Oil or fat	:	3 tsp

For jelling -

Boiled and cooked potatoes alongwith onions and peas.

Method

1. Prepare a hard dough with water. Knead well till soft.
2. Divide it into eight portions.
3. Roll each one into a round roti 15 cm in diameter.
4. Cut each into half.
5. Stiff each roti with prepared stuffing and shape into samosa.
6. Deep fry in hot oil or medium heat till golden brown.
7. Serve hot.

DALIA (BROKEN WHEAT PORRIDGE)

Ingredients :

Broken wheat	:	50 gms
Sugar	:	50 gms
Milk	:	500 ml

Method

Boil the milk and add broken wheat into it and pressure cook it on a slow fire for 5—10 minutes and then remove from the fire and add sugar in and cook for 2 minutes and serve hot.

PHULVARIAN

Ingredients :

Rice	:	100 gms
Water	:	for boiling rice
Salt	:	to taste
Chillies	:	to taste
Cumin powder	:	to taste

Method

1. Boil the rice.
2. Mash the boiled rice and add the spices.
3. Make a cone with hole and pur the mixture to it.
4. Pipe the phylvarian and dry then in sun.
5. Deep fry in oil, serve hot.

RICE KHICHRI

Ingredients :

Rice	:	150 gms
Moong Dal	:	30 gms

(Washed)		
Vegetable oil	:	1½ tsp.
Salt	:	1 tsp.
Cumin seeds	:	2 gms

Method

1. Clean and wash the rice and washed moong dal.
2. Add about 3 cups of water and salt.
3. Pressure cook it for 5 minutes.
4. Fry cumin seeds in ghee and add to the khichri.

SWEET RICE

Ingredients :

Rice	:	240 gms
Jaggery	:	150 gms
Water	:	450 ml
Sauf	:	15 gms
Ghee	:	30 gms

Method

Wash the rice and soak in water for 1—2 hrs. Make syrup of water and jaggery and strain. Put rice, ghee, sauf in syrup and cook on fire till rice is ready.

SUGARCANE JUICE KHEER

Ingredients :

Juice	:	200 ml
Rice	:	25 gms
Water	:	60 ml

Method

1. Clean and wash the rice.
2. Cook in water until half done.
3. Add sugarcane juice and keep on stirring. When the consistency becomes thick, remove it form fire.
4. Serve hot garnished with coconut and dry fruits.

PHIRNI

Ingredients :

Milk	:	1 lt.

Sugar	:	150 gms
Almonds	:	30 gms
Rice	:	40 gms

Method

Soak rice of good quality for about an hour* and then grind very fine with 4 to 5 tsp. Full of cold water. Mix the rice paste with the milk, cook on a medium heat and stir till the mixture is of creamy consistency. Remove from fire, add sugar and stir. Simmer till it is fully dissolved and then boil for 1 minutes. Add the shredded branched almond and serve.

PUFFED RICE LADDOO

Ingredients :

Puffed Rice	:	100 gms
Jaggery	:	200 gms
Ghee or Oil	:	30 gms

Method

1. Make syrup of one string consistency with jaggery and one cup of water.
2. Remove from fire.
3. Mix in puffed rice and fat.
4. Form into small balls.
5. For making marunda spread the mixture on a flat greased tray.

MARUNDA

Ingredients :

Puffed Rice	:	50 gms
Roasted Bengal Gram	:	25 gms
Roasted Peanut Kernels	:	25 gms
Jaggery	:	25 gms

Method

1. Make the thread syrup of jaggery
2. Add rice, grams and peanuts.
3. Prepare balls of mixture.

BLACK GRAM : (URAD) PAPPADS

Ingredients :

Powdered dal	:	1 kg
Chillies	:	100 gms
Salt	:	to taste

asafoetida dissolved in water

Method

1. Knead the flour with water.
2. Take a little and roll it in dry flour to form thin pappads.
3. Dry them in sun for 1 or 2 days.
4. Deep fry or roast them before serving.

VADIAN

Ingredients :

Green gram dal (split)	:	1 kg
Salt	:	to taste

Black pepper and cumin, coarsely ground, asafoetida dissolved in water.

Method

1. Soak dal for 4-5 hours.
2. Remove the husk and grind the dal.
3. Add salt, asafoetida, pepper and cumin and mix well.
4. Keep it over nigh for fermentation.
5. In the morning make small portions from the mixture and dry them in sun for 3-4 days.

BESAN POORA

Ingredients :

Besan	:	50 gms
Onion	:	10 gms
Green Chillies	:	5 gms
Salt	:	½ tsp
Coriander leaves	:	5 gms
Water	:	for making batter

Method

1. Sift the besan and salt.
2. Chop the onion, green chillies and coriander finely. Add the sieved ingredients.
3. Make a batter with water.
4. Spread the batter on a greased tava to form a round of about 12 cm diameter cook for 3 minutes, turn over.
5. Add the melted fat around the edges and little on top. Fry till crisp.

BESAN LADDOOS

Ingredients :

Besan	:	100 gms
Fat	:	100 gms
Sugar Powder	:	100 gms
Cardamum	:	3.5 gms

Method

1. Roast besan in fat till cream colour.
2. Remove pan from fire. Add powdered sugar and mix well.
3. Add crushed cardamum. Form into even shaped balls with wet hands.

PAKORAS

Ingredients :

Besan Salt Green Chillies Spinach Carrots Potatoes Onion Oil for frying	Finely chopped on granted

Method

1. Take besan in a bowl and add all spices.
2. Add vegetables.
3. Add water to make thick batter.

4. Heat oil in a deep pan.
5. Fry pakoras.

BHUGA

Ingredients :

Khoa	:	200 gms
Sesame	:	200 gms
Sugar	:	200 gms

Method

1. Grind sesame and sugar together.
2. Add khoa to it and mix well.
3. Make small balls and serve.

SESAME GACHAK

Ingredients :

Sesame	:	125 gms
Roasted peanuts	:	50 gms
Cardamon kernels	:	10 gms
Dry coconut powder	:	¼ cups
Sugar/jaggery	:	250 gms

Method

1. Roast sesame to light brown colour.
2. Cool and powder together with peanuts.
3. Prepare syrup of 1 strand consistency with one cup of water.
4. Mix all ingredients except coconut and keep stirring till the mixture leaves the sides of pan.
5. Grease a plate of spread mixture on it.

CHIKKI

Ingredients :

Jaggery	:	100 gms
Peanut kernels	:	30 gms
Water	:	1-2 tsp.

Method

1. Prepare two strand syrup of jaggery and water.
2. Add peanut kernels.

3. Grease a plate and pour syrup in it.
4. Keep it to eat. Cut into pieces.

GULGULAS

Ingredients :

Wheat flour	:	100 gms
Jaggery	:	100 gms
Water	:	Pinch
Oil for frying	:	Pinch
Metha Soda	:	Pinch

Method

1. Make thin syrup of jaggery with water.
2. Add soda to flour and make dough with syrup.
3. Serve it for some time.
4. Make small balls of the dough and deep fry then.

35

Dessert Powders and Puddings

GELATIN DESSERT POWDERS

Essentially, a gelatin dessert powder represents a mixture of gelatin and cane sugar, alone or combined with dextrose, powdered gelatin, natural or imitation fruit flavour, fruit acid such as citric or tartaric, and certified food colour.

Gelatin desserts are more popular today because of the constant striving of the manufacturer to improve the quality of the fruit flavour and to use a quality of gelatin as free as possible from bacteria, off odour and poor taste. The use of natural fruit flavour alone is incapable of producing that individual fruity taste, and, therefore, the addition of an imitation fruit flavour is necessary. To make a free-flowing gelatin dessert powder (one which will remain that way in the package) from 5 to 15% corn sugar must be used, to retard serious lumping. In the manufacture of pudding powders, the finest quality starch, low in moisture and bacteria content, should be employed. All products should be sifted after mixing and before final packaging.

Gelatin Dessert Powder

Formula No. 1

(For Bulk Sales)

Granulated Sugar	84	lb	Natural Fruit Flavor	1½lb
Gelatin Powder	12	lb	Imitation Fruit Flavour	To suit
Citric Acid Powder	2	lb	Certified Food Colour	To suit

Add 5 pints of boiling water to 17 ounces of above mixture. Stir until dissolved.

Formula No. 2

(For Package Sales)

Granulated Sugar	71	lb	Natural Fruit Flavour	3 lb
Gelatin Powder	12	1b	Imitation Fruit Flavour	To suit

Corn Sugar	13 lb	Certified Flood Colour	To suit
Citric Acid Powder	2 lb		

A 3¼ ounce-package of the above mixture added to 1 pint of boiling water, will make a gelatin dessert. If fruits, nuts, etc., are to be used, add after gelatin dessert is cold and set suf-ficiently to hold them in place.

FLAVOURS FOR GELATIN DESSERTS

Amount of Colour and Flavour for a 100 lb Batch

Strawberry

True Fruit Flavour	6 oz	Amaranth Colour Powder	4 oz
Imitation Fruit Flavour	1/7 oz	Orange I Colour Powder	1 oz

Raspberry

True Fruit Flavour	6 oz	Amaranth Colour Powder	6 oz
Imitation Fruit Flavour	1/3 oz		

Cherry

True Fruit Flavour	6 oz	Amaranth Colour Powder	6 oz
Imitation Fruit Flavour	1 oz		

Pineapple

True Fruit Flavour	6 oz	Tartrazine Colour Powder	4 oz
Imitation Fruit Flavour	1 oz		

Lemon

Lemon Oil	4 oz	Tartrazine Colour Powder	3 oz

Orange

Orange Oil	4 oz	Orange I Colour Powder	1 oz

Lime

Lime Oil	4 oz	Light Green S.F. Powder	3 oz
Tartrazine Colour Powder	½ oz		

Dissolve the colour in a minimum amount of hot water. Spray colour and flavour on gelatin batches during mixing operation.

Pudding Powders

Chocolate Flavour

Formula No. 1

(Average Quality)

Granulated Sugar	60 lb	Salt	1 lb
Cocoa Powder	15 lb	Vanillin	3 oz
Corn Starch	25 lb		

(Better Quality)

Formula No. 2

Granulated Sugar	53 lb	Ground Sweet Chocolate	9 lb
Corn Starch	22 lb	Salt	1 lb
Tapioca Starch	6 lb	Vanillin	2 oz
Cocoa Powder	9 lb		

Formula No. 3

Granulated Sugar	60 lb	Salt	1 lb
Corn Starch	23 lb	Vanillin	3 oz
Cocoa Powder	20 lb		

The above puddings are weighed up into 4 ounce-packages, cooked with one pint of water or milk, and stirred constantly until they reach the proper thickening point.

Vanillin Flavour

Formula No. 1

Granulated Sugar	64 lb	Vanillin	3 oz
Corn Starch	27 lb	Certified Food Egg	
Skimmed Milk Powder	8 lb	Colour	If desired
Salt	1 lb		

Weigh the above into 4 ounce-packages. Stir mixture into 1 pint of boiling water or milk.

Formula No. 2

Granulated Sugar	70 lb	Salt	1 lb
Corn Sugar	15 lb	Vanillin	2 oz
Corn Starch	30 lb		

Use 4 ounces to 1 pint of boiling milk.

Formula No. 3

Granulated Sugar	55	lb	Salt	1	lb
Corn Sugar	15	lb	Vanillin	2	oz
Corn Starch	30	lb			

Use 4 ounces to 1 pint of boiling milk.

Cocoanut Flavour Pudding

¹/Granulated Sugar	40	lb	Powdered Gelatin	2	lb
Corn Starch	38	lb	Fine Cut Cocoanut	10	lb
Skimmed Milk Powder	10	lb	Vanillin	2	oz

Use 4 ounces of the above mixture in one pint of boiling water or milk. Thicken in double boiler.

Maple-Flavor Powdered Pudding

Light Brown Sugar	65	lb	Powdered Caramel Color	1	oz
Corn Starch	25	lb	Maple Flavour	1	oz
Salt	2	lb	Skimmed Milk Powder	6	lb

Use 4½ ounces to 1 pint of boiling milk. Cook over moderate heat, to gloss (185 to 190°F).

Caramel, cocoanut and butterscotch-flavor pudding can be manufactured by a similar method.

Custard Pudding

Formula No. 1

Granulated Sugar	71	lb	Turmeric Powder	1	lb
Corn Starch	20	lb	Oil Bitter Almond	1½	oz
Gum Tragacanth	3	lb	Lemon Oil	⅛	oz

Use 4 ounces of the above to 1 pint of boiling milk. Then pour into dishes, and bake as custard.

Formula No. 2

Granulated Sugar	71	lb	Turmeric Powder	1	lb
Corn Starch	10	lb	Oil Bitter Almond	½	oz
Arrowroot Starch	10	lb	Oil Nutmeg	¼	oz

Use in same manner as Formula No. 1.

Formula No. 3

Granulated Sugar	70	lb	Salt	½ lb
Corn Starch	20	lb	Vanillin	2 oz
Whole Egg Powder	6	lb		

Use as above recipe.

Custard Cream

(French Style)

Granulated Sugar	60	lb	Shortening	4 lb
Corn Starch	18	lb	Salt	½ lb
Whole Milk Powder	18	lb	Vanillin	2 oz
Powdered Egg Yolk	4	lb		

Use 4 ounces of the above to 1 pint of boiling water. Then add to it 3 pints of cold water and whip up until mixture thickens.

Custard Filling for Pies

Formula No. 1

Granulated Sugar	70	lb	Powdered Whole Egg	5 lb
Whole Milk Powder	8	lb	Salt	1 lb
Corn Starch	16	lb	Vanillin	3 oz

Stir *2½* pounds of above in 1 pint of water. Pour this into 7 pints of boiling water and stir until it thickens. Use when cold.

Formula No. 2

Granulated Sugar	50	lb	Tapioca Starch	15 1b
Skimmed Milk Powder	20	lb	Vanillin	1 oz
Powdered Whole Egg	10	lb	Oil of Mace	¼ oz
Shortening	5	lb		

Whip 2 pounds of the above into a smooth paste with 1-½ pints of water. Add to 5 pints of boiling water and heat until it thickens. Use when cool.

Custard Pie—Rich and Non-Watering

Whole Milk Powder	30	oz	Powdered Whole Egg	15 oz
Granulated Sugar	43	oz	Salt	½ oz
Corn Starch	10	oz	Nutmeg	5 gms

Work the above ingredients into a smooth batter with about 2 pints of water. Pour this into 8 pints of boiling water, stir until it thickens. Then bake in individual pie plates at 425 to 450°F with good bottom heat.

Dry Vanilla Cream Powders

Formula No. 1

Granulated Sugar	30	oz	Corn Starch	11 oz
Powdered Egg Yolk	1	oz	Colour and Vanilla	
Salt	¼	oz	Flavour	If desired

Add the above to 1 quart of milk and mix until smooth. Then add gradually to 4 quarts of hot milk. Boil to 190°F, or until thick and glossy. A better product is obtained upon addition of 4 ounces of butter.

Formula No. 2

Granulated Sugar	41	oz	Corn Starch	16 oz
Powdered Skimmed Milk	27	oz	Colour and Vanilla	
Powdered Whole Egg	4	oz	Flavor	If desired
Salt	1	oz		

Add the above to 2 quarts of water. Mix into smooth paste. Then add gradually to 3 quarts boiling water. Boil to 190°F, or until thick and glossy.

36

Ice Cream

INTRODUCTION

ice cream as an industry in India is of comparatively recent origin and may be said to have started in the nineteen-sixties. Today ice cream may be considered a luxury food item, although its popularity is increasing rapidly. The production of ice cream in India in 1966 was estimated to be about 0.7 per cent of the total milk production and 1.3 per cent of the milk used for manufacture of dairy products (see Table 36.1).

DEFINITION

Ice cream may be defined as a frozen dairy product made by suitable blending and processing of cream and other milk products, together with sugar and flavour, with or without stabilizer or colour, and with the incorporation of air during the freezing process.

According to the PFA Rules (1976), ice cream is the frozen product obtained from cow or buffalo milk or a combination thereof or from cream, and or other milk products, with or without the addition of cane sugar, eggs, fruits, fruit juices, preserved fruits, nuts, chocolate, edible flavours and permitted food colours. It may contain permitted stabilizers and emulsifiers not exceeding 0.5 per cent by weight. The mixture must be suitably heated before freezing. The product should contain not less than 10 per cent milk fat, 3.5 per cent protein and 36.0 per cent total solids. However, when any of the aforesaid preparations contain fruits or nuts or both, the content of milk fat may be proportionately reduced but may not be less than 8 per cent by weight. Starch may be added to a maximum extent of 5 per cent, with a declaration to that effect on the label.

HISTORY AND DEVELOPMENT

The early history of ice cream manufacture is very scanty; however, the product is definitely known to have originated in Europe. Water ices were made in Southern Europe as early as the fifteenth century. The first printed record of 'Cream Ice' appeared in *The Experienced English House Keeper* in 1769, more than two hundred years ago. Since that time ice cream manufacture has continued to grow in popularity in England, though not nearly as rapidly as in the United States, where surveys indicate that ice cream forms a part of the daily diet and is the favourite American dessert.

Seme of the factors contributing to the development of the ice cream industry in developed dairying countries are: (i) the perfection of mechanical refrigeration and its application to the food industry; (ii) improved manufacturing methods and equipment such as homogenizers, over-run testers, continuous freezers, packaging machines, etc.; (iii) more and better ingredients and growth in knowledge concerning ice cream manufacture, resulting in a better product; (iv) lower manufacturing costs through mass production; (v) extensive advertising of the product; (vi) a realization of the high food value of ice cream; (vii) changing economic conditions, better wages, more purchasing power and a high standard of living among consumers; (viii) improved storage facilities for ice cream at home.

CLASSIFICATION

No standard classification of ice cream has yet been adopted by the industry, even in developed countries. However, some of the important frozen desserts can be classified as follows:

(i) *Plain :* An ice cream in which the colour and flavouring ingredients together amount to less than 5 per cent of the volume of the unfrozen ice cream. Examples: Vanilla and Coffee ice creams.

(ii) *Chocolate :* Ice cream flavoured with cocoa or chocolate.

(iii) *Fruit :* Ice cream containing fruits, with or without additional fruit flavouring or colour. Fruits such as strawberry, apricot, pineapple, mango, banana, etc., may be fresh, frozen-packed, can-ned or preserved.

(iv) *Nut :* Ice cream containing nuts, such as almonds, pistachio, walnuts, cashewnut, etc., with or without additional flavouring or colour.

(v) *Milk Ices or Milk Lollies.* According to the PFA Rules (1976), these refer to the frozen product obtained from milk, skim milk or milk products with or without the addition of cane sugar, eggs, fruits, fruit juices, nuts, chocolates, edible flavours, and permitted food colours. It may contain permitted stabilizers not exceeding 0.5 per cent of the product. The mixture should be suitably heat-treated before freezing. The product should contain not more than 2.0 per cent milk fat, not less than 3.5 per cent proteins and not less than 20.0 per cent total solids.

(vi) *Ices :* Made of fruit juice, sugar and stabilizer, with or without additional fruit acid, colour, flavouring or water, and frozen to the consistency of ice cream. Usually contain 28 to 30 per cent sugar, 20 to 25 per cent over-run and no dairy products.

(vii) *Sherbet :* Made of fruit juices, sugar, stabilizer, and milk products. It is similar to an ice except that milk, either whole, skim, condensed or powdered, or ice cream mix, are used in place of ail or part of the water in an ice.

(viii) *Fancy Moulded :* Moulded in fancy shapes and composed either of one colour and flavour of ice cream or a combination of colours and flavours, or especially decorated. Examples are: brick ice cream, cakes, cake roll, moulds representing fruits, etc.

(ix) *Novelties :* A Novelty ice cream or frozen confection is an especially shaped and usually a low-priced package containing an individual serving whose main appeal consists in its shape, size, colour or convenience for eating.

(x) *Soft Ice Cream (Softy) :* Sold as drawn from the freezer without hardening.

COMPOSITION

The composition of ice cream is usually expressed as a percentage of its constituents, i.e., a percentage of milk fat, milk-solids-not-fat (serum solids), sugar, stabilizer, total solids, etc. Its composition varies in different localities and in different markets. The best ice cream composition for a manufacturer to produce is often difficult to establish. After consideration of legal requirements, quality of product desired, raw materials available, plant procedures, trade demands, competition and cost, there is a choice of a product of minimum, average or high fat/solids composition. Some factories may choose to manufacture only one of these products, others two and still others all three, i.e., an economy-brand product, a good average composition product as a trade brand, or a deluxe high-quality product.

It may be inadvisable for a small manufacturer to produce more than one brand of ice cream. If only one composition is manufactured, it is extremely important that every effort be made to produce the best product possible.

In ice cream, the percentage of milk fat varies more than any other constituent. As the fat content is increased, the milk-solids-not-fat must be decreased so as to avoid 'sandiness' (i.e., the crys-tallization of milk sugar or lactose in the finished ice cream). Table 36.1 gives the composition of economy and good average ice creams.

Table 36.1 : Approximate composition of commercial ice cream (as a percentage).

Milk fat	Milk soiids-not-fat/ Serum solids	Sugar	Stabilizer and Emulsifier	Total solids
Economy Ice Cream				
10	10 to 11	13 to 15	0.30 to 0.50	35 to 37
Good Average Ice Cream				
12	11	15	0.30	37.5 to 39

SOURCE: *Ice Cream* by Arbuckle (1968).

The ISI specifications for ice cream *(IS: 2802,* 1964) are given in Table 36.2.

Table 36.2 : ISI specifications of ice cream.

Characteristics	Requirements
Weight (g/litre) (min.)	525
Total solids (% wt.) (min.)	36.0
Milk fat (% wt.) (min.)	10.0 (Tentative)
Acidity (% lactic acid) (max.)	0.25
Sucrose (% wt.) (max.)	15.0
Stabilizer/Emulsifier (% wt.) (max.)	0.5
Standard plate count (per g)	Not more than 2,50,000
Coliform count (per g)	Not more than 90
Pbosphatase test	Negative

Note: A satisfactory composition produces an ice cream which has the desired combinations of cost, food value, flavour, body and texture, cooling effect, colour scheme, viscosity, whipping ability (i.e., over-run) and freezing point. What is needed is a balanced mix, in which the proportions of the constituents and ingredients is such as will produce a fine and satisfactory ice cream.

FOOD AND NUTRITIVE VALUE

This depends not only on the composition of the ice cream but also upon the food and nutritive value of the products from which it is made. For instance, ice cream contains two to three times as much fat and slightly more protein than does milk. In addition, it may contain other food products such as fruits, nuts, eggs and sugar which en-hance its food value. However, like milk, it lacks iron, vitamin C and some of the trace minerals.

Among milk products, ice cream is also a rich source of calcium, phosphorus and other minerals of vital importance in building good bones and teeth. Being rich in lactose, ice cream favours greater assimilation of the calcium content in the diet. The protein content of ice cream also rates high, both in quantity and quality. The proteins are largely derived from milk, a small amount from stabilizer (gelatin) and from eggs when they are used in the mix. The milk and egg proteins are complete; that is, they contain all the amino-acids essential to animal life and are especially important sources of tryptophane and lysine which are lacking in many plan proteins. Ice cream provides these valuable proteins in a very palatable form. In fact, ice cream (without eggs and gelatin) is the most palatable source of milk proteins to vegetarians.

Ice cream is an excellent source of food energy. Having twice to three times the fat content of milk, and more than half its total solids being sugar (sucrose and lactose), the energy value of ice cream is very high. It is, therefore, a very desirable food item for growing children and persons who need to put on weight.

Like milk, ice cream is a rich source of many essential vitamins, without which normal health and growth cannot be maintained. Thus it is an excellent source of vitamin A, a good source of vitamins B (Thiamine) and G (Riboflavin), and a fairly good source of Niacin, vitamin E, and in fruit ice cream, of vitamin C. The digestibility and palatability of ice cream is also very high.

ROLE OF THE CONSTITUENTS IN ICE CREAM

(a) *Milk Fat* : This is high in food value, but expensive. It enriches and mellows the ice cream, giving it a full, rich, creamy flavour. If the milk fat is even slightly off-flavoured, the defect will be noticeable. The fat also contributes to the body and melting resistance of ice cream while producing a smoothness of texture. Fat gives stability to the ice cream but impairs whipping ability.

(b) Milk-solids-not-fat (MSNF) : Also known as serum solids, they consist of milk proteins, milk sugar and mineral matter. They are high in food value and also inexpensive. They add very little to the smell, but improve its body and texture. However, milk sugar adds to the sweet taste. The milk proteins help to make ice cream more compact and smooth. Milk-solids-not-fat should be added in as large a quantity as possible without risking the danger of sandiness.

(c) Sugar : The main function of sugar is to increase the acceptability of ice cream. The desired sweetening effect is only produced by sucrose. Sugars are usually the cheapest source of total solids in the mix.

(d) Stabilizers : These are used to prevent the formation of objectionably large ice crystals in ice cream, especially during storage. Since they are added in very small quantities, they have a negligible influence on food value and flavour.

(e) Emulsifiers : These are used mainly to improve upon and provide a uniform whipping quality to the mixture, and to produce a drier ice cream with smoother body and texture.

(f) Flavour and colour : Flavour increases the acceptability of ice cream, and colour its aesthetic appeal.

(g) Advantages and Limitations of Ice Cream Constituents : The advantages and limitations of the various ice cream constituents have been summarized by Sommer as follows:

I. *Milk Fat*

Advantages : (i) Enriches the flavour; (ii) produces a characteris-tic smooth texture; (iii) helps give body to the ice cream.

Limitations : (i) Cost; (ii) fat slightly hinders, rather than improves, whipping; (iii) high fat content may limit the amount of ice cream consumed; (iv) high calorific value.

II. *Milk-solids-not-fat*

Advantages. (i) Improve the texture; (ii) help to give body; (iii) a higher over-run without snowy or flaky texture; (iv) a comparatively cheap source of solids.

Limitations : (i) A high percentage causes 'sandiness'; (ii) the 'condensed milk' flavour may be objectionable; (iii) may cause salty or cooked flavour.

III. *Sugar*

Advantages : (i) Is usually the cheapest source of solids; (ii) improves the texture; (iii) enhances the flavour.

Limitations : (i) Excessively sweet; (ii) lowers whipping ability; (iii) requires a lower temperature for proper hardening.

IV. *Stabilizer*

Advantages : (i) Very effective in smoothening the texture; (ii) very effective in giving body to the product.

Limitation : Excess body and melting resistance.

V. *Emulsifier*

Advantages : (i) Improves whipping quality of mixture; (ii) gives smoother body and texture; (iii) reduces whipping time.

Limitations : (i) Homogenization of milk is essential; (ii) tends to favour 'shrinkage' defect; (iii) excess body and melting resistance.

VI. *Total Solids*

Advantages : (i) Smoother texture; (ii) better body; (iii) more nutritious; (iv) ice cream not as cold.

Limitations : (i) Heavy, soggy or pasty body; (ii) cooling effect insufficiently high.

VII. *Flavour*

Advantage : Increases acceptability.

Limitations : Harsh flavour less desirable; (ii) intense flavours provide immediate satisfaction.

VIII. *Colour*

Advantages, (i) Improves appearance; (ii) aids in identifying flavours.

Limitation, (i) Intense and 'unnatural' colours reduce consumer acceptability.

Properties of Mix

The properties of practical importance in the mix are: viscosity, acidity (lactic) and pH, mix stability, specific gravity, surface ten-sion, freezing point, and whipping rate.

A. *Viscosity :* This is defined simply as the resistance offered by liquids to flow. Viscosity is considered an important property of the ice cream mix, and a certain amount of it seems essential for proper whipping and the retention of air. Two types of viscosity exist in ice cream mixes: Apparent Viscosity, which is a thickened condition that disappears with agitation; and Basic Viscosity, which remains after the Apparent Viscosity disappears.

The viscosity of an ice cream mix is influenced by: (i) composition; (ii) kind and quality of ingredients; (iii) processing and handling of the mix; (iv) total solids concentration; and (v) temperature.

(i) *Composition :* Among the various mix ingredients, viscosity is more influenced by milk fat and stabilizer than the other ingredients. Gelatin affects viscosity to a gieat extent largely due to gel formation, while fat increases it slightly. Sugar, on the other hand, decreases the viscosity of the ice cream mix.

(ii) *Kind and Quality of Ingredients.* The kind of ingredient refers to whether it is a source of fat, serum-solids, sweetening, stabilizer, etc.; the quality indicates the emulsion stability of fat, colloidal stability of protein, etc. Those carrying the fat are especially important. Also, heat and salts (such as calcium, sodium, citrates, etc.), greatly affect the viscosity due to their effect on casein and other proteins. Among stabilizers, gelatin causes a decided increase in viscosity after ageing.

(iii) *Processing and Handling of the Mix.* These include: pasteurization, homogenization and ageing :

1. *Pasteurization :* At batch-holding temperatures followed by cooling, pasteurization causes a decrease in viscosity, while at higher temperatures it produces an increase in viscosity.
2. *Homogenization : If* the globules are small and individually dispersed, the basic viscosity of the mix remains at a minimum. However, the tendency of the sub-divided fat globules to clump or aggregate greatly increases.
3. *Ageing :* The ageing of mixes containing gelatin considerably increases their apparent viscosity. The increase is chiefly due to gel formation, but to some extent to the hydration of proteins and the clumping of fat globules. Aside from the increase in apparent viscosity, ageing causes an increase in basic viscosity as a result of a solidification of the butter fat and hydration of the milk proteins.

(iv) *Total Solids concentration :* As the liquid phase is replaced by a solid phase in a mixture such as ice cream mix, the viscosity usually increases. Consequently, as the solids content of the ice cream mix is raised, the viscosity increases although the effect of the different solids in this respect varies with the type and source of the solid. For example, slight increases in fat content may effect the mix viscosity to only a limited extent, whereas a slight increase in gelatin will affect the mix viscosity greatly. The extent to which the mix solids increase mix viscosity depends largely upon the phy-sical state of these solids. When the proteins are partially coagulated and when the fat globules form clumps, the mix viscosity increases on both counts.

(v) *Temperature :* With a lowering of temperature, the mix viscosity increases, and *vice versa.*

Note: It has not yet been determined how much viscosity is desirable in ice cream mix. A high viscosity was believed essential at one time, but for fast freezing (rapid whipping) in modern equipment, a lower viscosity seems desirable. In general, as viscosity increases, the resistance to melting and the smoothness of body increases, but the rate of whipping decreases. Viscosity is now considered a phenomenon that frequently accómpanies rather than causes good whipping, body and texture. Therefore the mix should be properly balanced (in regard to composition, concentration and quality of ingredients) and then properly processed to produce the desired whipping ability, body and texture. Under these conditions, a desirable viscosity is assured. The basic viscosity of mix ranges from 50 to 300 centipoise.

B. *Acidity (lactic) & pH. :* The normal acidity of ice cream mixes is dependent upon the serum solids content, and is calculated by the formula:

$$\% \text{ acidity of mix} = \% \text{ acidity of milk} \times \frac{\% \text{ serum solids in mix}}{\% \text{ serum solids in milk}}$$

A rule of thumb method to determine mix acidityis to multiply the serum solids by 2 and divide by 100. The normal pH of mix is about 6.3. Acidity and pH are related to the composition of the mix and an increase in milk-solids-not-fat raises the percentage acidity and lowers the pH. If fresh dairy products of excellent quality are used in preparing the mix, it may be expected to have a normal acidity. When acidity is above normal, it indicates that lactic acid is present in the dairy products used in the mix. A high acidity is undesirable as it contributes to excessive mix viscosity, a decreased whipping rate, an inferior flavour and a less stable mix resulting in cook on' or possible coagulation during the pasteurizing and processing stages.

If the mix acidity is higher than normal, it can be neutralized to the level of normal acidity. Over-neutralization (below 0.15 per cent titratable acidity) should be avoided as the ice cream will tend to have a flat (or neutralized) flavour and a dull or even greyish colour. When neutralizing, add the sugar at 32°C (90°F) and place all the ingredients in the mixing vat before the acidity test is run.. The neutralizer best suited to ice cream is sodium bicarbonate. Mix the neutralizer (1 kg neutralizer to 1 kg acid) with 10 times its weight of water. Heat the mix to 32°C (90°F), or slightly higher if butter is used. Keeping the agitator moving, add the neutralizer solution slowly so as to distribute it uniformly throughout the mix. The temperature should be maintained at 32°C (90°F) for at least 10 minutes before pasteurizing.

Note: It should be remembered that good ice cream cannot be made from a highly acidic mix.

C. *Mix Stability :* This refers to stability or resistance to separation by the 'milk proteins in an ice cream mix. Instability results in separation of milk proteins as coagulated or precipitated material in the mix, and the resulting ice cream has a curdled appearance on melting. This defect is caused by various factors which affect the colloidal stability of the milk proteins, such as high mix acidity, low citrate and phosphate content, a high calcium and magnesium content, high homogenizing pressure, high (pasteurizing) heat-treatment, low ageing time (resulting in poor hydration), destabilizing effect of freezing, etc. Particle size, charge, and hydration are important factors influencing the stability of an ice cream mix; the most stable mix particle is the hydrophillic suspension because it is çharged and hydrated; and the least stable suspension is that wherein the particle is neither hydrated nor carries a charge. It is the latter which results in instable mixes.

D. *Specific Gravity :* The specific gravity or density of an ice cream mix varies with its composition and may range from 1.05 to 1.12. It can be determined by using the following formula:

Sp. Gr. at 16°C(60°F)

$$= \frac{100}{\frac{\%\ \text{fat}}{0.93} + \frac{\%\ \text{Sugar} + \%\ \text{MSNF} + \%\ \text{Stabilizer}}{1.58} + \frac{\%\ \text{water}}{1}}$$

E. *Surface Tension.* This pertains to the attraction between the molecules of a liquid at its surface. The greater the attraction between the molecules, the higher the surface tension, and *vice versa.* The unit of measurement of surface tension is dyne.

Investigations on the surface tension of ice cream are limited. Studies indicate that increasing the surface tension above that of a freshly-made mix (made from fresh ingredients) is difficult, although it may be readily decreased by the addition of products such as emulsifiers and the like. Mixes with lower surface tension values (caused by the addition of excessive amounts of emulsifier *to* the mix) have shown excessive rates of whipping, fluffy short body characteristics, and susceptibility to the shrinkage defect. The normal surface tension values of ice cream mix may range from 48 to 53 dynes sq. cm. (At 20°C/68°F the surface tension of water is 72.75, and of milk, 40 to 60.)

F. *Freezing Point :* The freezing point of ice cream is dependent on the soluble constituents and varies with its composition. The mix constituents which affect the freezing point directly are sugar, milk sugar, milk salts, and any other substances that may have been added and are in true solution. Other mix constituents which affect the freezing point indirectly by replacing water are fat, protein and any other constituent not in true solution. Glucose depresses the freezing point almost twice as much as the same weight of sucrose, since the molecular weight of glucose is about one-half that of sucrose. On the other hand, corn syrup depresses the freezing point less than sucrose. In fruit ice cream, the freezing point will depend on the type of sugar used in fruit preparations (glucose or sucrose) and the extent to which the added sugar has undergone hydrolysis.

An average mix (containing 12 per cent fat, 11 per cent serum solids, 15 per cent sugar, 0.3 per cent stabilizer and 61.7 per cent water) has a freezing point of about 27.5°F. Mixes with high sugar and milk-solids-not-fat contents may range to 26.5°F; while high fat, low milk-solids-not-fat or low sugar content mixes may range to 29.5°F.

G. *Whipping Rate :* A high whipping rate means the ability to whip rapidly to a high over-run. It is now definitely known that the differences in whipping ability cannot be explained on the basis of viscosity. The present hypothesis is that whipping ability is based on tensile strength and the strength of the lamella (i.e., walls around the air cells). Whipping ability is improved by a high processing temperature, proper homogenization and ageing the mix for 2—4 hours.

Smaller fat globules and less clumping increase whipping ability. Mixes made with butter, butteroil, or frozen cream have a less satisfactory dispersion of fat and poor whipping ability. Egg yolk solids, regardless of their source, and fresh cream buttermilk solids, improve whipping ability. The usual variations in concentration of milk-solids-not-fat have no pronounced effect on whipping ability, but qualitative variations in the milk-solids-not-fat are important. Sugar decreases the whipping ability except wher. added after homogenization, in which case it increases it. Finally, the construction and operation of the freezer itself determine whether the maximum whipping ability of a given mix can be obtained.

The rate of whipping is measured by calculating the over-run at one-minute intervals while the mix is being frozen in a batch freezer. Normally, within 3 to 5 minutes after the freezing process starts, the mix is frozen and within 7 minutes an over-run of 90 per cent is obtained. In mixes which have a rapid whipping rate, 90 per cent over-run may be reached in 5 minutes or less. Mixes requiring 8 minutes or more to reach 90 per cent over-run are considered to have a slow whipping rate.

METHOD OF MANUFACTURE, PACKAGING, HARDENING AND STORAGE

A. *Flow Diagram of Manufacture*

Selection of ingredients

↓

Figuring the mix

↓

Making the mix

↓

Pasteurizing the mix (68°C/155°F for 30 min.)

↓

Homogenizing the mix (I stage 2,500 psi)

↓ (II stage 500 psi)

Cooling and ageing the mix (0—4°C/32—J0°F)

↓

Freezing the mix (-4 to -5°C/23 to 25°F)

↓

Packaging of ice cream

↓

Hardening and storage of ice cream

(-23 to -29°C/-10 to -20°F)

B. Details of Manufacture

(aa) *Selection of Ingredients :* The selection of ice cream ingredients depends on: (i) availability of milk products; (ii) perishability of the products; (iii) convenience in handling; (iv) effect on flavour, body and texture of ice cream; (v) cost, and (vi) equipment available. The selection of good ingredients is without doubt the most important factor in successful ice cream manufacture. A clean, fresh, creamy flavour in ice cream can be secured only by the use of products which have been carefully produced and handled.

Ice cream ingredients may be grouped into dairy and non-dairy products. Some dairy products supply the major source of fat, others the major source of milk-solids-not-fat and still others supply both fat and milk-solids-not-fat. The non-dairy products include sweetening agents, stabilizers and emulsifiers, flavours and colours, fruits and nuts, etc. The common ingredients used in each category have been listed below:

I. *Dairy Products*

Source of fat: (i) Sweet Cream—This is the most desirable concentrated source of fat for use in a mix; (ii) frozen cream; (iii) plastic cream; (iv) unsalted butter; (v) butter-oil.

Sources of Milk-solids-not Fat: (i) skim milk; (ii) skim milk powder—This is most frequently Used in the spray dried or flaked form; (iii) condensed skim milk (plain/sweetened); (iv) sweet cream butter-milk.

Sources of Both Fat and Milk-solids-not-fat: (i) whole milk; (ii) whole Milk powder; (iii) condensed whole milk (plains/weetened); (iv) evaporated milk.

II. *Non-dairy Products*

Sweetening Agents: (i) cane or beet sugar (sucrose)—most common; (ii) corn sugar (dextrose); (iii) corn syrup solids (dextrose + maltose); (iv) corn syrup; (v) invert sugar (glucose + fructose); (vi) saccharin.

Stabilizers: (i) gelatin of animal source; orthodox vegetarians object to its use in ice cream; (ii) sodium alginate/Dariloid (modified form)—this is of vegetable origin and widely used; (iii) guar gum—this is of Indian origin; (iv) others.

Emulsifiers: (i) mono-or di-glycerides of fat-forming fatty acids.

Flavours: (i) vanilla—this is the most popular flavour all over the world; (ii) chocolate; (iii) strawberry; (iv) pineapple; (v) lemon; (vi) banana; (vii) mango; (viii) orange, etc.

Colours: (i) yellow; (ii) green; (iii) pink, etc.

Egg Solids: Yolk solids—improve whipping ability.

Fruits and Nuts: (i) apple; (ii) banana; (iii) mango; (iv) pineapple; (v) grape; (vi) almond; (vii) pistachio; (viii) cashewnut; (ix) walnut, (x) groundnut.

(a) *Dairy Products :* These constitute the basic materials for ice cream preparation and have either been discussed in the preceding chapters, or shall be so discussed in the succeeding ones.

(b) *Sweetening Agents :* Many kinds of sweeteners are used in ice cream. These include: cane and beet sugar, corn sweeteners, brown sugar, honey, invert sugar and sugar substitutes. Cane or beet sugars are most commonly used. One-fourth to one-third of cane or beet sugar may be replaced by corn sugar with good results. The use of a combination or blend of sugars in either dry or liquid forms is a popular practice; sugar blends usually consist of 70 per cent sucrose and 30 per cent corn sweeteners. The different kinds of sugars do not produce an equal sweetening effect. Apart from sweetening, sugars affect the properties of the mix and the finished product. Sugars depress the freezing point of the mix, produce a thinner mix with a slower whipping rate, and an ice cream with a smoother body and texture with faster melting qualities. The different sweeteners commonly used are as follows:

(i) *Sucrose :* Commonly known as granulated cane or beet sugar, this is the most widely accepted source of sugar throughout the world. It depresses the freezing point of ice cream.

(ii) *Corn Sweeteners :* These may be: refined corn sugar (dextrose) —a dry crystalline product; dried corn syrup or corn syrup solids; and corn syrup—a liquid.

Refined Corn Sugar : Dextrose is 80 per cent as sweet as sucrose. It has a lower freezing point than sucrose and can therefore be used to about 25 per cent of the total desired sugar.

Dried Corn Syrup Solids : Contain dextrose and maltose together with dextrin. Usually added to the extent of not more than one-third of the total sweetener.

Corn Syrup—Contains variable amounts of dextrose and maltose.

(ill) *Invert Sugar :* Mixture of different parts of glucose and fructose (resulting from hydrolysis of sucrose) and generally obtained in the form of syrup. Sweeter than sucrose. Depresses the freezing point and hence should be used to supply not more than one-fourth to one-third of the total sugar in the mix.

(iv) *Saccharin :* Artificial sweetener. Sweetening effect up to 550 times that of sucrose. Used in 'diabetic ice cream*. Causes problems of low total solids and low over-run. (Continued consumption of 0.3 g. per day is liable to impair digestion, because of its antiseptic properties and preservative action. Lately, it has been suggested that it might be a cause of cancer.)

Note : Use of lactose as sweetener has the following problems: lactose is one-sixth as sweet as sucrose and is less soluble; moreover the crystals are hard and have sharp edges. When the water portion of the mix contains as much as 9 per cent lactose, the lactose may form crystals large enough to be discernible, and leave an undesirable 'sandy' taste in the mouth. This property definitely limits the concentration of lactose in ice cream mix. Since the source of lactose is milk-solids-not-fat of dairy products and about 54 per cent of milk-solids-not-fat is lactose, the maximum concentration of lactose that can be safely used is directly related to the maximum concentration of milk-solids-not-fat.

(c) *Stabilizers :* These may be defined as substances which help to preserve emulsions. Although added in small amounts, they per-form a very important role. Stabilizers are added in ice cream to produce smoothness in body and texture, retard or reduce ice crystal growth during storage, and provide uniformity in the product and resistance to melting. Stabilizers function through their ability to form gel structures in water or combine with water as water of hydration.

Among the stabilizers which are permitted and used in making ice cream are: gelatin, sodium alginate, carageenan, agar agar, carboxy methyl cellulose, pectin; guar gum, and other gums. These are discussed below:

(i) *Gelatin :* Of animal origin, it was one of the first of the commercial stabilizers, and is still used. Its advantage lies in its ability to form a gel in the mix during the ageing period as well as during the freezing process, and even after the frozen product is placed in the hardening room. Its peculiar gel structure and its great affinity for water prevent the formation of large ice crystals in ice cream, and contribute to the smoothness in texture and firmness in body of the frozen product.

The amount of gelatin to be used depends on several factors such as the source of gelatin, whether from calf, pork skins or bone material;

its gel strength as measured by the Bloom Test; its viscosity value; the composition of the mix, etc. In general, the amount to be used is approximately the amount required to produce a meltdown (in evenly melted ice cream) of about the same con-sistency as aged 40 per cent sweet cream. This amount is usually between 0.25 and 0.5 per cent for a 250 Bloom gelatin. The ice cream mix stabilized with gelatin usually requires about 4 hours of ageing to develop complete stabilizing properties, while other stabilizing materials do not require an ageing period.

Note: Several tests have been developed to determine gel strength and to serve as the guidelines to the amount to be used in the mix. Among these are the Bloom Test (by a Bloom Gelometer) for gel strength. Other factors being equal, the gelatin that carries the greatest gel strength per unit of cost is the one to select. Good quality gelatin should have a low bacterial count and should be practically odourless and colourless.

(ii) *Sodium Alginate :* Of vegetable origin; it is also sold under the trade name of 'Dariloid'. The basic stabilizing principle, algin, is extracted from a giant ocean kelp (seaweed) growing on the shores of California and Japan. This product improves whipping ability and leaves a slightly cleaner flavour in the mouth. It dissolves properly only when added to the mix at about 68 to 71°C (155 to 160°F). A slightly smaller amount is needed to produce the same stabilizing effect as gelatin.

(iii) *Carageenan :* This is extracted from Carageen (Irish Moss), a seaweed growing on the coast of Ireland, etc. It is used together with gum stabilizers.

(iv) *Agar Agar :* This is a product extracted from red algae (seaweed) growing on the Pacific Coast. More useful for sherbets and ices.

(v) *CMC (Carboxy Methyl Cellulose) :* This has a high water-hold-ing capacity and can be easily dissolved in the mix. Also acts as an emulsifier. Slightly less of it is to be used than gelatin. It does not form as firm a gel as gelatin and some of the vegetable stabilizers, but seems to be good for use in ice cream.

(vi) *Pectin :* This is a carbohydrate obtained mainly from citrus fruits. Not satisfactory as a stabilizer for ice cream, although suitable for sherbets and ices.

(vii) *Guar Gum.* This is a carbohydrate obtained from Indian legume. Often used in combination with carageenan. It is readily soluble in cold solutions and used as stabilizer for mixes to be pasteurized by HTST or continuous pasteurization methods.

(viii) *Other Gums* (such as Tragacanth, Arabic, Karaya, or India gums) : These are exudates from incisions made in the bark of certain trees and plants growing usually in tropical countries. More useful for sherbets and ices.

Note: (i) The selection of a suitable stabilizer for use in the mix is dependent on several factors, such as: adaptability to the particular need of the plant; personal preference; availability; cost; freedom from toxicity; effect of stabilizer on the properties of the mix; whether or not an ageing period is necessary; kind of product being manufactured and method of processing adopted in the plant; effect on flavour and body and texture characteristics; and effect on melting and storage properties of the ice cream.

(ii) The amount of stabilizer used depends on the kind of stabilizer and the quality necessary to produce the desired stabilizing effect in the product being manufactured. There are four common ways of determining the amount of stabilizer to be used in the ice cream mix: the fat content of the mix; the total solids content of the mix; the kind of freezer used; and the use of a constant amount which may range from 0.15 to 0.50 per cent.

(iii) The method of incorporating stabilizers (and emulsifiers) in the ice cream mix is as follows: Mix with 4 to 5 parts of sugar and add before or during the heating process, disperse by gently adding to the mix without special handling, suspend in cold water and add them to the mix when mix temperature is 71°C (160°F) in the case of sodium alginate or use a hopper and pump or some other special arrangement. When the batch method of pasteurization is employed, the stabilizer may be added to the cold or hot mix. This method gives greater latitude for the selection of a stabilizer. In the HTST pasteurization process, the stabilizer must be added to the cold mix ingredients and should disperse readily at a low temperature; the algin, guar and CMC type of products are commonly used in this processing method.

(d) *Emulsifiers :* These may be defined as substances which help to form emulsions. The value of emulsifying agents in the manufacture of ice cream lies mainly in the improved whipping quality of the mix, the production of a drier ice cream with a smoother body and texture, in their superior drawing qualities at the freezer, and the possibility of maintaining more precise control over the various manufacturing processes.

There are two kinds of emulsifiers used in the manufacture of ice cream, viz., mono- and di-glycerides derived by the chemical reaction of naturally occurring glycerides and polyoxyethylene derivatives of hexahydric alcohols, glycol and glycol esters. The mono-glycerides improve fat dispersion and whipping ability and have a moderate effect on stiffness and the melting rate. The poly-derivatives are effective in producing dryness, stiffness and increasing the melting time.

Emulsifiers are available in liquid, semi-solid and powder forms and may include glycerides, lecithin and fatty acid esters. In general, emulsifiers have little effect on the acidity, pH or viscosity of the ice cream mix. A significant reduction in whipping time is encountered when any emulsifier is used. The use of emulsifiers decreases the melting rate in the finished ice cream. Emulsifiers seem to produce somewhat smaller ice crystals which are more evenly distributed, and smaller air cells that result in a smoother ice cream. Several factors may affect the action of an emulsifier. Among these are: ingredients of the mix; procedure of processing, freezing and hardening; and the amount of emulsifier used. Some disadvantages in the use of emulsifiers are: homogenization of the mix is essential in order to obtain good results and they seem to favour the development of a 'shrinkage' defect. Excessive use of emulsifiers may cause a short body and poor texture, slow melting, and a curdy meltdown in the finished ice cream.

Note: Excellent ice cream, and considerable amounts of it, are made without adding stabilizer or emulsifier. Since milk and milk products contain natural stabilizing and emulsifying materials, viz., milk protein, fat, lecithin, phosphates and citrates, mixes of a certain composition and processing treatment may be stabilized by the effect of these natural materials. Further, egg yolk products are high in lecithin and have long been used in ice cream. These products produce results similar to, but not as pronounced as, those caused by commercial stabilizers and emulsifiers.

(e) *Flavours :* The two most popular flavours, viz., vanilla and chocolate, have been discussed in detail below :

Vanilla

Introduction : Vanilla is undoubtedly the most popular flavour for ice cream throughout the world. In the United States of America, records show that about 75 per cent of all ice cream produced contains vanilla flavouring. It may be kept in mind that vanilla is often used in combination with other flavours or as a background flavour in many ice creams.

Vanilla flavouring is obtained from the perennial climbing plant, *Vanilla Planifolia Andrews,* a member of the orchid family. It is a native of Mexico and was introduced to the civilized world by the great Spanish explorer, Hernando Cortez, in 1528. The above plant and its related types have been introduced to other tropical regions such as the Madagascar Islands (now providing 80% of the world's supply), Indonesia (Java), certain islands in the West Indies, Mauritius, parts of Central and South America, etc.

Vanillin is the principal flavouring material in vanilla. However, there is no free vanillin in the beans when they are harvested, and the typical vanilla flavour is developed by fermenting the bean. Artificial or synthetic vanilla is a product of a slightly different flavour than the natural one.

Curing or Fermentation. The vanilla plant can be grown only in tropical regions where climate, moisture and soil conditions are just right. The plant flowers during the second year, when the finest ones are promptly fertilized by hand. The development of the fruit or bean-pod follows. The mature fruit has little flavour and is yellow in colour; when ripe, they are harvested and sold to the curer.

Although the curing or fermentation process differs in different countries, it usually consists of a process called 'sweating' in which the beans are alternately dried in the sun and wrapped up in blankets at night so that they heat and ferment. This sweating process continues for approximately 4 weeks to 4 months. In the course of this process, an enzymatic reaction takes place and the complex fats, resins, tannins, essential and fixed oils, vanillin and other aromatic compounds are formed. (At least 28 distinct components have been isolated from the vanilla aroma, most of them still unidentified.) At the end of the curing period, the pods are carefully sorted out into various grades based on their quality. The colour now ranges from chocolate to almost black. They are then packed and shipped to their final destination where extraction will take place.

Extraction : Extraction of the vanilla flavour from cured beans is a delicate process, and much depends on the skill of the person carrying out the operation. Unless correctly treated at this stage, the true flavour of the vanilla from the beans will be ruined. The beans are first chopped by extra-fine knives. A solvent such as dilute ethyl alcohol must be used for extraction. The alcohol content of the extract varies between 35 to 50 per cent. The extract is obtained through a process of percolation, which consists in continuous circulation of the alcohol-water mixture (with or without sugar and glycerine) over the chopped beans, under precisely controlled conditions, until the extraction is completed.

Classification : Vanilla flavourings may be grouped under the following general classes: true vanilla flavourings; compound vanilla flavourings and imitation vanilla flavourings.

1. *True Vanilla flavourings :* These may be sub-graded as:

True Vanilla Extract : This is prepared by the extraction of finely cut vanilla beans by a solution containing not less than 35 per cent ethanol. A standard single-strength pure vanilla extract contains soluble matter to the extent of 13.35 ounces of the vanilla beans (with or without added sugar glycerine or colouring matter) per gallon of extract. These true vanilla extracts are generally of such a strength that only 5 or 6 oz., of the extract are required to flavour 5 gallons of ice cream mix.

Concentrated Vanilla Extrac : This is obtained by distilling off a large part of the solvent until the strength reaches the desired concentrations, which is then specified as 'two-fold (or double strength)', 'three-fold', etc. A two-fold extract would be twice as strong as the single-strength extract, and would therefore contain the extractives from 26.70 oz. of vanilla beans per gallon.

True Vanilla Powders : These are made either by mixing finely ground vanilla beans with sugar, or by incorporating the vanilla extractives with a dry carrier, evaporating and drying the solvent. The amount used would correspond by weight to the number of ounces used of a standard strength extract.

Vanilla Paste : This is made by mixing the concentrated extractives with a dry carrier to form a paste. The amount used would be the same as for powders.

True Vanilla Flavour : This conforms to the same standards as for vanilla extract, except that it contains less than 35 per cent alcohol, propylene glycol or some other solvent being used as the carrier.

2. *Compound Vanilla Flavourings*

Reinforced Vanilla : Not less than one-half of the flavour may be derived from the vanilla bean content. Not more than one ounce of vanillin should be used in conjunction with 13.35 oz., of vanilla beans. This type is also available in various degrees of concentration.

3. *Imitation Vanilla Flavourings*

Blends : These are composed of true vanilla extract, flavour or powder with added synthetics where less than half of the flavour is derived from the vanilla beans.

Synthetics : These are preparations that contain no vanilla bean extractives and are made up entirely of one of several combinations of substances, such as synthetics and natural extractives derived from sources other than vanilla beans. These preparations may contain added water, alcohol, propylene glycol, vanillin, caramel, colour, etc.

Usage : The amount of vanilla used in flavouring ice cream depends on the concentration of the vanilla flavouring material and the composition of ice cream. Vanilla flavouring is available in liquid or powder forms such as pure vanilla, reinforced vanilla with vanillin, and imitation vanilla. Concentration ranges from single strength (extractive from 13.35 oz., of vanilla beans per gallon extract) to a ten-fold or higher concentrate. Vanilla may be used at rates ranging from J oz., to 5-6 oz. per 10 gallons of ice cream, depending upon the extract concentration. The amount of vanilla required decreases with decrease in the fat content of the mix and a low sugar level requires a higher vanilla level. An adequate amount of the best quality flavouring material should always be used. The vanilla flavour in the mix should not be too pronounced.

Chocolate

Introduction : Chocolate and cocoa rank second only to vanilla as flavouring for ice cream. They are obtained from cacao beans, the fruit of the perennial tree *Theobroma cocoa,* growing in such tropical regions as Mexico, Ghana, Brazil, Venezuela, Nigeria, Ecuador, the West Indies, the African Gold Coast, the East Indies, etc. The origin of the cacao tree is in dispute. Like vanilla, it was introduced to the civilized world by Cortez in 1528. The cacao tree is a strictly tropical plant thriving only in hot, humid climates. As with vanilla beans, cacao beans must be subjected to a fermentation process before the characteristic flavour develops. Besides fermentation, a rather extensive processing of the bean is necessary before the flavour can be used in food products.

Fermentation : The cacao trees of most strains will bear a full crop in the fifth year. The tree trunk and older branches bear pods, and there will be 25 to 40 beans per pod. The ripened pods, which are a rich golden red in colour, are cut from the tree, gathered in piles and left to ripen further for about 48 hours. The pods are then slashed open, the beans removed and placed in bags for about 10 days to undergo fermentation, after which the characteristic flavour and rich brown colour develop. The beans are then washed, cleaned, dried (either artificially or under the sun) sufficiently to prevent mould growth, sorted and graded prior to shipment to manufacturers of chocolate and cocoa.

Processing : At the factory the beans are first mechanically cleaned. Then they are roasted at a temperature of 121°C (250°F) or above for 30 minutes to 2 hours to eliminate the moisture and bring out the special chocolate flavour and aroma. The roasted beans are then quickly cooled by forced air, and run through a winnowing machine which crushes them into small pieces and separates the shells from the nibs (i.e., the seed part which is made into chocolate or cocoa).

Types : There are several types of chocolate flavouring used in ice cream:

1. *Chocolate Liquor.* This is a high-fat product. It is the trade name for the liquid chocolate which is produced by crushing the nibs between heavy stone grinders or mills which reduce them to a liquid (by heat generated by the friction of milling). It contains about 50 per cent fat and little flavouring material.

2. *Cocoa Powder (Natural Process).* This is a low-fat product. It is made from chocolate liquor by subjecting the liquid to high pressure in hydraulic presses. This process removes a large amount of the cocoa-fat, usually about 38—40 per cent of the total, and leaves a hard dry cake which normally contains 10 to 24 per cent fat (average 22). It also contains nearly all the flavouring material from the cacao bean. This cocoa cake is then cooled, pulverized and sifted into cocoa powder.

3. *Chocolate Blends.* These are combinations of liquor and powder. The fat content ranges from 36 to 40 per cent.

4. *Dutch Process Cocoa Powder :* This is made as per the Natural process, except that the cacao beans are treated with certain alkalis at the time of roasting to break up the cell structure. This alkali treatment makes the cocoa more soluble and gives it the desired dark colour, which distinguishes the Dutch process from Natural cocoa. It also helps to bring out the fully fine chocolate flavour when the cocoa is used in the finished product. Because the alkali counteracts the puckery acid taste which is found in Natural cocoa, Dutch process cocoa leaves no bitter taste when used as flavouring in ice cream.

Usage : Chocolate products used in flavouring ice cream are:

1. Cocoa powder (20—25 per cent cocoa fat);
2. Chocolate liquor (50—53 per cent cocoa fat);
3. Chocolate blends (36—40 per cent cocoa fat);
4. Chocolate syrups.

The amount of cocoa or chocolate liquor/blends to be used in ice cream depends upon several factors, such as consumer preference, colour desired in ice cream, strength of flavour, etc. The usual recommendation varies from as much as 4 kgs of cocoa (or 6 kgs of chocolate liquor) to 100 kgs of mix. Extra sugar should be added to compensate for the bitterness of the cocoa or chocolate, the usual recommendation being to use the same weight of sugar as of cocoa or chocolate.

Preparing Chocolate Syrup : The small manufacturer usually prefers to flavour chocolate ice cream by adding syrup at the freezer. Favourable results may be expected by using a formula of 20 kgs i cocoa, 20 kgs sugar and enough water to make 38 kgs of finished syrup; 5 to 7 kgs of this syrup may be used to 19 kgs of mix. The syrup should be made in a chocolate kettle or double boiler. Mix the sugar and cocoa/chocolate together and add enough water to make a heavy paste. Heat gradually and add water slowly as necessary. (The final syrup should contain enough water for it to pour when cooled.) The syrup should be heated to boiling point and cooled before use so as not to prolong the freezing operation.

Adding the Cocoa/Chocolate : Whenever possible, an entire chocolate mix should be made by adding the cocoa (or chocolate) and extra sugar to the mix, along with the other dry ingredients, before pasteurization. The temperature of pasteurization is sufficient to incorporate the flavour properly. A chocolate mix made in this way whips more rapidly than plain mix plus syrup at the freezer and gives a better-flavoured, more uniform product, free of dark specks.

The best chocolate ice cream is made when the chocolate mix is compounded and processed. A typical formula is as follows: fat—10 per cent, milk-solids-not-fat—10 per cent, sugar—18 per cent, cocoa —2.5 per cent, chocolate liquor—1.5 per cent, stabilizer—0.2 per cent and total solids—42.2 per cent.

Freezing Characteristics : Chocolate ice cream is one of the most difficult to freeze because it whips very slowly. This is due to the fact that chocolate ice cream is very viscous. The viscosity may be reduced and whipping time improved by adding one kgs of citrate or phosphate to 1,000 kgs of mix.

(f) Colours : Only harmless, edible, permitted food colours should be used. Generally, colours are matched with the flavours added.

(g) Egg Solids : Frozen and powdered egg yolks are used by many ice cream manufacturers. Usually not more than 0.5 per cent of egg yolk solids are added to the mix. Egg yolk solids improve the whipping quality of the mix. They are especially desirable in mixes in which butter or butter-oil constitute the main source of fat.

(h) *Fruits and Nuts :* The fruits in ice cream may be fresh, frozen or canned. Fresh fruits must be considered the best source of flavour when available at low prices; they should be thoroughly washed and peeled or hulled before use. Fruits may be used whole, sliced or crushed. It is better to mix fruits with sugar in the ratio of 2—7 kgs fruit to 1 kgs sugar and hold them at about 5°C (40°F) for 12—24 hours before using @ 15—20 per cent of the mix. In India, pieces of chopped mango, banana, etc., are added towards the end of the freezing process @ 7-8 per cent of the mix. Care should be taken to exclude inedible and fibrous parts.

Nuts should be sound, clean, and free from rancid flavours. Considerable care should be taken to prepare them for the ice cream mix so that there are no foreign materials. To make them safe, nuts are dry-heated to pasteurizing temperatures or above; they may also be fried in oil or dipped in a boiling, slightly salted, sugar solution for a few seconds. All nuts should be chopped into very small pieces before they are added to the mix at 1—3 per cent.

(bb) *Figuring the Mix :* A knowledge of calculation of ice cream mix is helpful in properly balancing a mix, in establishing and maintaining uniform quality and in producing ice cream that conforms to legal standards. Ice cream mix may be divided into two groups, namely simple and complex. Simple mixes require the least calculation and are made of ingredients each of which supplies one constituent. Complex mixes are more difficult to calculate. They include mixes where at least one constituent is obtained from two or more products. (Complex mixes require the use of the Pearson's Square, the Serum Point or Algebra method.) Before a mix can be calculated, it is necessary to:

(i) decide upon the composition of the mix to be made;

(ii) decide on the amount of mix to be made in the batch at one time. (Whatever the amount, it may be calculated on the basis of 100 *kgs,* if so desired.)

(iii) choose from the available ingredients those that will give the desired quality characteristics and composition at the lowest cost;

(iv) be familiar with the composition (i.e. the analysis) of ingredients to be used.

Since ice cream contains a higher percentage of fat than fluid milk, one of the mix ingredients must be high in fat. Cream, plastic cream, or butter is usually used for this purpose. Ice cream also contains more solids-not-fat than milk; and a source high in these solids, such as condensed skim milk, condensed whole milk or (preferably skim) milk powder is needed. Fluid milk is usually used as the basic ingredient in ice cream mix. Calculation of the mix involves finding the required weights of these ingredients along with the necessary sugar and stabilizer.

The calculations are simplified by first finding the weights of the ingredients needed to make 100 kgs of the desired mix. With the algebraic method, symbols such as *X, Y, Z* are used to represent the weights of dairy ingredients required for a 100 kgs batch of mix. These symbols are then used in writing the three equations that express the weights of fat, serum solids (solids-not-fat) and the total weight of,dairy ingredients needed for 100 kgs of mix. The method is applicable to all types of mix problems. A typical problem and its solution follows:

Problem: Prepare an ice cream mix containing fat—10 per cent, serum solids—11 per cent, sugar—14.5 per cent and stabilizer—0.3 per cent. Given: whole milk testing 6.8 per cent fat and 9.6 per cent serum solids, cream testing 40 per cent fat and 5.4 per cent serum solids, skim milk powder testing 0.5 per cent fat and 97 per cent serum solids, sugar and stabilizer (cent per cent dry matter).

Solution: Let

whole milk required = X kg

cream required = Y kg

and, skim milk powder required = Z kg

Hence,

$$X\left(\frac{6.8}{100}\right)+Y\left(\frac{40}{100}\right)+Z\left(\frac{0.5}{100}\right)=10 \quad \text{. . . I (Flat Equation)}$$

$$X\left(\frac{9.6}{100}\right)+Y\left(\frac{54}{100}\right)+Z\left(\frac{97.0}{100}\right)=11 \quad \text{. . . II (S.S. Equation)}$$

$$X+Y+Z+14.5+0.3=100 \quad \text{. . . III (Weight Equation)}$$

Solving the above,

$$\left.\begin{aligned} X &= 67.9 \\ Y &= 13.4 \\ Z &= 3.9 \end{aligned}\right\} Ans.$$

Note : For other problems using different kinds of ingredients, see standard text books

(cc) *Making the Mix.* In order to make good ice cream, the milk products and other ingredients must first be selected and combined so as to produce the desired body and a delicately blended flavour. Obviously the selection of good, wholesome ingredients and calculation of a satisfactory composition precede the mixing of the ingredients in a vat, where they can be heated to facilitate dissolving, blending and pasteurizing. The mixing process may range in scope from the small batch operation, where each ingredient is weighed or measured into the pasteurizing vat, to the large automatic continuous operation where many of the ingredients are metered into the batch. Continuous mix-making procedures may be quite variable and some such operations may actually be modifications of the batch operation. (Modern electronic computers can be used to control the cost and quality of ice cream mixes by the mathematical technique known as linear programming.)

The order in which ingredients are added is as follows: all liquid ingredients are placed in the jacketed vat provided with a power stirrer, and the agitation and heating started at once. The dry ingredients, including skim milk powder, sugar and stabilizer (with a few exceptions), are added while the liquid material is agitated and before the temperature reaches 49°C/120°F. Proper suspension to avoid lumpiness of the dry ingredients may be obtained by either mixing the dry material thoroughly with part of the sugar before slowly adding it to the liquid, or by sifting/slowly adding these substances to the liquid.

If gelatin is the stabilizer used, it is best added after it is thoroughly mixed with an equal volume of sugar, and before the liquid material reaches 49°C (120°F); alternatively, it can be sprinkled on the surface of the cold liquid and allowed to soak before the mixture is heated, or soaked in water and then the mixture heated to completely dissolve the gelatin, which is usually added to a warm (38—49°C/100—120°F) mix.

If sodium alginate (Dariloid) is used, it should not be added until the temperature of the liquid material has reached at least 66°C (150°F).

The dry Dariloid is not allowed to soak but is stirred up with cold water and immediately dumped into the hot mix.

When butter, plastic cream, frozen cream or other frozen products are used, they should be cut into fairly small pieces and added after time has been given to allow for complete melting before the pasteurizing temperature is reached. With a few exceptions, colouring and flavouring materials are added when the mix is frozen.

Pasteurizing the Mix : Proper pasteurization of all ice cream mixes should be compulsory because this process destroys all pathogenic or disease-producing bacteria, thereby safeguarding the health of the consumer. Pasteurization has come to be considered as highly desirable and requires only slight additional expense, since the homo-genization process can be best accomplished at the pasteurization temperature level. The advantages of pasteurization are:

(i) it renders the mix completely free of pathogenic bacteria;

(ii) it dissolves and helps to blend the ingredients of the mix;

(iii) it improves flavour;

(iv) it improves keeping quality; and

(v) it produces a more uniform product.

Proper pasteurization consists in rapidly heating the mix to a definite temperature, holding it at that temperature for a definite minimum period of time and then rapidly cooling it to below 5°C (40°F). The ISI specifications *(IS: 2802,* 1964) for pasteurization temperature-time combination for ice cream mix are as follows:

Batch Method—68.5°C (155°F) for not less than 30 min.

HTST Method—80.0°C (175°F) for not less than 25 sec.

There is a trend towards the higher temperature process. In the batch system, the mix is usually heated and held before going to the homogenizer and from there passes over a cooler. The heating and holding may be accomplished in the vat used for mixing the ingredients.

(ee) *Homogenizing the Mix :* Homogenization of the ice cream mix is essential. The main purpose of homogenization is to make a permanent and uniform suspension of the fat by reducing the size of the fat globules to a very small diameter, preferably not more than 2 microns. The advantages of homogenization are:

(i) it prevents fat separation during ageing;

(ii) produces more uniform ice cream with a smoother texture;

(iii) improves whipping ability;

(iv) shortens ageing period;

(v) decreases the risk of churning occurring in the freezer, and

(vi) leads to the use of slightly less stabilizer.

Note: Butter, butter-oil, plastic cream and frozen cream can be used in the mix only when the latter is homogenized.

The mix is usually homogenized at temperatures from 63° to 77°C (145° to 170°F). At low temperatures, homogenization increases the formation of clumps of fat globules, as also the viscosity and the freezing time in batch freezers. The pressure required for homogenization depends upon several factors: desired viscosity; composition of the mix; stability of the mix; temperature used; and construction of the homogenizing machine. A pressure of 2,500 to 3,000 psi with one valve, or 2,500 to 3,000 psi at the first stage and 500 psi at the second will usually give good results for an average mix (with 3 to 12 per cent fat).

(ff) *Cooling and Ageing the Mix :* Cooling the mix immediately after homogenization to 0—5°C (32—40°F) is essential, after which it should be held in ageing tanks until used. Coolers of the surface or cabinet types are generally used for this purpose. Ageing the mix before freezing has been .practised since the inception of the ice cream industry. Ageing refers to holding the mix at a low temperature for a definite time before freezing. The ageing temperature should not exceed 5°C (40°F). The ageing time under average commercial conditions may be 3 to 4 hours, except for sodium alginate which requires no ageing. Ageing produces the following results:

(i) it improves the body and texture of ice cream;

(ii) improves whipping capacity of mix;

(iii) increases maximum over-run;

(iv) increases melting resistance.

(gg) *Freezing the Mix :* When the mix has been properly aged, it is ready for the freezing process, which follows immediately. Freezing is one of the most important operations in the making of ice cream for upon it depends the quality, palatability and yield of the finished product.

The freezing process may, for convenience, be divided into two parts: 1. The mix, with the proper amount of colour and flavouring materials generally added at the freezer, is quickly frozen while being agitated to incorporate air in such a way as to produce and control the formation of small ice crystals—so necessary to give smoothness in body and texture, palatability and satisfactory over-run in the finished ice cream. 2. When the ice cream is partially frozen to a certain consistency, it is drawn from the freezer into packages and quickly transferred to cold storage rooms, where the freezing and hardening process is completed without agitation.

Note: Although the general procedure of the freezing process is easily learnt, the correct handling of the details to produce a uniform product requires expert judgement and almost split-second timing—a technique acquired only through experience guided by continual and careful study.

(a) *Classification of Freezers :* Freezers may be classified as follows:

(i) *Batch Freezer :* Horizontal, Direct Expansion (Freon or Ammonia).

(ii) *Continuous Freezer :* Horizontal, Direct Expansion (Freon or Ammonia).

(iii) *Soft Serve Freezer :* Batch and Automatic Continuous Freezers of the Direct Expansion type.

(b) *Importance of Rapid Freezing :* Rapid freezing is essential for a smooth product because ice crystals that are formed quickly are smaller than those formed slowly. Therefore, it is desirable to freeze and draw the mix from the freezer in as short a time as possible. A continuous freezer accomplishes this in a few seconds, while batch freezers take 6 to 10 minutes, depending on several factors. Also, since freezing continues after the ice cream is placed in the hardening rooms, the ice crystals formed during the hardening period are larger because they are formed more slowly than in the freezer. For this reason, it is desirable to freeze the ice cream as stiffly as possible and yet have it liquid enough to be able to draw it out of the freezer.

(c) *Factors Influencing Freezing Time* :

I. *Mechanical*

(i) type and make of freezer;
(ii) condition of freezer wall and blades;
(iii) speed of dasher;
(iv) temperature of refrigerant;
(v) velocity of refrigerant passing around freezing chamber;
(vi) over-run desired;

(vii) temperature at which ice cream is drawn;
(viii) rate at which freezer is unloaded.

II. *Character of Mix* :
(i) composition of the mix;
(ii) freezing point of the mix;
(iii) acidity content of ingredients;
(iv) kind of ingredients, particularly those carrying fat;
(v) methods by which the mix is processed;
(vi) kind and amount of flavouring materials added.

Note: The influence of type of freezer on the freezing time and temperature is shown in Table 36.3.

Table 36.3 : Freezing time and drawing temperature for different freezers.

Approximate	Approximate freezing time (to 90 per cent overrun)	Approximate drawing temperature	
		°C	°F
Batch	7 min.	-4 to -3	24 to 26
Continuous	24 sec.	-6 to -5	21 to 22

(d) *Changes which take place during the Freezing Process :*

The function of the freezing process is to freeze a portion of the water of the mix and to incorporate air into the mix. This involves: lowering the temperature of the mix from ageing temperature to the freezing point, freezing a portion of the water in the mix, incorporating air into the mix, and cooling the ice cream from the temperature at which it is drawn from the freezer to hardening-room temperature.

The temperature of the mix which is put into the freezer drops very rapidly while the sensible heat is being removed and before any ice crystals are formed. This process takes less than a minute or two. Meanwhile, the rapid agitation reduces the viscosity by partially destroying the gel structure and by breaking up the fat-globule clusters. The gel structure may restore itself partially during the hardening process in the hardening room. Also, the rapid agitation hastens incorporation of air into the mix.

When the freezing point is reached, the liquid water changes to ice crystals which appear in the mix. These ice crystals are practically pure water in a solid form, and thus the sugar as well as the other solutes become more concentrated in the remaining liquid water. Increasing the concentration of these solutes slightly depresses the freezing point of the liquid portion, so that the temperature must be lowered before any more ice crystals will form. Thus, in freezing ice cream, the freezing point is continually being lowered by the formation of ice crystals; and while the temperature drops, more ice crystals are formed, increasing the concentration of sugar and other solutes in the remaining liquid water until the concentration is so great that further freezing will not occur. Thus all the water does not freeze even after long periods in the hardening room.

Table 36.4 shows the approximate percentage of water frozen in the mix at various drawing temperatures.

Table 36.4 : Percentage water frozen in ice cream mix at different drawing temperatures

Temperature (°C/°F)	Percentage water frozen	Temperature (°C/°F)	Percentage water frozen
—4/25	33	—7/20	59
—4-5/24	41	—7.5/19	62
—5/23	47	—8/18	64
—5 5/22	52	—8.5/17	67
—6/21	56	—26/-15	90

The first phase of the freezing process accounts for the freezing of 33 to 67 per cent of the water, depending on the drawing temperature. The second phase, i.e., the hardening process, may then account for freezing another 23 to 57 per cent, depending on the drawing temperature.

(e) *Batch Freezing :* The Batch Freezer consists mainly of a freezing chamber and a dasher. The dasher consists of two parts, viz., scraper blades and the beater. The dasher performs the following functions: aids in transmission of refrigeration by keeping the mix in continuous contact with the freezer walls, scrapes freezer walls free of ice crystals; beats in air and continually pushes mix forward, which is essential for unloading the freezer. (It is important that the dasher be in proper alignment, and the blades sharp.)

Note: The temperature of the refrigerant is rather important and may vary from —23 to —29°C (—10 to — 20°F) to ensure rapid formation of ice crystals, which results in a smoother ice cream. However, the freezing should be slow and ought to permit incorporation of the desired amount of air, since this affects the body and texture of ice cream as well.

The freezing procedure in the batch freezer consists of: (i) *Preparation of the freezer.* The freezer parts should be inspected to ensure that they are clean and dry. Then they should be assembled in accordance with the instructions from the manufacturer. The operator's hands should be clean. After the freezer is assembled, it should be sanitized either by running hot water at 82°C/180°F followed by a cold water rinse; or by a cold solution of a chemical sanitizing agent (such as chlorine solution containing 100 to 200 ppm available chlorine). After the addition of hot water, cold water or chlorine solution, the dasher should be revolved a few times and the particular liquid drained out. (ii) *Adding the Mix :* It is always desirable that the temperature of the mix be below 5°C (40°F) when it goes into the freezer. Colour and flavour should be accurately measured, and poured into the mix. The total volume of the mix, flavour and colour should be about half the total capacity of the freezing chamber. The flavour and colour must be so added as to be uniformly distributed. Acid, fruits, nuts, etc., should be added only after some ice crystals have formed. The freezer should be operated uniformly as to speed, refrigerant, temperature, etc. (iii) *Freezing and Incorporation of Air :* The mix should now run into the freezer, the dasher should be started and then the refrigerant turned into the freezing chamber. This sequence must be preserved to avoid damage to the machine. To prevent the scraper blades from becoming blunt and wearing out rapidly, the dasher must never be operated when there is no mix in the freezer; neither should the refrigerant be turned on unless the dasher is in motion. This order of operation and these precautions apply to all freezers, regardless of size, type, or installation, (iv) *Drawing of Ice Cream :* When ice cream is drawn from the freezer, it should be sufficiently stiff to 'ribbon' or almost hold its shape, and yet soft enough to 'settle' or lose its shape within a minute or two. The container or package into which the ice cream is drawn should be cooled sufficiently to prevent the ice cream melting. This melting may cause a coarse and icy texture around the edge of the package and also loss of over-run. Formation of air-pockets within the container should also be avoided. The freezer should be emptied rapidly to prevent wide fluctuations in over-run in the packages. Therefore, avoid filling small packages directly from the batch freezer.

Note: When the freezer is not going to be used for 2 hours or more, it should be taken apart, cleaned and sanitized.

(f) *Continuous Feezing :* Continuous freezers are of two types in the market today: 1. One of these has two pumps just behind the freezer barrel. One pump pulls the mix from the supply tank and pumps it to the second one. This second pump operates at a speed approximately twice as great as that of the first pump. This has the effect of creating a partial vacuum between the two pumps. The valve device in the piping between the pumps allows for air to be sucked in. The amount of air incorporated can be regulated very accurately, and once it is in the system, it cannot get out provided the machine is operating normally. The mix and air are pumped into the freezing barrel by the second pump. As the mix freezes, semi-frozen ice cream is forced out from the front of the machine. 2. The second type operates in a very similar fashion as the first. However, here the two pumps are at the front. One pump pushes the mix into the rear end of the freezer and the other helps to pull out the semi-frozen ice cream from the freezer. There is a separate air pump that forces air directly into the freezer barrel. This second kind of continuous freezer is just as versatile as the first one.

Some important advantages of the continuous freezing method are:

(i) less stabilizer is needed;

(ii) a shorter ageing time is possible;

(iii) less flavouring material is needed;

(iv) smoother ice cream is obtained;

(v) tendency towards development of sandiness decreases;

(vi) a more uniform yield is obtained with less variation between packages.

Some disadvantages are:

(i) great care must be taken in handling the parts of the machine which fit with very small clearance;

(ii) operators and mechanics must have special experience and traning in order to avoid operational difficulties and possible damage to the equipment;

(iii) it is difficult to prevent excessive over-run;

(iv) there is a greater tendency for ice cream to shrink in volume after hardening;

(v) initial cost of the equipment is high.

Note: The processing procedures in the manufacture of ice cream have become fully mechanized in developed countries and various degrees of automation of these processes are now common.

(hh) *Over-run in Ice Cream.* Over-run is usually defined as the volume of ice cream obtained in excess of the volume of the mix. It is usually expressed as a percentage. This increased volume is composed mainly of the air incorporated during the freezing process. The amount of air which is incorporated depends upon the composition of the mix and the way it is processed; and is regulated so as to give that percentage of over-run or yield which will give the proper body, texture and palatability necessary to a good quality product. Too much air will produce a snowy, fluffy, unpalatable ice cream while too little, a soggy, heavy product. In order to secure uniform overrun and yield, the following points should receive attention:

(i) uniformity in refrigerant temperature and rate of flow of refrigerant;

(ii) the use of overrun testers;

(iii) uniform make, etc., of freezer for the operator;

(iv) not too many freezers per operator;

(v) hopper system for filling containers if batch freezers are used.

The control of overrun is very important and should be as nearly constant as possible from batch to batch and from day to day. The correct overrun percentage depends upon the kind and composition of product and freezing equipment. The desirable percentage overrun in different ice creams is given in Table 36.5.

Table 36.5 : Percentage overrun in ice creams.

Products	Percentage overrun
Ice cream, packaged	70 to 80
Ice cream, bulk	90 to 100
Soft ice cream (softy)	30 to 50

There are two basic or fundamental methods for calculating percentage over-run, viz., by volume and by weight:

$$\text{(i) \% overun} = \frac{(\text{volume of ice cream}) - (\text{volume of mix})}{\text{volume of mix}} \times 100$$

$$\text{(ii) \% overrun} = \frac{\begin{pmatrix}\text{weight of unit} \\ \text{volume of mix}\end{pmatrix} - \begin{pmatrix}\text{weight of unit} \\ \text{volume of ice cream}\end{pmatrix}}{\text{weight of unit volume of ice cream}} \times 100$$

(jj) *Packaging of Ice Cream :* When ice cream is drawn from the freezer, it is usually collected in containers which give it the desired shape or size for convenient handling during the hardening and marketing processes. The chief requirements for packages of ice cream are: protection against contamination; an attractive appearance; ease of opening and reclosure; and ease of disposal. Protection against moisture loss and temperature fluctuations is also desirable: Broadly speaking, ice cream packages are of two types, viz., multi-service and single-service:

(i) *Multi-service :* This type of container is seldom used in modern operations; a tinned-steel can is an example. They are cleaned, sanitized and used repeatedly.

(ii) *Single Service :* This type of package has met with increasing favour, especially during recent years. The quantity filled may be for bulk or retail sale. Most bulk ice cream is packaged in fibre board cartons coated with wax or polythene-wax blends for protection against moisture and oxygen. The most recent trend for such factory-filled carry-home packages is the all-plastic cylindrical container with a recloseable lid. Retail ice cream may be packaged in cups, stick or bars. Cups may be of paper or cardboard, treated as above to make them impervious to moisture. The recent trend is towards multi-packs (such as six packs) in polythene bags, multi-bars in foil cartons, etc.

(kk) *Hardening and Storage of Ice Cream :* When ice cream is drawn from the freezer and put into the container to be placed in the hardening room, it has a semi-fluid consistency not stiff enough to hold its shape. The freezing process is, therefore, continued without agitation during hardening until the temperature of the ice cream reaches -18°C (0°F) or below. Here, as in the freezer, quick hardening is desirable, since slow hardening favours large ice crystals and coarseness. Most operators allow a hardening time of 12 hours. The factors affecting hardening time are: (i) size and shape of the ice cream package; (ii) speed of (cool) air circulation; (iii) temperature of cooling air; (iv) section of the hardening room; (v) temperature of ice cream drawn from the freezer: (vi) composition of mix, and (vii) percentage over-run in the ice cream being hardened.

The different hardening systems are given in Table 36.6.

Table 36.6 : Ice cream hardening systems.

Hardening systems	Temperature maintained	
	°C	°F
Hardening rooms	—12 to —45	10 to —50
Hardening tunnels	—34 to —45	—30 to —50
Hardening cabinets	—23 to —26	—10 to —15

After the ice cream is hardened, it may be immediately marketed, or it may be stored for a week or two at the most. The operation of storage rooms is the same as for the hardening room with two exceptions: the temperature should be maintained uniformly at a point between -23°C to -18°C (-10°F to 0°F) and the packages should be piled very close, to delay changes in ice cream temperature.

Some precautions to be observed in the operation of hardening/ storage rooms are:

(i) provide facilities for calling for aid, should the operator accidentally be trapped inside;

(ii) keep both an axe and a sledge hammer in a definite place just inside the door;

(iii) avoid fluctuations in temperature.

Distribution

When ice cream is marketed, the manufacturer usually transports it to the retailer under refrigeration at the same temperature as is maintained in the retailer's cabinet. The various means of refrigerating the distribution vehicle are:

(a) *'Dry Ice[1] Refrigeration :* Dry ice is solid carbon dioxide with a freezing point of — 78°C (— 109°F); it is used extensively for package deliveries. It is cut into pieces of an appropriate size, which are wrapped in paper to delay rapid evaporation, and then placed around the package of the ice cream inside an insulated packer or in a single service type packer. The latter is usually a cardboard box insulated with corrugated cardboard and is used especially for the carryout package. This system is popular for retailing ice cream in push carts in large Indian cities.

Advantages : (i) It is neither moist nor messy; (ii) the package is neat in appearance; (iii) it does not waterlog the insulation, and (iv) it is very light.

Disadvantages : (i) At present, it is expensive and availability is limited; (ii) loss during handling and storage (up to 10 to 15%); (iii) danger of burns to 'handler' and (iv) greater opportunity for heat-shock, which may injure the texture of the ice cream.

(b) *Refrigerated Truck :* This is the most commonly used means of transportation for ice cream in developed countries. The truck is refrigerated over-night, and loaded with hardened ice cream the following morning.

(c) *Frozen Brine :* Jacketed metal containers, known as Eutectic pads, which contain calcium chloride (brine) solution of specific gravity of about 1.1, are refrigerated in a similar brine tank whose specific gravity is about 1.26, at a temperature of — 32°C (—25°F). The containers attain a temperature of — 21°C (—5°F) and are then placed around the packaged ice cream. This arrangement is used by a few ice cream factories for air-lifting ice cream in this country.

SOFT ICE CREAM (SOFTY)

There is a marked demand for the form of ice cream which has generally come to be known as 'softy'. This term has been applied largely because this product is marketed in a soft condition and is ready for consumption shortly after it is drawn from the freezer. The problems involved in the preparation of softy ice creams are somewhat different from those encountered in the manufacture of regular ice cream. The composition of soft ice cream has been given in Table 36.7.

Table 36.7 : Composition of soft ice cream.

Constituent	Percentage
Fat	3 to 6
Milk-solids-not-fat	11 to 14
Sugar	12 to 15
Stabilizer and emulsifier	0.4 to 0.6

Note: Soft ice cream is usually drawn from the freezer at around -8 to -7°C (18 to 20°F). The over-run may be in the range of 30 to 50 per cent.

JUDGING AND GRADING OF ICE CREAM

A. *Score Card :* This is given in Table 36.8.

Table 36.8 : Score card of ice cream (ADSA).

Items	Perfect score
Flavour	45
Body and texture	30
Bacteria	15
Colour and package	5
Melting quality	5
	100

B. *Procedure of Examination :*

(a) *Sampling :* Taken at random for ice cream cups but at a later stage for bigger lots.

(b) *Tempering ice cream :* Generally, temperatures from — 15°C to — 12°C (5°F to 10°F) are satisfactory. This is best done by taking the ice cream out of the hardening room and placing it in a dispensing cabinet several hours prior to judging.

(c) *Sequence of Observations :* Since the condition of ice cream changes rapidly when exposed to room temperature, one should be alert and observant during sampling, so as not to miss any of its true characteristics, particularly of body and texture. Proceed in the following order:

(i) *Examine Container :* Note the type and condition of container and presence of any package defects.

(ii) *Note Colour of Ice Cream :* Observe the colour of ice cream, its intensity and uniformity, and whether the colour matches its flavour.

(iii) *Sample the Ice Cream :* While using the dipper for sampling, note the following: the manner in which the product cuts, the evenness of cutting, the resistance offered during cutting, the presence of ice particles, whether the ice cream is heavy or soggy, light or fluffy, etc. Set aside a sample in a petri plate/ dish for observing the melting characteristics.

(iv) *Begin Judging :* After obtaining the sample, take a small spoonful or bite of the frozen product, and taste. Quickly manipu-late the sample between teeth and tongue and note the body and texture and flavour characteristics. (Expect delayed taste reaction.)

Note: Rinse mouth with saline water frequently.

(v) *Note the Melting Qualities :* Observe whether the melted liquid is creamy, curdled, foamy or watery.

(vi) Determine the bacterial count.

C. *Requirements of high grade ice cream.* An ideal ice cream should be packaged in an attractive container, possess a typically pleasant and desirable flavour, have a close, smooth and uniform body and texture, have desirable melting properties, possess an uniform natural colour, and have a low bacterial count.

DEFECTS IN ICE CREAM, THEIR CAUSES AND PREVENTION

Defects in ice cream may arise due to low quality ingredients, improper mixing, or faulty methods of manufacture and storage. The common defects in ice cream, their causes and prevention are given in Table 36.9.

Table 36.9 : Defects in ice cream, their causes and prevention.

	Name of defect	Causes	Prevention
(a)	*Flavour*		
	High	Addition of excessive amount of flavour.	Addition of correct amount of flavour.
	Low	Addition of inadequate amount of flavour.	-do-
	Acid/sour	Presence of excessive (developed) acidity due to: use of sour dairy products, slow cooling of mix and storage of mix at higher temperatures.	Control over developed acidity by: using fresh and sweet dairy products, prompt and efficient cooling of milk and storage of mix at 0—5°C.
	Bitter	Using, low quality ingredients, especially flavour, dairy products, etc.	(i) Using true flavour extract (ii) Using fresh, sweet dairy products.
	Cooked	Over-heating of mix during pasteurization.	Proper heating of mix during pasteurization.
	Flat	Addition of inadequate amount of sugar.	Addition of correct amount of sugar.
	Unnatural	Addition of not-so-typical (ice cream) flavour.	Addition of typical (ice cream) flavour.
	Rancid	Fat hydrolysis due to lipase action in the individual fat-rich ingredients or in the mix.	Inactivating lipase by proper pasteurization of the individual fat-rich ingredients or mix.

Name of defect	Causes	Prevention
Oxidized/Oily/ Metallic/Tallowy	Fat oxidation due to: direct contact of individual fat-rich ingredients or mix with copper or iron, exppsure to sunlight, etc.	Storage of individual fat-rich ingredients or mix in tinned/aluminium alloy/ stainless steel vessels,
(b) *Body*		
Crumbly	(i) Low solids content (ii) Low stabilizer content (iii) Excessive over-run (iv) Improper homogenization	(i) Optimum solids content (ii) Optimum stabilizer content (iii) Correct over-run (iv) Proper homogenization.
Soggy	(i) Low overrun (ii) High sugar content (iii) Excessive stabilizer content	(i) Optimum over-run (ii) Optimum sugar conten! (iii) Optimum stabilizer content.
Weak	(i) Low solids content . (ii) Low stabilizer content.	(i) Optimum solids content (ii) Optimum stabilizer content.
(c) *Texture*		
Buttery	Inadequate homogenization.	Adequate homogenization.
Coarse/Icy	(i) Low solids content (ii) Low stabilizer content (iii) Inadequate ageing (iv) Slow freezing (v) Slow hardening (vi) Heat-shock (vii) Long storage.	(i) Optimum solids content (ii) Optimum stabilizer content (iii) Adequate ageing (iv) Rapid freezing (v) Rapid hardening (vi) Avoiding heat-shock (vii) Short storage.
Fluffy	(i) Excessive over-run (ii) Low solids content (iii) Excessive emulsifier content.	(i) Optimum over-run (ii) Optimum solids content (iii) Optimum emulsifier content.
Sandy	(i) High MSNF/lactose content (ii) Temperature fluctuation in retail cabinet (iii) Long storage period.	(i) Optimum MSNF/lactose content (ii) Avoiding temperature fluctuation in retail cabinet (iii) Short storage period.
(d) *Melting quality*		
Curdy meltdown	Using high-acid mix.	Using fresh, sweet mix.
Foamy meltdown	(i) Excessive over-run (ii) Excessive emulsifier content.	(i) Optimum over-run (ii) Optimum emulsifier content.
Slow melting	(i) Excessive stabilizer content. (ii) Inadeauate homogenization	(i) Optimum stabilizer content. (ii) Adequate homogenization.
(e) *Colour*		
Unnatural	Wrong colour.	Proper colour.
(f) *Miscellaneous*		
Shrinkage	(i) Temperature fluctuation during storage (ii) Excessive over-run (iii) Rough transportation.	(i) Constant temperature during storage (ii) Optimum over-run (iii) Avoiding rough transportation.

USES OF ICE CREAM

(i) direct consumption as frozen dessert;

(ii) as a topping for fruit pies and fruit salad.

ALL FOLLOWING PROJECT REPORTS ARE READILY AVAILABLE

- Steel Furnitures And Electrical Appliances
- Steel Furniture And Fire Fighting Equipments
- Steel Furniture And Room Cooler
- Steel Wire Drawing And Galvanizing
- Steel Wire/Rod
- Steel Wool
- Ston Scrusher And Screening Plant
- Submerged Arc Welded Pipes
- Submersible Pump Manufacturing
- Super Enamelled Copper Wire
- Super Enamelled Copper Wire (From Copper Cathode Rod)
- Three Wheelers
- Tie-Rod Ends
- Tin Containers
- Toolroom And Sheet Metal Products
- Trolley (Shopping) For Carrying Of Stores At Super Market And Ware Houses
- Tractor Trailers
- Transmission Power Fitting
- Tubular Poles
- Tyre Retreading By Cold Process
- Super Enamelled Copper Wires
- Trolley (Shopping) For Carrying Of Stores At Super Market & Ware Houses
- Tmt Bars
- Tubular Poles For Electrical Transmission (By Fabrication Process)
- Tubular Poles Of M.S. & High Tensile Steel
- V- Belt
- Vacuum Cleaners
- Vacuum Flask (Stainless Steel)
- Valves For Refrigeration And Air-Condition
- Vehicle Welding & Painting
- Venetion Blind
- Washing Machines (Automatic & Computerised)
- Water Controller (Automatic)
- Watch Straps/Chains/ Bracelets/Belt Brass & Stainless Steel
- Water Coolers
- Welded Wire Mesh
- Welding Electrodes
- Wheel Barrow
- Wick Stoves
- Wind Mill Window Frame (Ferrous & Non-Ferrous)
- Wrist Watch

CHEMICALS (ORGANIC & INORGANIC) WITH PETROLEUM PRODUCTS

- Acetic Anhydride
- Acetic Acid (Glacial)
- Acetic Acid From Ethanol
- Acetone
- Acetylene Black
- Acetyl Chloride
- Acetylene Gas
- Acetylene Gas & Oxygen Gas (Integrated Unit)
- Acid Black Dye
- Acid Slurry
- Activated Alumina
- Activated Bleaching Earth (Activated Fullers Earth)
- Activated Carbon From Cashewnut Shell
- Activated Carbon From Rice Husk
- Activated Carbon From Rice Husk, Coconut Shell & Coconut Powder
- Activated Carbon From Wood
- Activated Carbon Powder & Granules From Coconut Shell
- Activated Carbon & Sodium Silicate From Paddy & Rice Husk
- Alcohol From Broken Rice
- Alum For Water Treatment
- Adhesive (Fevicol Type)
- Aerosol Insecticides Spray (Baygon, Hit, Mortein Type)
- Agarbatti Synthetic Perfumery Compounds
- Alcohol From Potato
- Alcohol From Rice Grains
- Alcohol From Rice Husk
- Alcohol From Molasses
- Alcohol, Beer, Starch, Liquid Glucose, Dextrose, Sorbitol, Vitamin-C,
- Alcoholic Beverages And Vinegar From Coconut Water
- Germ Oil, Cattle Feed Etc. From Maize
- Alkyd Resin
- Alkylated Phenol Likenonyl Phenol, Dodecyl Phenol
- Alum (Non Ferric)
- Alum (Ferric)
- Aluminium Chloride From Aluminium Ore
- Alum Cake
- Alum From Aluminium Hydrate
- Aluminium Ingot By Bauxite
- Aluminium Phosphide
- Aluminium Phosphate
- Aluminium Sulphate (Non Ferric Alum) 17% - 18% Alumina Content In Granules (2 Mm To 4 Mm) And Flakes
- Amines & Allied Products
- Amino Acid
- Ammonia Gas
- Ammonia Gas Bottling
- Ammonia Liquor
- Ammonium Nitrate
- Ammonium Chloride (Pure & Technical)
- Ammonium Sulphate
- Annato Seed Extraction And Processing
- Anti Corrosion Chemicals
- Anthranilic Acid From Phthalic Anhydride
- Anesthesia (All Types) Used In Hospitals
- Aniline
- Argon Gas
- Ariel Type Detergent Powder
- Anthraquinone
- Antimony Trioxide
- Atenolol
- Auramine "O"
- Azodicarbonamide
- Baking Soda From Ash
- Barium Carbonate
- Barium Compounds
- Barium Nitrate
- Barium Peroxide
- Barium-Thio-Sulphate Banzene
- Baryte Powder
- Bar Soap (All Varieties) Using Soap Noodles
- Beer Plant
- Belt Paste
- Beneficiation Of Chromite Ore Processing Charge Chrome
- Benzyl Acetate, Benzyl Benzoate, Benzyl Alcohol
- Beta Naphthol
- Bentonite Powder
- Benzoic Acid
- Benzidine
- Biofertiliser From Mother Culture
- Bio Oil For Power Generation From Coffee Husk
- Bio Gas Plant
- Bio Gas Filling In Cylinder
- Bio Tech Unit
- Bi-Chromate Of Sodium, Potassium & Ammonium
- Bi-Functional Black Mfgr.Reactive Dye (Dye From Cotton Yarn Dyeing)
- Bio-Fuel (Jatropha Cultivation And Extraction)
- Bituminous Roademulsion
- Black Phenyl
- Black Sulphur
- Bleaching Powder (Stable)
- Blue Detergent Powder
- Bone Crushing Plant
- Bone Meal (Calcined) Enrichment With Calcium & Phosphorus
- Boric Acid
- B.O.N. Acid
- Bromine Gas Plant
- Brandy
- Butanol
- Butyl Rubber For The Manufacture Of Tubes For Truck And Car Tyres
- 1,4, Butanediol
- Butyl Acetate
- Caffein From Tea Waste
- Calcined Lime (Dead Burnt Dolomite)

Market Survey Cum Detailed Techno Economic Feasibility Report on all Projects are available Contact.
"ENGINEERS INDIA RESEARCH INSTITUTE", 4449, Nai Sarak (D), Main Road, Delhi-110006 (India)
Ph.: [illegible], 91-11-23918117, 23916431, 45626431, 64727385 Fax : 91-11-23916431
E-mail: [illegible]@gmail.com, eiribooks@yahoo.com • website: www.eiri.in, www.eiriindia.org

FLORICULTURE HAND BOOK
(Hand book of flowers growing technology)

ISBN 81-86732-72-1
Rs. 1000/- or US $ 110/-

Carnation, ChinaAster, Dahlia, Gladiolus, Gerbera, Gloriosa, Jasmine, Lilium, Lotus, Marigold, Orchids, Rose, Tuberose, Other flowers, Gypsophila, Statice, Zantedeschia, Gaillardia, Sweet Sultan, Solidago, Plant Economics of various floriculture projects etc.

HAND BOOK OF ICE CREAM TECHNOLOGY & FORMULAE

ISBN. 81-86732-70-5 ★ Rs. 525/-

Composition of Ice Cream Mixes, Manufacturing Process, Ice Cream Freezing, Ice Cream Mix Calculations, Packaging of Ice Cream, Frozen Dairy Products and Formulations, Laboratory Tests, Project Profiles, Suppliers of Machineries etc.

BOOKS ON RUBBER CHEMICALS & RUBBER GOODS

TECHNOLOGY OF RUBBER & RUBBER GOODS INDUSTRIES

ISBN. 81-86732-59-4 ★ Rs. 900/-

The book cover natural rubber, Classification, Properties, Uses and Manufacture, Latex processing and applications, Chemical aspects of rubber technology, Physical aspects of rubber technology, Styrene Butadiene Rubber (SBR), Processing and curing of Polybutadiene and Polyisoprene, Manufacture and Processing of EPDM, Butyl and Halobutyl Rubbers, Nitrile & Polyacrylic Rubber, Neoprene (Polychloroprene) & Hypalon Rubber, Silocone Rubber, Reclaimed Rubber, Latex & Foam Rubber, Vulcanisation, Manufacturing Techniques of Rubber Products, Recycling of Wastes from Rubber & Plastic, Quality control in Rubber Industry etc.

RUBBER CHEMICALS & PROCESSING INDUSTRIES

ISBN. 81-86732-15-2
 # Rs. 400/- US$50

The book covers Technology of Rubber Chemicals and Manufacturing of Rubber Products/Goods. Various Project Profiles are given, Suppliers of Raw Materials and Machinery, Natural Rubber, Synthetic & Acrylic Rubber, Butyl Rubber, Silicon & Nitrile Rubber, Rubber Powder etc.

BOOKS ON PAINT VARNISH LACQUER SOLVENTS, COATING, RESINS & INKS INDUSTRIES

PAINT VARNISH SOLVENTS AND COATING TECHNOLOGY

ISBN. 81-86732-44-6
 # Rs. 750/- or US$ 75/-

Introduction, General Pigments Physical Properties, Pigments Processing, Plasticizers and Solvents, Synthetic Resins, Varnishes, Pigmentation, Paints (Decorative & Building), Coatings, Industrial Paints & Coatings, Industrial Finishes, Miscellaneous Coatings and Ancillary Materials, Testing and Evaluation, Miscellaneous Formulae, Project Profiles, Suppliers of Raw Materials & Plant and Machinery, Present Manufacturers etc.

PAINT PIGMENT VARNISH & LACQUER MANUFACTURING

ISBN. 81-86732-16-0
 # Rs. 450/- or US$ 50/-

The Book covers Process, Formulations, Technology, Project Profiles on various Paint, Varnish, Lacquer manufacturing industries. Suppliers of Plant, Equipments and Machinery with Raw Materials have also been incorporated etc.

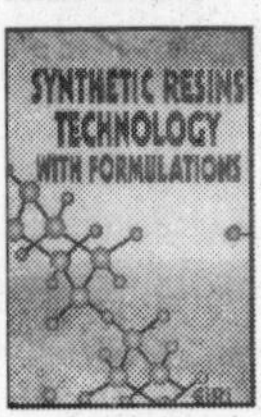

SYNTHETIC RESINS TECHNOLOGY WITH FORMULATIONS

ISBN. 81-86732-40-3
 # Rs. 800/- or US$ 80/-

Latest technology to manufacture various Synthetic Resins with formulae including epoxy resin, alkyd resins, acrylics, ion-exchange resin, melamine formaldehyde resin, phenol formaldehyde resin, polyester resin, polyvinyl acetate, polyvinyl alcohol, pvc resin & plastisol, silicones, urea formaldehyde resins etc. Suppliers of Machinery and Raw Materials etc.

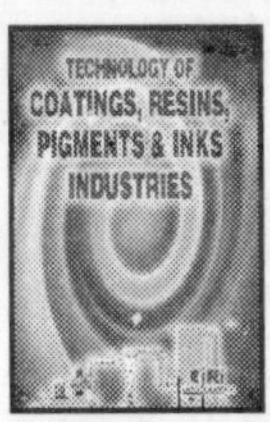

TECHNOLOGY OF COATINGS, RESINS, PIGMENTS AND INKS INDUSTRIES

ISBN. 81-86732-64-0
 # Rs. 975/- or US$ 100/-

Introduction, PU Coatings, Powder Coatings, Antifouling Coatings, UV Curable Powder Coatings, Polyurethane Coating, Colour of Pigments, Caprolactone Modification of Polyester Resins, Acrylics, Additives in Paints, Polyester- based Water- borne and Solvent-borne Coil Coatings, Zinc Dust Pigment, Alkyd Manufacturing, Calcium Carbonate Extenders, Pigments for Paints Inks & Plastics, Design of Paint Formulations, Polyester Resin etc.

MODERN INKS FORMULAES & MANUFACTURING INDUSTRIES

ISBN. 81-86732-17-9
 # Rs. 325/- or US$50/-

Colour Matching, Raw Materials, Waxes & Additives, Typographic Inks, Formuations, Photogravure Inks Screen Process Inks, Ball Point Pen Inks, Testing of Finished Inks, Formulae, Toner Inks, Printing Inks, Screen & Offset Printing Inks, Stamp Pad Inks,

PROFITABLE SMALL SCALE MANUFACTURE OF SOAPS & DETERGENTS

ISBN. 81-86732-25-X # Rs. 375/-

Raw materials, soap manufacture, soap from non edible oil, soap from soap stock, Medicated soap, Shaving soap, shaving creams, synthetic detergent powder, detergent cake and powder, Enzyme detergent powder, Project Profiles on various Soap and Detergent projects, Suppliers of Plant and Machinery and raw materials etc.

ENGINEERS INDIA RESEARCH INSTITUTE Mobile : 9811437895

4449, Nai Sarak, Main Road, Delhi - 110 006 (INDIA) Ph./Fax : 91-11- 23918117, 23916431, 43626431